Active Directory Administration:

The Personal Trainer

Windows Server 2008 & Windows Server 2008 R2

William R. Stanek

PUBLISHED BY

Stanek & Associates
PO Box 362
East Olympia, WA 98540-0362

Cover Design: Creative Designs Ltd.
Editorial Development: Andover Publishing Solutions
Technical Review: L & L Technical Content Services

You can provide feedback related to this book by emailing the author at
williamstanek@aol.com. Please use the name of the book as the subject line.

Contents at a Glance

Table of Contents

Introduction

Active Directory Administration: The Personal Trainer for Windows Server 2008 & Windows Server 2008 R2 is the authoritative quick reference guide to Active Directory and is designed to be a key resource you turn to whenever you have questions about Active Directory. To this end, the book zeroes in on the key aspects of Active Directory that you'll use the most.

Inside this book's pages, you'll find comprehensive overviews, step-by-step procedures, frequently used tasks, documented examples, and much more. One of the goals is to keep the content so concise that the book remains compact and easy to navigate while at the same time ensuring that the book is packed with as much information as possible—making it a valuable resource.

What's This Book About?

Active Directory Administration: The Personal Trainer for Windows Server 2008 & Windows Server 2008 R2 is designed to be used in the daily administration of Active Directory. In this book, I teach you how features work, why they work the way they do, and how to customize them to meet your needs. I also offer specific examples of how certain features can meet your needs, and how you can use other features to troubleshoot and resolve issues you might have. In addition, this book provides tips, best practices, and examples of how to fine-tune all major aspects of Active Directory.

What Do I Need to Know?

This book covers Active Directory for small, medium, and large organizations. To get practical and useful information into your hands without the clutter of a ton of background material, I had to assume several things. If you are reading this book, I hope that you have basic networking skills and a basic understanding of Windows Server operating systems, and that Windows Server is already installed on your systems. With this in mind, I don't devote entire chapters to understanding Windows Server architecture, installing Windows Server, or Windows networking. I do, however, provide complete details on the components of Active Directory networks and how you can use these components. I cover installing domain controllers, configuring Active Directory sites, and much more.

How Is This Book Organized?

Making this book easy to follow and understand was my number one goal! I really want anyone, skill level or work schedule aside, to be able to learn how to effectively manage Active Directory.

To make the book easy to use, I've divided it into 9 chapters. In Chapters 1 and 2, you'll roll up your sleeves and dive right in to the good stuff while also learning how Active Directory works. Chapter 1 provides an overview of tools, techniques, and concepts related to Active Directory. Chapter 2 discusses installing forests, domain trees, and child domains.

Chapter 3 details techniques for deploying writable domain controllers and the tasks you'll need to perform to set up domain controllers. Chapter 4 covers the deployment of read-only domain controllers. Together, these chapters provide the detailed information you need to configure domains and forests, whether you are deploying Active Directory Domain Services for the first time or extending your existing infrastructure.

In addition to their standard roles, domain controllers can also act as global catalog servers and operations masters. Chapter 5 explores techniques for configuring, maintaining, and troubleshooting global catalog servers. Chapter 6 examines how you manage operations masters. Chapter 7 describes your work with Active Directory sites, subnets, and replication. You'll learn the essentials for creating sites and associating subnets with sites. You'll also learn advanced techniques for managing site links and replication.

Chapter 8 describes how to manage trusts and authentication. You'll learn how Active Directory authentication works within domains, across domain boundaries, and across forest boundaries. You'll also learn how trusts are used and established. Chapter 9 provides techniques you can use to maintain, monitor, and troubleshoot Active Directory infrastructure. In addition to learning techniques for backing up and recovering Active Directory, you'll also learn how to perform essential maintenance tasks and how to configure related options and services, including Windows Time service.

Finally, Appendix A provides a quick reference for command-line utilities you'll use when working with Active Directory.

What Conventions Are Used in This Book?

I've used a variety of elements to help keep the text clear and easy to follow. You'll find code terms and listings in monospace type, except when I tell you to actually enter a command. In that case, the command appears in bold type. When I introduce and define a new term, I put it in italics.

This book also has notes, tips and other sidebar elements that provide additional details on points that need emphasis.

Other Resources

Although some books are offered as all-in-one guides, there's simply no way one book can do it all. This book is intended to be used as a concise and easy-to-use resource. It covers everything you need to perform core tasks for Active Directory, but it is by no means exhaustive.

As you encounter new topics, take the time to practice what you've learned and read about. Seek additional information as necessary to get the practical experience and knowledge that you need.

I truly hope you find that *Active Directory Administration: The Personal Trainer for Windows Server 2008 & Windows Server 2008 R2* helps you manage Active Directory successfully and effectively.

Thank you,

William R. Stanek

(williamstanek@aol.com)

Chapter 1. Active Directory Essentials

Whether you are a skilled administrator who has worked with Windows networks for years or a novice with a basic understanding, your long-term success in the ever-changing technology landscape increasingly depends on how well you understand Active Directory. *Active Directory* is an extensible directory service that enables centralized management of network resources. It allows you to easily add, remove, or relocate accounts for users, groups, and computers as well as other types of resources. Nearly every administrative task you perform affects Active Directory in some way. Active Directory is based on standard Internet protocols and has a design that helps you clearly identify the physical and logical components of your network's structure.

Understanding Directory Services

Active Directory provides the necessary infrastructure for designing a directory that meets the needs of your organization. A *directory* is a stored collection of information about various types of resources. In a distributed computing environment such as a Windows network, users must be able to locate and use distributed resources, and administrators must be able to manage how distributed resources are used. This is why a directory service is necessary.

A *directory service* stores all the information needed to use and manage distributed resources in a centralized location. The service makes it possible for resources to work together. It is responsible for authorizing access, managing identities, and controlling the relationships between the resources. Because a directory service provides these fundamental functions, it must be tightly integrated with the security and management features of the network operating system.

A directory service provides the means to define and maintain the network infrastructure, perform system administration, and control the user experience. Although users and administrators might not know the exact resources they need, they should know some basic characteristics of the resources they want to use. If so, they can use the directory service to obtain a list of resources that match the known characteristics. As illustrated in Figure 1-1, they can use the directory service to query the directory and locate resources that have specific characteristics. For example, users can search the directory to find a color printer in a particular location or to find a color printer that supports duplex functionality.

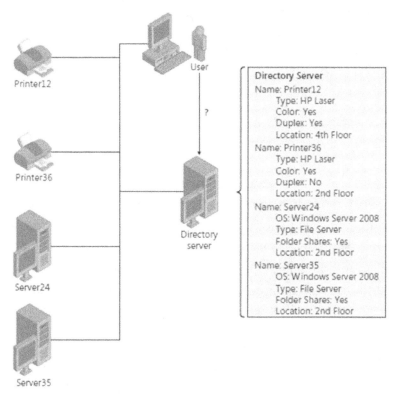

Figure 1-1 Working with directory services.

Because a directory service is a tool for both administrators and standard users, administrators can also use the directory to locate resources. For example, an administrator could locate file servers running Windows Server 2008 R2. As an organization grows and its network grows with it, there are more and more resources to manage, and the directory service becomes increasingly important.

Introducing Active Directory

Active Directory is the directory service included with Windows Server. Active Directory includes the directory that stores information about your distributed resources as well as the services that make the information useful and available. All current versions of Windows Server support Active Directory.

Active Directory Domains

Windows domains that use Active Directory are called *Active Directory domains*. In an Active Directory domain, your data resides in a single, distributed data repository that requires less administration to maintain while also allowing easy access from any location on the network. Using the physical and logical structures provided by Active Directory, you can scale the directory to meet your business and network requirements whether you have hundreds, thousands, or millions of resources.

Active Directory is designed to interoperate with other directory services and to accept requests from many different clients using a variety of interfaces, as shown in Figure 1-2. The primary protocol Active Directory uses is Lightweight Directory Access Protocol (LDAP) version 3, an industry-standard protocol for directory services. When working with other Windows servers, Active Directory supports replication through the REPL interface. When working with legacy messaging clients, Active Directory supports Messaging Application Programming Interface (MAPI). Active Directory also supports the Security Accounts Manager (SAM) interface.

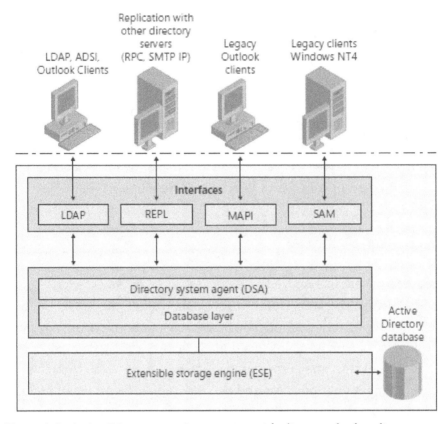

Figure 1-2 Active Directory can interoperate with clients and other directory services.

Active Directory authentication and authorization services use Kerberos version 5 and other industry-standard protocols to provide protection for data by default while maximizing flexibility. For example, by default Active Directory signs and encrypts all communications that use LDAP. Signing LDAP communications ensures data comes from a known source and has not been modified.

Active Directory is integrated with Windows Server security. As with files and folders, you can control access to distributed resources in the directory by using a granular set of permissions. You also can control access to the properties of distributed resources. Additionally, Active Directory provides security groups for administration at various levels throughout the enterprise.

In Active Directory, group policies are used to define permitted actions and settings for users and computers. Policy-based management simplifies many administration tasks. Group policies can be applied in many different ways. One way is to use security templates to configure the initial security of a computer.

DNS Domains

Active Directory uses the Domain Name System (DNS). DNS is a standard Internet service that organizes groups into a hierarchical structure. Although implemented for different reasons, Active Directory and DNS have the same hierarchical structure. The DNS hierarchy is defined on an Internet-wide basis for public networks and an enterprise-wide basis for private networks. The various levels within the DNS hierarchy identify individual computers and the relationship between computers. The relationship between computers is expressed by using domains. Computers that are part of the same DNS domain are closely related. Domains used within organizations are *organizational domains*. Domains at the root of the DNS hierarchy are *top-level,* or *root,* domains.

Active Directory clients use DNS to locate resources. DNS translates easily readable host names to numeric Internet Protocol (IP) addresses. Each computer in a domain has a fully qualified domain name (FQDN), such as server34.microsoft.com. Here, *server34* represents the name of an individual computer, *microsoft* represents the organizational domain, and *com* is the top-level domain.

Top-level domains (TLDs) are at the base of the DNS hierarchy. TLDs are organized geographically by using two-letter country codes, such as *CA* for Canada; by organization type, using codes such as *com* for commercial organizations; and by function, using codes such as *mil* for U.S. military installations.

Like top-level domains, DNS domains within an organization can be structured in many ways. Normal domains, such as microsoft.com, are also referred to as parent domains. They have this name because they're the parents of an organizational structure. You can divide parent domains into subdomains, which you can then use for different offices, divisions, or geographic locations. For example, the FQDN for a computer at Imagined Land's Denver office could be designated as workstation11.denver.imaginedlands.com. Here, *workstation11* is the computer name, *denver* is the subdomain, and *imaginedlands.com* is the parent domain. Another term for a subdomain is *child domain*.

Updates to DNS are handled through a single authoritative DNS server. This server is designated as the primary DNS server for the particular domain or area within a domain called the *zone*. The primary DNS server stores a master copy of DNS records and a domain's configuration files. Secondary DNS servers provide additional services for a domain to help balance the workload. Secondary servers store copies of DNS records obtained from a primary server through a process called a *zone transfer*. Secondary servers obtain their DNS information from a primary server when they're started, and they maintain this information until the information is refreshed or expired.

In Figure 1-3, the primary DNS server is responsible for DNS domains imaginedlands.com, data.imaginedlands.com, and recs.imaginedlands.com. Secondary DNS servers in the data.imaginedlands.com and recs.imaginedlands.com domains obtain their DNS information from this primary server through periodic zone transfers.

Active Directory depends so much on DNS that you should either configure DNS on the network before you install Active Directory or allow the Active Directory Installation wizard to install DNS for you. Configuring DNS requires installing and configuring DNS clients and DNS servers. All Windows operating systems include DNS clients and can be configured with fully qualified host names. Any computer running the Windows Server operating system can be configured as a DNS server.

When you configure Active Directory on your network, you can automatically install DNS as part of Active Directory installation. You can also specify whether DNS and Active Directory should be integrated partially or fully. As integration with Active Directory changes the way DNS works, understanding the integration options is very important.

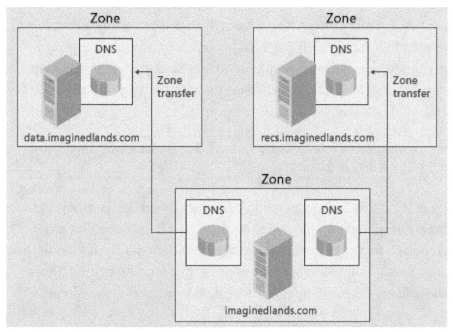

Figure 1-3 A DNS environment with zones.

With partial integration, the domain uses standard file storage, and updates to DNS are handled exactly as discussed previously. The domain has a single primary server and one or more secondary DNS servers. Secondary DNS servers obtain their DNS information from the primary DNS server.

With full integration, DNS information is stored directly in Active Directory. Because the information is part of Active Directory, you gain all the benefits of Active Directory and your domain uses Active Directory to update and maintain DNS information.

Domain Controllers

When you install Windows Server on a computer, you can configure the computer as a stand-alone server, a member server, or a domain controller.

A *domain controller* (DC) is a computer that hosts an Active Directory directory. If you are using Windows Server 2008 or Windows Server 2008 R2, you install Active Directory in two steps. First you add the Active Directory Domain Services role to the server by using the Add Role Wizard. Then you run the Active Directory Installation Wizard. If DNS isn't installed already, you are prompted to install DNS. If there isn't an existing domain, the wizard helps you create a domain and configure Active Directory in the new domain. The wizard can also help you add child domains to existing domain structures.

> **Note** Unlike earlier releases of Windows Server, Windows Server 2008 R2 runs only on 64-bit hardware.

Unlike early Windows Server operating systems, current versions of Windows Server do not designate primary or backup domain controllers. Instead, Windows Server supports a multimaster replication model. In this model, as shown in Figure 1-4, any domain controller can process directory changes and then replicate those changes to other domain controllers automatically.

This differs from the Windows NT single-master replication model, in which the primary domain controller stores a master copy and backup controllers store backup copies of the master. In addition, Windows NT distributed only the Security Accounts Manager (SAM) database, but current releases of Windows Server distribute the entire directory of information regarding distributed resources.

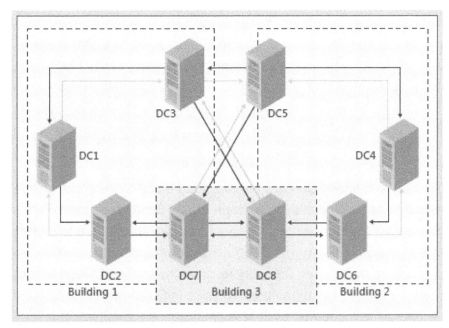

Figure 1-4 Any domain controller can replicate changes.

Real World   Because some changes are impractical to perform in multimaster fashion, Active Directory also uses single-master replication. Here, one or more domain controllers, designated as operations masters, are assigned to perform operations that are not permitted to occur at different places on the network at the same time.

Active Directory uses a multimaster approach to provide many performance and availability benefits. Multimaster replication allows you to update the directory at any domain controller. That domain controller in turn replicates the changes to other domain controllers. When you have multiple domain controllers deployed, replication continues even if any single domain controller fails.

Although Active Directory domains can function with only one domain controller, you can and should configure multiple domain controllers in your domains. This way, if one domain controller fails, you can rely on another domain controller to handle authentication and other critical tasks.

Domain controllers manage all aspects of a user's interaction with Active Directory domains. They validate user logon attempts, locate objects, and much more. Within Active Directory, directory information is logically partitioned. Each domain controller stores a copy of all pertinent partitions. The pertinent partitions for a particular domain controller are determined by where the domain controller is located and how the domain controller is used.

Domain controllers manage changes for information they store and replicate changes to other domain controllers as appropriate. Because of how replication works, a conflict can occur if an attribute is modified on a domain controller, because a change to the same attribute on another domain controller is propagated. Active Directory resolves the conflict by comparing each attribute's property version number (a value initialized when an attribute is created and updated each time an attribute is changed) and replicating the changed attribute with the higher property version number.

Normally domain controllers are readable and writable. However, Windows Server 2008, Windows Server 2008 R2 and later also support read-only domain controllers. A *read-only domain controller* (RODC) is a domain controller that hosts a read-only replica of a domain's directory. By default, RODCs store no passwords or credentials besides those used for their own computer account and the Kerberos Target (krbtgt) account. This makes RODCs ideal for branch offices where a domain controller's physical security cannot be guaranteed.

Figure 1-5 shows an RODC deployed to a branch office. Here the main office has multiple domain controllers with writable data. The branch office has an RODC with read-only data. The RODC is placed at the branch office because the physical security of the server cannot be guaranteed.

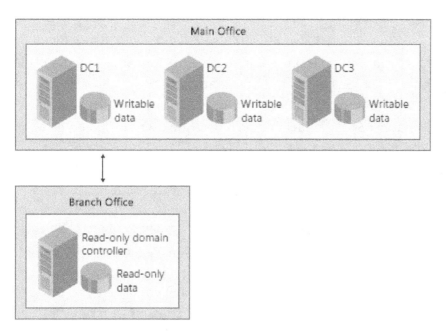

Figure 1-5 A read-only domain controller deployed to a branch office.

> **Tip** Except for passwords, RODCs store the same objects and
> attributes as writable domain controllers. These objects and attributes
> are replicated to RODCs by using unidirectional replication from a
> writable domain controller that acts as a replication partner. Although
> RODCs can pull information from domain controllers running Windows
> Server 2003, RODCs can pull updates of the domain partition only from
> a writable domain controller running Windows Server 2008 or later in
> the same domain.

RODCs pull user and computer credentials from a writable domain controller
running Windows Server 2008 or later. Then, if allowed by the Password
Replication Policy that is enforced on the writable domain controller, RODCs
cache credentials as necessary until the credentials change. Because only
subsets of credentials are stored on RODCs, the credentials that can possibly
be compromised are limited.

Active Directory Objects

Resources that you want to represent in Active Directory are created and stored as objects. Objects have attributes that define the kinds of information you want to store about resources. For example, the User object in Active Directory has attributes that help describe users, including first name, middle initial, last name, and display name. The Computer object in Active Directory has attributes that help describe computers, such as the computer's name, description, location, and security identifier.

Objects in the directory are either leaf objects or container objects. Objects that can't contain other objects are *leaf objects,* or simply *leafs*. Objects that hold other objects are referred to as *container objects,* or simply *containers*. The directory itself is a container that contains other containers and objects. In Figure 1-6, the Users object is a container that contains User objects, the Computers object is a container that contains Computer objects, and the Printers object is a container that contains Printer objects.

Each object created within the directory is of a particular class. The Active Directory schema defines the available object classes and provides rules that determine how you can create and use objects. Available object classes include User, Group, Computer, and Printer.

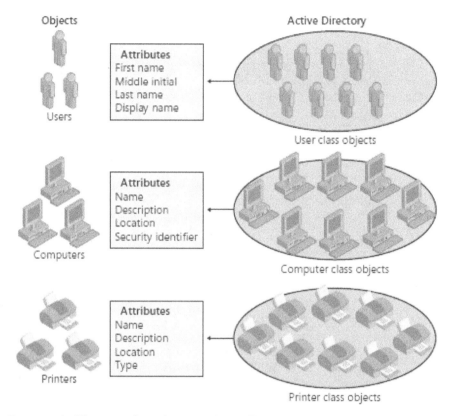

Figure 1-6 Objects and attributes in Active Directory.

Active Directory Schema

Essentially, the *schema* is a list of definitions that determines object classes and the types of information about the object classes that can be stored in the directory. The schema definitions themselves are stored as one of two types of objects:

- Schema class objects, or simply schema classes
- Schema attribute objects, or simply schema attributes

As shown in Figure 1-7, schema class objects and attribute objects are defined separately in the directory. You can refer to both sets of objects collectively as *schema objects.*

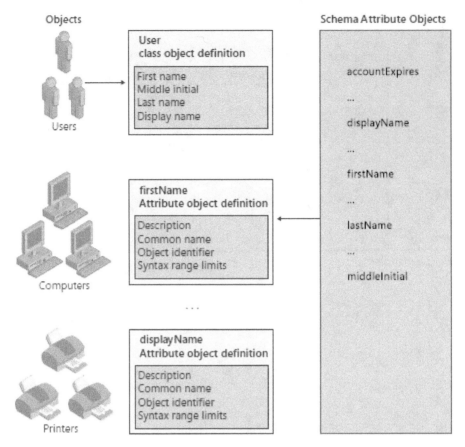

Figure 1-7 Objects within a schema.

Schema class objects describe the objects you can create. They function as templates for creating new objects. Within a particular schema class, the schema attributes store the information that describes related objects. For example, the User, Group, Computer, and Printer classes are composed of many schema attributes. The User class has attributes that describe users. The Group class has attributes that describe groups of users. The Computer class has attributes that describe computers. The Printer class has attributes that describe printers.

> **Tip** Each schema attribute is defined only once and can be used in multiple schema classes. For example, the Description attribute is defined only once in the schema but is used in the User, Group, Computer, and Printer classes as well as other classes.

A core set of schema classes and attributes is included with Active Directory. Because the directory is extensible, other application and server products can dynamically extend the schema. For example, when you install Microsoft Exchange Server in the enterprise, Exchange Server extension classes and attributes are added to the directory. Any new extensions to the directory are replicated automatically as appropriate.

> **Note** Experienced developers and administrators can extend the schema as well. However, extending the schema is an advanced procedure that should be planned and tested carefully before it is implemented. Also, keep in mind that once defined, the extended schema classes and attributes can be deactivated but cannot be deleted. You cannot deactivate or delete schema objects that are part of the default schema that ships with Active Directory.

Active Directory Components

You can use a variety of Active Directory components to define the structure of the directory. These components are organized into physical and logical layers. Physical layer components control how directory information is structured and stored. Logical layer components control how users and administrators see information in the directory and also control access to that information. The physical and logical layers are completely separate.

Physical Components

The physical components of Active Directory are sites and subnets. A *site* is a combination of one or more IP subnets connected by highly reliable links. A *subnet* is a group of network IP addresses. You use sites and subnets to create a directory structure that mirrors the physical structure of your organization.

You use sites to map your network's physical structure. As shown in Figure 1-8, a site typically has the same boundaries as your local area networks (LANs). Because site mappings are separate and independent from logical components in the directory, there's no necessary relationship between your network's physical structures and the logical structures in the directory.

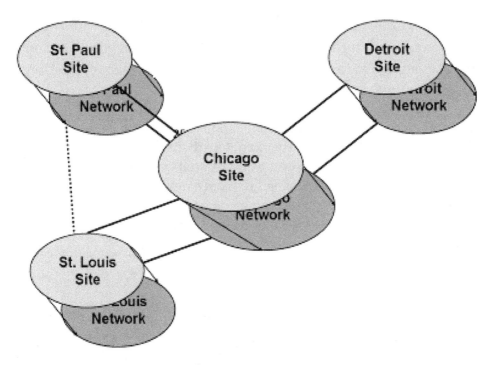

Figure 1-8 Mapping sites to network structure.

Whereas sites can be associated with multiple IP address ranges, each subnet has a specific IP address range. Subnet names are shown in the form *network/bits-masked*, such as 10.1.11.0/24. Here, the network address 10.1.11.0 and network mask 255.255.255.0 are combined to create the subnet name 10.1.11.0/24. Figure 1-9 shows the related subnets for several LANs. Each LAN is associated with two subnets. For example, the St. Paul network is associated with the 10.1.11.0/24 subnet and the 10.1.12.0/24 subnet.

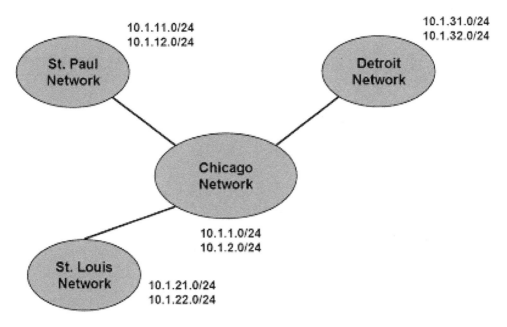

Figure 1-9 LANs within a WAN and their related subnets.

Ideally, when you group subnets into sites, you should ensure that all subnets are well connected. *Well connected* means that the subnets are connected by reliable, fast connections. Generally, fast network connections are at least 512 kilobits per second (Kbps). To also be reliable, the network connections must always be active, and there must be available bandwidth for directory communications above the normal network traffic load.

In Figure 1-10, the Detroit and St. Louis networks are connected to the Chicago network using a 512 Kbps connection and therefore are considered to be well connected. Because of this, all three networks can be part of the same site. On the other hand, the St. Paul network is connected to the Chicago network with a 256 Kbps connection and to the St. Louis network with a 128 Kbps connection. Because of this, the St. Paul network is not considered well connected and should not be part of a site that includes the other networks.

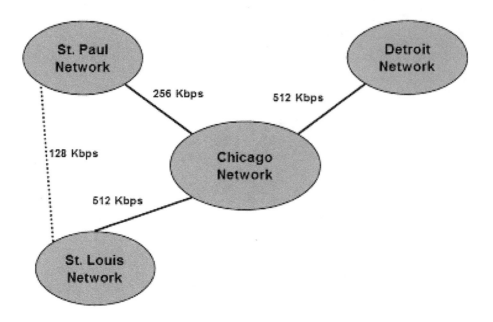

Figure 1-10 LANs within a WAN and the related connection speeds.

When you browse Active Directory, you see the logical components rather than the physical components. The reason for this is that sites and subnets are not part of the normal Active Directory namespace. Sites contain only computer objects and connection objects. These objects are used to configure replication between sites. Computers are assigned to sites based on their location in a subnet or a set of subnets.

As an administrator, you must create sites and subnets as appropriate for your organization. You must place domain controllers within sites to optimize authentication and replication.

Logical Components

The logical components of Active Directory are domains, domain trees, domain forests, and organizational units (OUs). These components help you organize resources in a logical structure. This logical structure is what is presented to users.

Domains

Domains are logical groupings of objects that share common directory databases. In the directory, domains are represented as container objects. Within a domain, you can create accounts for users, groups, and computers as well as for shared resources such as printers and folders.

In Figure 1-11, a domain object is represented by a large triangle, and the objects it contains are shown within it.

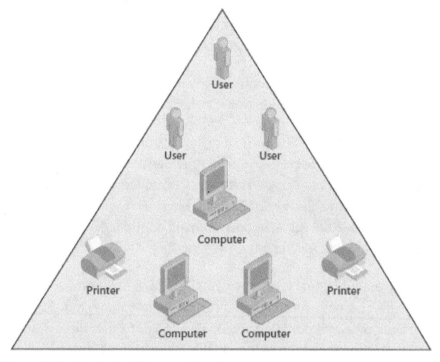

Figure 1-11 An Active Directory domain.

A domain can store millions of objects and is the parent object of all objects it stores. Keep in mind, however, that a domain stores information only about the objects it contains and that access to domain objects is controlled by security permissions. The security permissions assigned to an object determine which users can gain access to an object and what type of access any particular user has.

The directory can contain one domain or many domains. Each domain name must be unique. If the domain is part of a private network, the name assigned to a new domain must not conflict with any existing domain name on the private network. If the domain is part of the public Internet, the name assigned to a new domain must not conflict with any existing domain name throughout the Internet. Because of this, you must register public domain names through a designated registrar before using them. You can find a current list of designated registrars at InterNIC (*http://www.internic.net*).

Because a domain can span more than one physical location, a domain can span one or more sites. A single site also can include resources from multiple domains. Each domain has its own security policies and settings.

Domain functions are limited and controlled by the domain functional level. Several domain functional levels are available, including the following:

- **Windows Server 2003**   Supports domain controllers running Windows Server 2003, Windows Server 2008, Windows Server 2008 R2 and later.
- **Windows Server 2008**   Supports domain controllers running Windows Server 2008, Windows Server 2008 R2 and later.
- **Windows Server 2008 R2**   Supports domain controllers running Windows Server 2008 R2 and later.

You set the domain functional level when you install the first domain controller in a new domain. Although you can raise the domain functional level, you cannot lower the domain functional level. For further discussion of domain functional levels, see the section titled "Establishing Functional Levels" in Chapter 2, "Installing New Forests, Domain Trees, and Child Domains."

Trees

Although domains are important building blocks for implementing Active Directory structures, they are not the only building blocks. Other important building blocks are domain trees. *Domain trees* are logical groupings of domains.

> **Note**   Within the directory, the tree structure represents a hierarchy of objects, showing the parent-child relationships between the objects. The domain at the top of the tree is the root domain. The root domain is the first domain created in a new directory tree, and it is the parent of all other domains for that particular domain tree. Other domains that you create in the domain tree are child domains.

As an administrator, you create domain trees to reflect your organization's structure. Domains in a tree share a contiguous namespace. The domain name of a child domain is the relative name of the child name appended to the name of the parent domain.

In Figure 1-12, imaginedlands.com is the parent of tech.imaginedlands.com and sales.imaginedlands.com. The tech.imaginedlands.com domain has related subdomains: eng.tech.imaginedlands.com and dev.tech.imaginedlands.com. This makes tech.imaginedlands.com the parent of the child domains eng.tech.imaginedlands.com and dev.tech.imaginedlands.com.

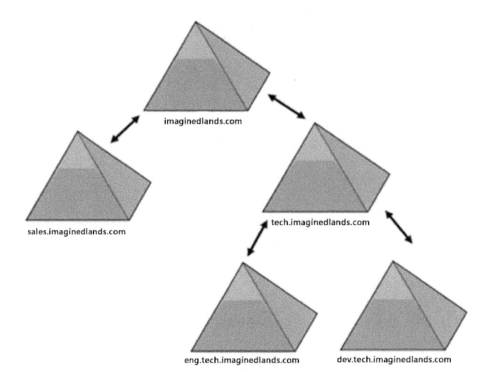

Figure 1-12 A domain tree.

Forests

Domain forests are logical groups of domain trees. Domain trees in a domain forest are separate and independent. As such, domain trees that are members of a forest do not share a contiguous namespace. In fact, when you add a new domain to Active Directory that is part of a different namespace, the domain is added as part of a new tree in the forest. For example, if Active Directory has a single tree as shown in Figure 1-12, and you add the domain reagentpress.com to the directory, the domain is added as part of a new tree in the forest, as shown in Figure 1-13. This domain becomes the root domain for the new tree.

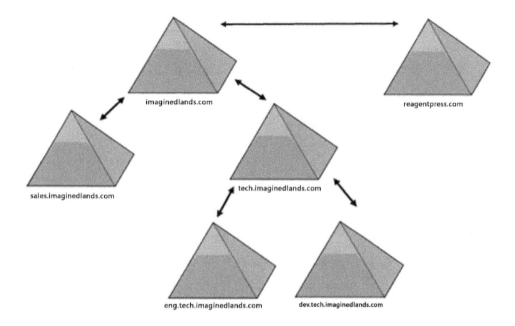

Figure 1-13 A domain forest with two domain trees.

As an administrator, you create domain forests to reflect your organization's structure. Domains in a forest operate independently but share a common schema. The forest enables communication across member domains. Like domain trees, domain forests have root domains. The first domain created in a new forest is the forest root domain. The first domain created in any additional tree within the forest is the root domain only for the additional tree. In Figure 1-14, imaginedlands.com and reagentpress.com are the root domains for their respective domain trees, but because imaginedlands.com was the first root domain created, it is the forest root domain.

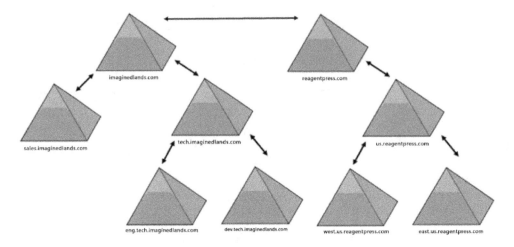

Figure 1-14 An extended domain environment.

> **Tip** Domains in a forest are connected through implicit two-way
> transitive trusts. A trust is a link between two domains in which one
> domain (referred to as the *trusting domain*) honors the logon
> authentication of another domain (referred to as the *trusted domain*).
> Trusts join parent and child domains in the same domain tree and join
> the roots of domain trees. The default protocol used for trusts is
> Kerberos version 5. For more information, see Chapter 8, "Managing
> Trusts and Authentication."

Forest functions are limited and controlled by the forest functional level.
Several forest functional levels are available, including:

- **Windows Server 2003** Supports domain controllers running Windows
  Server 2003, Windows Server 2008, Windows Server 2008 R2 and later.
  When all domains within a forest are operating in this mode, you see
  improvements in both global catalog replication and replication
  efficiency for Active Directory data. Because link values are replicated,
  you might see improved intersite replication as well. You can deactivate
  schema class objects and attributes; use dynamic auxiliary classes;
  rename domains; and create one-way, two-way, and transitive forest
  trusts.

- **Windows Server 2008**   Supports domain controllers running Windows Server 2008, Windows Server 2008 R2 and later. When all domains within a forest are operating in this mode, you see improvements in both intersite and intrasite replication throughout the organization. Domain controllers can use Distributed File System (DFS) rather than File Replication Service (FRS) for replication as well. Further, Windows Server 2008 security principals are not created until the primary domain controller (PDC) emulator operations master in the forest root domain is running Windows Server 2008. This requirement is similar to the Windows Server 2003 requirement.
- **Windows Server 2008 R2**   Supports domain controllers running Windows Server 2008 R2 and later. When a forest is operating at this level and using domain controllers running Windows Server 2008 R2 and later, domain controllers support several functionality and performance enhancements specific to the R2 release, including Deleted Object Recovery, Managed Service Accounts, and Offline Domain Join.

Organizational Units

Organizational units (OUs) are logical containers used to organize objects within a domain. Because OUs are the smallest scope to which you can delegate authority, you can use OUs to help manage administration of accounts for users, groups, and computers and for administration of other resources such as printers and shared folders.

By adding OUs to other OUs, you can create a hierarchy within a domain. Because every domain in a domain forest has its own OU hierarchy, the OU hierarchy of a domain is independent from that of other domains.

Ideally, you create OUs to make administration easier. You can use OUs to:

- Reflect the way resources and accounts are managed.
- Reflect the department structure within the organization.
- Reflect the geographic locations for business units.
- Reflect cost centers within the organization.

Following this, you might create OUs for each division or business unit within the organization. This would allow you to delegate authority to unit-level administrators who would have permissions to manage accounts and resources only within a particular business unit. If a unit-level administrator later needs permissions in another business unit, you can grant the administrator the appropriate permissions for the additional OU.

By default, all child OUs inherit permissions from parent OUs. Because of this, an administrator who has permissions for a parent OU can also manage the accounts and resources of any child OUs of that parent. For example, if North America is the parent OU and the child OUs are United States and Canada, an administrator who has permissions for North America would by default also have permissions for United States and Canada.

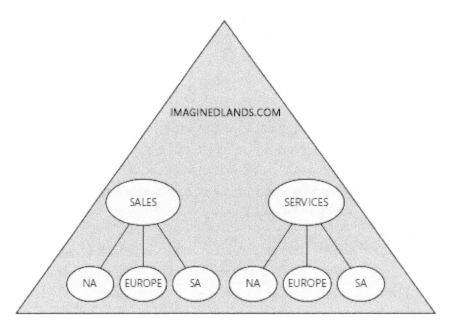

Figure 1-15 Organizational units within a domain.

In Figure 1-15, the imaginedlands.com domain uses the organization of a sales and services company with global operations in North America, Europe, and South America. Sales and Services are top-level OUs. Sales has three nested OUs: NA, Europe, and SA. Services has three nested OUs: NA, Europe, and SA. In this environment, administrators can have several levels of responsibility.

Domain administrators have permissions for the domain and all OUs. Administrators for the Sales OU have permissions for the Sales OU and its nested OUs but do not have permissions for the domain, the Services OU, or any OUs nested within the Services OU. Within the Sales OU, subadministrators for NA, Europe, or SA have permissions only for that OU.

Managing Active Directory

Administrators spend a lot of time managing Active Directory. I discuss basic tools and techniques in this section.

Working with Active Directory

When you establish domains and forests by installing domain controllers, Active Directory creates default user accounts and groups to help you manage the directory and configure access controls. Important default users and groups include:

- **Administrator** A default user account with domainwide access and privileges. By default, the Administrator account for a domain is a member of these groups: Administrators, Domain Admins, Domain Users, Enterprise Admins, Group Policy Creator Owners, and Schema Admins.
- **Administrators** A local group that provides full administrative access to an individual computer or a single domain, depending on its location. Because this group has complete access, you should be very careful about adding users to it. To make someone an administrator for a local computer or domain, all you need to do is make that person a member of this group. Only members of the Administrators group can modify this account. Default members of this group include Administrator, Domain Admins, and Enterprise Admins.

- **Domain Admins**   A global group designed to help you administer all the computers in a domain. Members of this group have administrative control over all computers in a domain because they are members of the Administrators group by default. To make someone an administrator for a domain, make that person a member of this group.
- **Enterprise Admins**   A global or universal group designed to help you administer all the computers in a domain tree or forest. Members of this group have administrative control over all computers in the enterprise because the group is a member of the Administrators group by default. To make someone an administrator for the enterprise, make that person a member of this group.
- **Group Policy Creator Owners**   A global group designed to help you administer group policies. Members of this group have administrative control over Group Policy.
- **Schema Admins**   A global group designed to help you administer Active Directory schema. Members of this group have administrative control over schema.

Whenever you work with Active Directory, be sure that you are using a user account that is a member of the appropriate group or groups.

Active Directory Administration Tools

You can manage Active Directory by using both graphical administration tools and command-line tools. The graphical tools are the easiest to work with, but if you master the command-line tools, you will often be able to accomplish tasks more quickly. When you use the command-line tools with the Task Scheduler, you might even be able to automate routine tasks.

Graphical Administration Tools

The graphical administration tools for working with Active Directory are provided as snap-ins for the Microsoft Management Console (MMC). You can access these tools directly on the Administrative Tools menu or add them to any updateable MMC. If you're using another computer with access to a Windows Server domain, the tools won't be available until you install them. One technique for installing these tools is to use the Add Feature Wizard.

Graphical tools you can use to manage Active Directory include:

- **Active Directory Domains And Trusts** Used to manage and maintain domains, domain trees, and domain forests. See Figure 1-16.

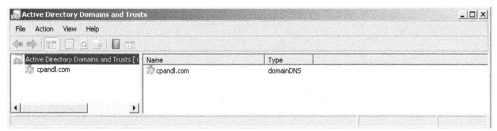

FIGURE 1-16 Active Directory Domains And Trusts.

- **Active Directory Sites And Services** Used to manage and maintain sites and subnets. See Figure 1-17.

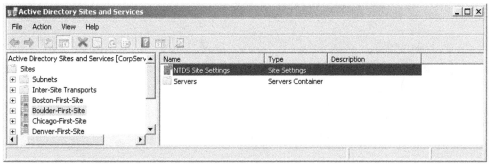

FIGURE 1-17 Active Directory Sites And Services.

- **Active Directory Users And Computers**   Used to manage and maintain accounts for users, groups, and computers. Also used to manage and maintain OUs. See Figure 1-18.

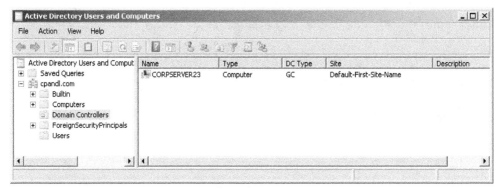

FIGURE 1-18   Active Directory Users And Computers.

- **Active Directory Schema**   Used to view and manage the schema in Active Directory. You work with object classes and attributes separately. See Figure 1-19.

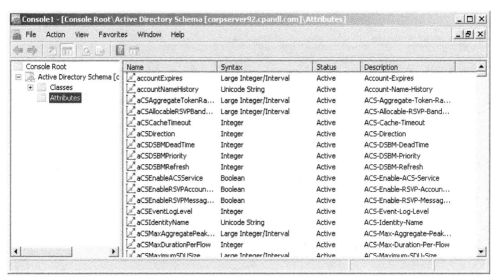

FIGURE 1-19   Active Directory Schema.

- **ADSI Edit** Used to edit the ADSI (Active Directory Service Interfaces). This low-level editor lets you manipulate objects and their attributes directly. See Figure 1-20.

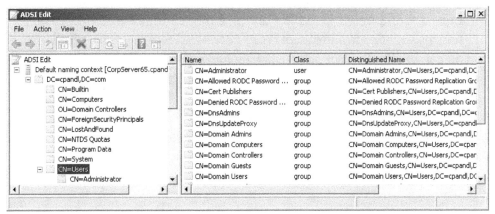

FIGURE 1-20 ADSI Edit.

Windows Server 2008 R2 includes Active Directory Administrative Center. Active Directory Administrative Center allows you to perform common Active Directory administrative tasks using an integrated console. Behind the scenes, the console uses PowerShell cmdlets to handle the administrative tasks. The same cmdlets that the console uses are available for your use at a Windows PowerShell prompt.

Although each tool has a different purpose, you can perform some common editing tasks using similar techniques. You can:

- Drag resources to new locations by selecting the objects you want to move and then pressing and holding down the left mouse button while moving the mouse.
- Edit and set properties of multiple resources by selecting the objects you want to work with, right-clicking, and then selecting the operation, such as Add To Group, Disable Account, or Properties.
- Select a series of resources at once by holding down the Shift key, selecting the first object, and then clicking the last object.
- Select multiple resources individually by holding down the Ctrl key and then clicking the left mouse button on each object you want to select.

> **Tip** Windows Firewall can affect remote administration with some MMC tools. If Windows Firewall is enabled on a remote computer and you receive an error message stating that you don't have appropriate rights, the network path isn't found, or access is denied, you might need to configure an exception on the remote computer for incoming Transmission Control Protocol (TCP) port 445. To resolve this problem, you can enable the Windows Firewall: Allow Remote Administration Exception policy setting within Computer Configuration\Administrative Templates\Network\Network Connections\Windows Firewall\Domain Profile. For more information, see Microsoft Knowledge Base Article 840634 (*http://support.microsoft.com/default.aspx?scid=kb;en-us;840634*).

Command-Line Tools

You also can manage Active Directory from the command line. Command-line tools you can use include:

- **ADPREP** Used to prepare a forest or domain for installation of domain controllers. Use **adprep /forestprep** and **adprep /domainprep** to prepare a forest or a domain, respectively. Use **adprep /domainprep /gpprep** to prepare Group Policy for the domain.
- **DSADD** Used to add computers, contacts, groups, organizational units, and users to Active Directory. Enter **dsadd objectname /?** at the command line to display Help information on using the command, such as **dsadd computer /?**.
- **DSGET** Used to display properties of computers, contacts, groups, organizational units, users, sites, subnets, and servers registered in Active Directory. Enter **dsget objectname /?** at the command line to display Help information on using the command, such as **dsget subnet /?**.
- **DSMOD** Used to modify properties of computers, contacts, groups, organizational units, users, and servers that already exist in Active Directory. Enter **dsmod objectname /?** at the command line to display Help information on using the command, such as **dsmod server /?**.

- **DSMOVE**   Used to move a single object to a new location within a single domain or to rename the object without moving it. Enter **dsmove /?** at the command line to display Help information on using the command.
- **DSQUERY**   Used to find computers, contacts, groups, organizational units, users, sites, subnets, and servers in Active Directory using search criteria. Enter **dsquery /?** at the command line to display Help information on using the command.
- **DSRM**   Used to remove objects from Active Directory. Enter **dsrm /?** at the command line to display Help information on using the command.
- **NETDOM**   Used to manage domain and trust relationships from the command line.
- **NTDSUTIL**   Used to view site, domain, and server information; manage operations masters; and perform database maintenance of Active Directory. Enter **ntdsutil /?** at the command line to display Help information on using the command.
- **REPADMIN**   Used to manage and monitor replication using the command line.

Chapter 2. Installing New Forests, Domain Trees, and Child Domains

Whether you are implementing Active Directory Domain Services (AD DS) for the first time or extending your existing Active Directory infrastructure, you should begin with a detailed design plan. At a minimum, your plan should list any prerequisites, necessary postinstallation changes, and overall impact on your network. Once you complete your planning, you will be ready to modify your infrastructure as discussed in this chapter.

To ensure your success, you must familiarize yourself with the various installation and removal methods available so that you can choose the method or methods that best meet your needs in a particular situation. For example, when you are working with a Server Core installation of Windows Server, you install from the command line or an answer file instead of using the graphical interface. The command line and answer file options are very different from the graphical interface options.

Verifying your work is a key part of the process as well. You'll need to ensure the installation or modification turned out the way you intended. If necessary, you must be able to use the available tools to troubleshoot problems you encounter.

Preparing for Active Directory Installation

Preparing for your Active Directory implementation or modification is essential. When you are adding domain controllers to install a new forest, domain tree, or domain, there are some initial decisions you'll have to make. The same is true when you are adding or removing domain controllers within existing domain structures.

In the Active Directory database, stored data is represented logically using objects. Every object in the directory has a name relative to the parent container in which it is stored. This relative name, which is simply the name of the object, is referred to as an object's common name (CN) and is stored as an attribute of the object. Because this name must be unique for the container in which it is located, no two objects in a container can have the same common name. However, two objects in different containers could have the same common name. In this case, the CN of the two objects would be the same within their respective domains, but the complete name in the directory would be different. Why? Because in addition to a common name, directory objects also have a distinguished name (DN).

An object's DN describes the object's place in the directory tree, from the highest container of which it is a member to the lowest. As the name implies, DNs are used to distinguish like-named objects. No two objects in the directory can have the same distinguished name.

The root of the directory tree is referred to as the rootDSE. The rootDSE represents the top of the logical namespace for a directory. Although the rootDSE itself has no parent, all other objects in the directory have a parent. Because it specifically relates to the domain controller on which the directory is stored, the rootDSE will have a slightly different representation on each domain controller in a domain. Below the rootDSE, every directory tree has a root domain. The root domain is the first domain created in a forest and is also referred to as the forest root domain. After you establish the forest root domain, the root never changes, even if you add new trees to the forest.

When you install Active Directory on the first domain controller in a new forest, three containers are created below the rootDSE:

- Forest Root Domain container, which is the container for the objects in the forest root domain

- Configuration container, which is the container for the default configuration and all policy information
- Schema container, which is the container for all objects, classes, attributes, and syntaxes

Active Directory uses object names to group objects into logical categories that can be managed and replicated as appropriate. The largest logical category is a directory partition. All directory partitions are created as instances of the domainDNS object class. The Forest Root Domain container, the Configuration container, and the Schema container each exist in separate Active Directory partitions.

Within Active Directory, domains themselves are simply containers of objects that are logically partitioned from other container objects. When you create a new domain in Active Directory, you create a new container object in the directory tree, and that container is in turn contained by a domain directory partition for the purposes of management and replication.

Logically apportioning data using partitions simplifies the process of distributing forestwide, domainwide, and application-specific data. Forestwide data is replicated to every domain controller in a forest. Domainwide data is replicated to every domain controller in a particular domain. Application-specific data is replicated to domain controllers that maintain a particular application partition. For example, when you integrate Active Directory with Domain Name System (DNS), domain controllers that are also DNS servers will have the default application partitions used with your DNS zones.

When you need to make changes to Active Directory, you can do so on any domain controller, and you can rely on the Active Directory built-in replication engine to replicate the changes to other domain controllers as appropriate. You can do this because every domain controller deployed in the organization is autonomous, with its own copy of the directory.

At a minimum, every domain controller stores:

- The domain directory partition for the domain of which it is a member
- The schema partition for the forest of which it is a member
- The configuration partition for the forest of which it is a member

Data in a domain directory partition is replicated to every domain controller in the domain as a writable replica. Forestwide data partitions are replicated to every domain controller in the forest. The configuration partition is replicated as a writable replica. The schema partition is replicated as a read-only replica, and the only writable replica is stored on a domain controller that is designated as having the schema operations master role. Other operations master roles are defined as well.

In addition to full replicas that are distributed within domains, Active Directory distributes partial replicas of every domain in the forest to special domain controllers designated as global catalog servers. The partial replicas stored on global catalog servers contain information on every object in the forest and are used to facilitate searches and queries for objects in the forest. Because only a subset of an object's attributes is stored, the amount of data replicated to and maintained by a global catalog server is significantly smaller than the total size of all object data stored in all the domains in the forest.

Establishing or Modifying Your Directory Infrastructure

You install new forests, domain trees, and domains by installing domain controllers in the desired namespace. Whether you are planning to establish or modify your organization's Active Directory infrastructure, there are some initial decisions you'll have to make. The same is true when you are adding or removing domain controllers within existing domain structures. Start by reviewing your organization's Active Directory infrastructure plan with regard to:

- Forests and domains
- Organizational units (OUs)
- Sites and subnets

Regarding forests and domains, it is important to keep in mind how trusts work. A trust is a link between two domains, in which one domain (referred to as the trusting domain) honors the logon authentication of another domain (referred to as the trusted domain). Within a forest, two-way, implicit trusts join parent and child domains in the same domain tree and join the roots of domain trees. Between forests, no default trusts exist. Every forest is separate and distinct from every other forest by default, and you must explicitly establish trusts between forests.

You'll want to try to limit your Active Directory infrastructure to one forest. Otherwise, you'll have to maintain multiple schemas, configuration containers, global catalogs, and trusts, and users will have additional required steps when working with the directory. However, you might need multiple forests when your organization has autonomous business units; when you need to isolate the schema, configuration container, or global catalog; or when there is a need to limit the scope of trust relationships within the organization. For example, you might want the members of your research and development unit to be able to access resources in other business units but not want to allow anyone outside the research and development unit to access its resources.

In some situations, you might not have control over whether your organization has multiple forests. For example, as the result of a merger or acquisition, your organization might gain one or more new forests. In this case, you'll probably need to configure the forests to work with each other by establishing the appropriate trust relationships between the forests.

With multiple forests, you no longer have a single top-level unit for sharing and managing resources. You have separate structures that are autonomous and isolated from one another. By default, forests do not share schema, configuration information, trusts, global catalogs, or forestwide administrators.

You can join forests using cross-forest trusts. Unlike interforest trusts, which are two way and transitive by default, cross-forest trusts are either two way or one way. With a two-way trust, users in either forest have access to resources in the other forest. With a one-way trust, users in one forest have access to resources in the other forest but not vice versa.

When you're establishing a new forest, the first domain you install becomes the forest root domain. The forest root domain can be either a nondedicated root or a dedicated root. A nondedicated root is used as a normal part of the directory. It has user and group accounts associated with it and is used to assign access to resources. A dedicated root, also referred to as an *empty root,* is used as a placeholder to establish the directory base. No user or group accounts are associated with it other than accounts created when the forest root is installed and accounts that are needed to manage the forest. Because no additional user or group accounts are associated with it, a dedicated root domain is not used to assign access to resources.

When you plan to have multiple domains, using a dedicated root domain makes sense. An empty root is easier to manage than a root domain that contains user accounts and resources. It allows you to separate the root domain from the rest of the forest. This is important because the forest root domain cannot be replaced. If the root domain is destroyed and cannot be recovered, you must re-create the entire forest.

> **Tip** The forest root domain contains the forestwide administrator accounts (Enterprise Admins and Schema Admins) and the forestwide operations masters (domain naming master and schema master). It must be available when users log on to domains other than their home domain and when users access resources in other domains.

Within a forest, you define a domain hierarchy by determining the number of domain trees, designating tree root domains, and defining the hierarchy of any required subdomains. You name domains by assigning a DNS name to the forest root domain of each forest, to the tree root domain of each tree, and to each remaining subdomain. Once you create a domain and establish a new namespace, you cannot easily restructure or rename it.

> **Real World**   Using the Domain Rename utility (Rendom.exe), which is now included with Windows Server, you can rename domains. However, you cannot use the Domain Rename utility to change which domain is the forest root domain. Although you *can* change the name of the forest root domain so that it is no longer the forest root logically, the domain remains the forest root domain physically in Active Directory.

Before adding a domain tree or child domain to an existing forest, you'll want to consider the increased overhead and hardware costs. The reason for using multiple domains should not be based solely on the number of users, groups, and other objects. Although the number of objects is a factor to consider from a manageability standpoint, a single domain can have millions of objects.

To ensure availability and allow for disaster recovery, every domain should have two or more domain controllers. Some reasons you might want to create additional domains are to:

- Establish distinct namespaces.
- Optimize replication traffic.
- Meet special security or administrative requirements.

Regardless of whether your forest uses a single namespace or multiple namespaces, additional domains in the same forest have the following characteristics:

- **Share common forestwide administrators**   All domains in the forest have the same top-level administrators: Enterprise Admins, who are the only administrators with forestwide privileges; and Schema Admins, who are the only administrators with the right to modify the schema.
- **Share a common global catalog**   All domains in the forest have the same global catalog, and it stores a partial replica of all objects in the forest.

- **Share a common trust configuration**   All domains in the forest are configured to trust all the other domains in the forest, and the trust is two way and transitive.
- **Share a common schema**   All domain controllers in the forest have the same schema, and a single schema master is designated for the forest.
- **Share a common configuration directory partition**   All domain controllers share the same configuration container, and it stores the default configuration and policy information.

With multiple locations, domain changes need to be replicated to all domain controllers, and geographic separation is often a deciding factor. Primarily, this is because there is less replication traffic between domains than within domains (relatively speaking). Therefore, if business locations are geographically separated, it makes sense to limit the replication traffic between locations if possible, and one way to do this is to create multiple domains.

Even within a single business location, the need to limit replication traffic can be a deciding factor for using multiple domains. For example, a large organization with users in multiple buildings in a campus setting may find that the connection speed between locations isn't adequate, and it may be necessary to use multiple domains to limit replication traffic.

As part of establishing forest and domain structures, you'll also have to determine the placement of DNS servers. To ensure proper name resolution, your Active Directory forest will need to have authoritative DNS servers for each domain. If you allow DNS to be configured automatically when you install Active Directory, the new domain controller is automatically set to meet the DNS requirements for joining Active Directory. However, if you installed DNS manually or if your architecture doesn't allow dynamic DNS updates, you'll need to:

- Ensure the _ldap._tcp.dc._msdcs.*DNSDomainName* (SRV) resource record exists in DNS, where *DNSDomainName* is the DNS name of the Active Directory domain.

- Ensure a host (A) resource record for the DNS name of the domain controllers is specified in the data field of the SRV resource record.

Before you install Active Directory, you should ensure the server has a static IP address. If DNS is already set up and the server won't also act as a DNS server, you'll want to designate preferred and alternate DNS servers. If the domain controller will also act as a DNS server, you can set the preferred DNS server to the local loopback address 127.0.0.1 and remove any alternate DNS server (or allow the setup process to do this for you when you install Active Directory).

After reviewing your organization's forest and domain plans, you should review your organizational unit (OU) plan. Within domains, you use OUs to help manage administration of accounts for users, groups, and computers and for administration of other resources such as printers and shared folders. The result of your planning should be a diagram of OU structures for each domain and a list of user groups in each OU.

In a manner similar to the way you use OUs to group users and resources, you use sites to group computers. However, whereas forests, domains, and OUs are logical groupings, sites are physical groupings. Sites reflect the physical structure of your organization's network and are used to optimize network traffic. You define a site for each LAN or set of LANs connected by a high-speed backbone. Any location that is not well connected or is reachable only by SMTP e-mail should be in its own site.

> **Tip** As you design your sites, you also want to determine how other network resources fit into this architecture. You should design sites with Domain Name System (DNS), Dynamic Host Configuration Protocol (DHCP), Distributed File System (DFS) file shares, certificate authorities, Microsoft Exchange servers, and other essential services in mind. Ideally, you want to configure sites so that client queries for a particular network resource can be answered within the site. If every client query for a network resource has to be sent to a remote site, there could be substantial network traffic between sites, which could be a problem over slow WAN links. However, the ideal configuration

isn't always possible or practical, and you'll need to carefully evaluate the placement of each resource separately.

Within sites, you'll want to place domain controllers strategically because the availability of Active Directory depends on the availability of domain controllers. A domain controller must always be available so users can be authenticated. For optimum availability and response time, you'll want to ensure the following:

- Each site has at least one domain controller.
- Each domain has at least two domain controllers.

Because replication between sites occurs over site links, you'll want to ensure site links are configured properly. An effective strategy ensures efficient replication and fault tolerance. If a link to a site is unreliable, intermittent, or saturated, you'll want to consider placing additional domain controllers in the site.

Every domain must have at least one global catalog server. By default, the first domain controller installed in a domain is set as that domain's global catalog server. You can change the global catalog server, and you can designate additional servers as global catalog servers as necessary.

When you are configuring sites, designate global catalog servers as necessary to accommodate forestwide directory searching and to facilitate domain client logons when universal groups are available. When universal groups are available in a domain, a domain controller must be able to locate a global catalog server to process a logon request.

For remote locations, you should determine whether read-only domain controllers (RODCs) are appropriate. Additionally, if the wide area network (WAN) link between the remote site and the hub site is limited, you can use universal group membership caching in the remote site to accommodate the logon needs of users in the site. Do not place the global catalog on a domain controller that hosts the infrastructure operations master role in the domain (unless all domain controllers in the domain are global catalog servers or the forest has only one domain).

Establishing Functional Levels

Functional levels affect the inner workings of Active Directory and are used to enable features that are compatible with the installed server versions of the Windows operating system. Each forest and each domain within a forest can be assigned a functional level.

The functional level for a domain within a forest is referred to as the *domain functional level*. When you set a domain's functional level, the level of functionality applies only to that domain. Other domains in the forest can have a different functional level.

Domain functional levels available include:

- **Windows Server 2003 mode**   Supports domain controllers running Windows Server 2003, Windows Server 2008, Windows Server 2008 R2 and later. A domain operating in Windows Server 2003 mode can use universal groups, group nesting, group type conversion, easy domain controller renaming, update logon time stamps, and Kerberos KDC key version numbers.
- **Windows Server 2008 mode**   Supports domain controllers running Windows Server 2008, Windows Server 2008 R2 and later. Also supports additional Active Directory features, including the DFS replication service for enhanced intersite and intrasite replication.
- **Windows Server 2008 R2 mode**   Supports domain controllers running Windows Server 2008 R2 and later. Also supports additional Active Directory features, including the Active Directory Recycle Bin.

Raising the functional level changes the operating systems that are supported for domain controllers and supported Active Directory features. Although you can raise the domain functional level, you cannot lower it when you are working with any of the previously listed functional levels.

When the domain functional level is Windows Server 2003, File Replication Service (FRS) is used to replicate the SYSVOL. FRS enables interoperability with Windows 2000 Server and Windows Server 2003 but does not support the latest replication enhancements. When the domain functional level is Windows Server 2008 or later, Distributed File System (DFS) can be used to replicate the SYSVOL, and the latest replication enhancements are available, including replication of changes only within files, bandwidth throttling, and improved replication topology.

Domains in Windows Server 2003 mode can use many improved Active Directory features, including group nesting, group type conversion, universal groups, easy domain controller renaming, update logon time stamps, migration of security principals, and Kerberos KDC key version numbers. Applications can use constrained delegation to take advantage of the secure delegation of user credentials through the Kerberos authentication protocol. Authorization Manager can store its authentication policies in Active Directory. You can redirect the Users and Computers containers to define a new well-known location for user and computer accounts. You also can implement selective authentication by specifying users and groups from a trusted forest who are allowed to authenticate to resources in a trusting forest.

Windows Server 2008 domain functional level adds features beyond those available with Windows Server 2003. Distributed File System Replication for SYSVOL provides more robust and granular replication of SYSVOL, including replication of only the changes within files, bandwidth throttling, and improved replication topology. Advanced Encryption Standard (AES) support allows user accounts to use AES 128-bit or AES 256-bit encryption. Last interactive logon information displays the time of the last successful interactive logon for a user, the number of failed logon attempts since the last logon, and the time of the last failed logon. Fine-grained password policies make it possible for password and account lockout policy to be specified for user and global security groups in a domain.

The functional level for a forest is referred to as the *forest functional level.* Forest functional levels available include:

- **Windows Server 2003**   Supports domain controllers running Windows Server 2003, Windows Server 2008, Windows Server 2008 R2 and later.
- **Windows Server 2008**   Supports domain controllers running Windows Server 2008, Windows Server 2008 R2 and later.
- **Windows Server 2008 R2**   Supports domain controllers running Windows Server 2008 R2 and later.

As with the domain functional level, you can raise the forest functional level, but you cannot lower it. When you raise the forest functional level to Windows Server 2008, all domains using the Windows 2000 native domain functional level or higher are automatically raised to the Windows Server 2008 domain functional level.

Forests operating in Windows 2000 mode can't use many current Active Directory features and have a limited capability. They cannot use extended two-way trusts between forests, domain rename, domain restructure using renaming, or any of the replication enhancements introduced with Windows Server 2003. On the other hand, Windows Server 2003 forest functional level supports all of these features, including:

- Linked-value replication, which improves the replication of changes to group memberships.
- Improved Knowledge Consistency Checker (KCC) algorithms and more efficient generation of complex replication topologies.
- Improved Intersite Topology Generator (ISTG) algorithms and more efficient scaling across all sites in a forest.
- Ability to create application group groups and query groups for role-based authorization.
- Ability to deactivate and redefine classes and attributes in Active Directory schema.
- Ability to convert inetOrgPerson objects to User object instances and vice versa.

- Ability to set the userPassword attribute as the effective password on inetOrgPerson and User objects.
- Ability to deploy read-only domain controllers running Windows Server 2008.

The Windows Server 2008 forest functional level offers incremental improvements over the Windows Server 2003 forest functional level in Active Directory performance and features. When all domains within a forest are operating in this mode, you'll see improvements in both intersite and intrasite replication throughout the organization. Domain controllers can use Distributed File System (DFS) replication rather than File Replication Service (FRS) replication as well. In addition, Windows Server 2008 security principals are not created until the primary domain controller (PDC) emulator operations master in the forest root domain is running Windows Server 2008.

Active Directory Domain Service in Windows Server 2008 R2 has many new features that give administrators additional options. When you have deployed Windows Server 2008 R2 or later on all domain controllers throughout the domains in your Active Directory forest, your domains can operate at the Windows Server 2008 R2 domain functional level, and the forest can operate at the Windows Server 2008 R2 forest functional level. These operating levels allow you to take advantage of Active Directory enhancements that improve manageability, performance, and supportability, including:

- **Active Directory Recycle Bin** Allows administrators to undo the accidental deletion of Active Directory objects in much the same way as they can recover deleted files from the Windows Recycle Bin.
- **Authentication Mechanism Assurance** Improves the authentication process by allowing administrators to control resource access based on whether a user logs on using a certificate-based logon method. This allows an administrator to specify that a user has one set of access permissions when logged on using a smart card and a different set of access permissions when not logged on using a smart card.

- **Managed service accounts**   Introduces a special type of domain user account for managed services that reduces service outages and other issues by having Windows manage the account password and related Service Principal Names (SPNs) automatically.
- **Managed virtual accounts**   Introduces a special type of local computer account for managed services that provides the ability to access the network with a computer identity in a domain environment.

> **Note**   Although you can use managed service accounts and managed virtual accounts in a mixed-mode domain environment, there are several important caveats. First, you must update the Active Directory schema for Windows Server 2008 R2. Second, you must manually manage SPNs for managed service accounts.

Other improvements for Windows Server 2008 R2 don't require that you raise domain or forest functional levels, but they do require that you use Windows Server 2008 R2. These improvements include:

- **Active Directory Administrative Center**   Provides a task-orientated interface for managing Active Directory. A related option is on the Administrative Tools menu.
- **Active Directory module for Windows PowerShell**   Provides cmdlets for managing Active Directory when you are working with Windows PowerShell. A related option is on the Administrative Tools menu.
- **Active Directory Web Services**   Introduces a Web service interface for Active Directory domains.
- **Offline domain join**   Allows administrators to preprovision computer accounts in the domain to prepare operating systems for deployment. This allows computers to join a domain without having to contact a domain controller.

Deploying Windows Server 2008 and R2

Before you deploy Windows Server 2008 or Windows Server 2008 R2 for the first time, there are preparations you must make. First, you should run

Adprep to prepare the forest schema before you can install the first domain controller that runs Windows Server 2008 or Windows Server 2008 R2.

After you prepare the forest schema, you must verify that the domain naming master operations master role is hosted on a domain controller that runs either Windows Server 2003, Windows Server 2008 or later. Then you need to prepare the domain schema for any domain where you plan to install a domain controller that runs Windows Server 2008 or Windows Server 2008 R2.

Windows Server 2008 and later support both writable and read-only domain controllers. If you plan to install an RODC in the forest after you install the initial Windows Server 2008 or Windows Server 2008 R2 domain controller, you must also prepare the forest for RODCs. You only need to prepare a forest one time for RODCs

You can prepare a forest by completing the following steps:

1. Log on to the schema master using an account that is a member of Enterprise Admins and Schema Admins. Additionally, the account must be a member of Domain Admins for the domain that contains the schema master.

2. As appropriate, insert the Windows Server 2008 or Windows Server 2008 R2 DVD into the DVD drive.

3. Start an elevated, administrator command prompt by clicking Start, right-clicking Command Prompt, and then clicking Run As Administrator.

4. Type the following command, and then press Enter: **D:\sources\adprep\adprep /forestprep** where D: is the drive designator of the DVD drive.

5. If you plan to install an RODC in any domain in the forest, type the following, and then press Enter: **D:\sources\adprep\adprep /rodcprep** where D: is the drive designator of the DVD drive.

6. Wait for the operation to complete, and then wait for the changes to replicate throughout the forest before you prepare your domains.

> **Note** Unlike adprep /forestprep, which must be run on the schema master, you can run adprep /rodcprep on any computer in the forest. Note any errors. If you receive a message that says that not all application partitions have been updated, you'll need to rerun the adprep /rodcprep command.

You can prepare a domain by completing the following steps:

1. Log on to the infrastructure master using an account that is a member of the Domain Admins group.

2. As appropriate, insert the Windows Server 2008 or Windows Server 2008 R2 DVD into the DVD drive.

3. Start an elevated, administrator command prompt by clicking Start, right-clicking Command Prompt, and then clicking Run As Administrator.

4. Type the following command, and then press Enter: **D:\sources\adprep\adprep /domainprep** where D: is the drive designator of the DVD drive.

5. Wait for the operation to complete, and then wait for the changes to replicate before you install your domain controllers.

Creating Forests, Domain Trees, and Child Domains

Any server running Windows Server can act as a domain controller. You configure a server as a domain controller by installing the necessary binaries for the Active Directory Domain Services (AD DS) and then configuring AD DS using the Active Directory Domain Services Installation Wizard (Dcpromo.exe).

When you are creating a domain controller in a new forest, domain tree, or domain, you should log on to the local machine using either the local Administrator account or an account that has administrator privileges on the local machine. Then start the installation. The Administrator account will be created as a user account in the new domain, with full administrator permissions. This means the account will be a member of the Users, Domain Users, and Domain Admins groups.

As you are creating the new forest, the server should have a static IP address. After you install DHCP servers in the new forest, you can assign the domain controller a dynamic IP address. However, domain controllers that also act as DNS servers should not have dynamic IP addresses. The reason for this is that the IP address of a DNS server should be fixed to ensure reliable DNS operations.

Installing the AD DS Binaries

The AD DS binaries include the Windows components that enable servers to act as domain controllers as well as the related administration tools. You can install the Active Directory binaries by entering the following command at an elevated command prompt: **servermanagercmd –install adds-domain-controller**. This installs the AD DS binaries, which enables the Active Directory Domain Services role on the server.

You also can use the Add Role feature in Server Manager to perform this procedure. Follow these steps:

1. Start Server Manager by clicking Start and then clicking Server Manager.
2. In Roles Summary, click Add Roles. As necessary, review the Welcome page and then click Next.
3. On the Select Server Roles page, select Active Directory Domain Services, and then click Next. As necessary, review the Start page and then click Next.
4. On the Confirm Installation Selections page, click Install. When the installation completes, click Close.

Real World   Before starting an Active Directory installation, you should examine local accounts and check for encrypted files and folders by using the EFSInfo utility. Because domain controllers do not have local accounts or separate cryptographic keys, making a server a domain controller deletes all local accounts and all certificates and cryptographic keys from the server. Any encrypted data on the server, including data stored using the Encrypting File System (EFS), must be decrypted before installing Active Directory, or it will be permanently inaccessible.

Creating New Forests

You can create a new forest by installing a domain controller in the desired namespace by using these steps:

1. Start the Active Directory Domain Services Installation Wizard by clicking Start, typing **dcpromo** in the Search box, and pressing Enter. Before the wizard starts, it checks to ensure the AD DS binaries are installed. If you haven't installed the AD DS binaries, the wizard installs them. After installing the AD DS binaries as necessary, the wizard displays an introductory page.

2. By default, the wizard uses Basic Installation mode. If you want to set the NetBIOS name of the domain, select Use Advanced Mode Installation, as shown in Figure 2-1, before clicking Next to continue.

FIGURE 2-1 Set the installation mode.

3. If the Operating System Compatibility page is displayed, review the warning about the default security settings for domain controllers and then click Next.

4. On the Choose A Deployment Configuration page, select Create A New Domain In A New Forest, as shown in Figure 2-2, and then click Next.

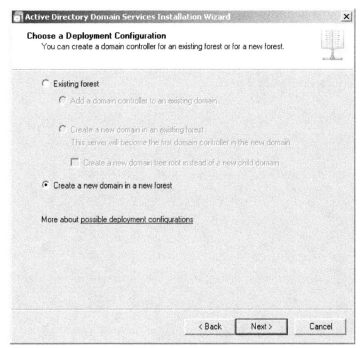

FIGURE 2-2 Create a new domain in a new forest.

5. On the Name Of The Forest Root Domain page, enter the full DNS name for the first domain in the new forest, as shown in Figure 2-3, and then click Next. Domain names are not case sensitive and use the letters A to Z, the numerals 0 to 9, and the hyphen (-) character. Each component of the domain name must be separated by a dot (.) and cannot be longer than 63 characters.

6. The wizard determines whether the name you've entered is already in use on your network. If the name is already in use, you will need to enter a different name or go back and make a different configuration selection. Once the wizard validates the domain name, it uses the name to generate a default NetBIOS name. If you are using advanced installation mode or the wizard has detected a conflict, you will be able to accept the wizard-generated name or enter a new NetBIOS name of up to 15 characters, as shown in Figure 2-4, and then click Next to continue.

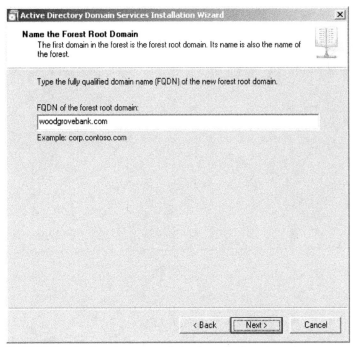

FIGURE 2-3 Set the name of the forest's first domain.

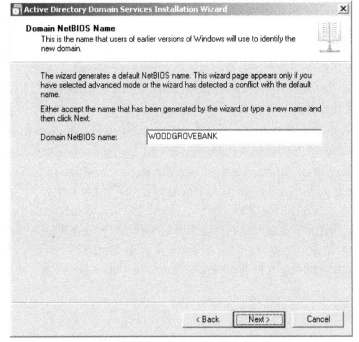

FIGURE 2-4 Set the NetBIOS name for the domain.

7. On the Set Forest Functional Level page, choose the desired functional level for the new Active Directory forest, as shown in Figure 2-5, and then click Next. As discussed previously in "Establishing Functional Levels," the forest functional level can be set to Windows Server 2003, Windows Server 2008 or Windows Server 2008 R2.

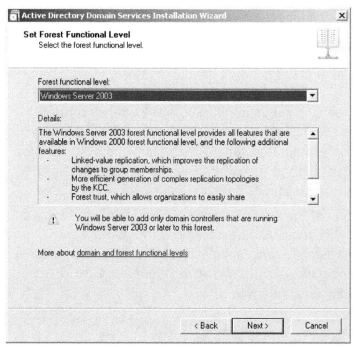

FIGURE 2-5 Set the forest functional level.

8. If you set the forest functional level to Windows 2008 or Windows Server 2008 R2, the domain functional level is set automatically to Windows Server 2008 or Windows Server 2008 R2 and you do not see the Set Domain Functional page. Otherwise, on the Set Domain Functional Level page, choose the desired functional level for the new domain and then click Next. The domain functional level can be set to Windows 2003, Windows 2008 or Windows Server 2008 R2.

9. The wizard examines the network environment and attempts to register the domain and the domain controller in DNS. If the wizard detects that no DNS server is available, DNS Server will be selected as an additional option on the Additional Domain Controller Options page, and the descriptive text also will recommend that you install the

DNS Server service. If you plan to use Active Directory–integrated DNS, ensure the DNS Server option is selected. If you have an existing DNS infrastructure and you do not want this domain controller to be a DNS server, clear the DNS Server check box. Because the first domain controller in a new forest must be a global catalog and cannot be a read-only domain controller, the global catalog option is selected and cannot be cleared, and the read-only domain controller option is dimmed. Click Next.

10. If you choose to let the wizard install the DNS Server service, note the following:

   a. The DNS Server service will be installed, and the domain controller will also act as a DNS server. A primary DNS zone will be created as an Active Directory–integrated zone with the same name as the new domain you are setting up. The wizard will also update the server's TCP/IP configuration so that its primary DNS server is set to itself.

   b. During installation of the operating system, Windows Setup installs and configures IPv4 and IPv6 if networking components were detected. If you've configured dynamic IPv4, IPv6, or both addresses, you'll see a warning message, as shown in Figure 2-6. Click Yes to ignore the warning and continue.

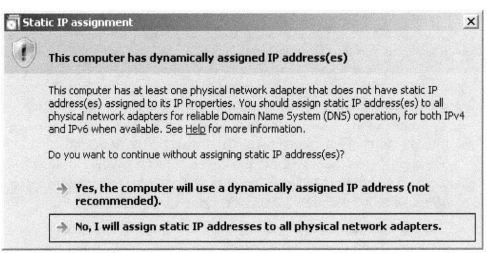

FIGURE 2-6 Determine whether the server should have static or dynamic IP addressing.

c. If you want to modify the TCP/IP configuration, click No to return to the Additional Domain Controller Options page, and then make the appropriate changes to the system configuration before clicking Next to continue. If you configure a static IPv4 address but do not configure a static IPv6 address, you'll also see the warning. To ignore the warning and continue with the installation, click Yes.

Note   At a minimum, you should configure a static IPv4 address before continuing. Click Start, type **ncpa.cpl** in the Search box, and then press Enter. In Network Connections, double-click Local Area Connection. In Local Area Connection Properties, click Properties and then double-click Internet Protocol Version 4 (TCP/IPv4), make any necessary changes, and then click OK. If you also want to configure a static IPv6 address, double-click Internet Protocol Version 6 (TCP/IPv6), make any necessary changes, and then click OK. If you decide not to configure a static IPv6 address, you may need to make changes to DNS records later if your organization starts using IPv6 addresses.

d. The wizard next attempts to register a delegation for the DNS server with an authoritative parent zone. If you are integrating with an existing DNS infrastructure, you should manually create a delegation to the DNS server and then click Yes to continue. Otherwise, you can ignore this warning and click Yes to continue.

11. If you choose to not let the wizard install the DNS Server service, the wizard next attempts to register a delegation for the DNS server with an authoritative parent zone. If the wizard cannot create a delegation for the DNS server, it displays a warning message, as shown in Figure 2-7, to indicate that you must create the delegation manually. Click No to return to the Additional Domain Controller Options page so you can select and install DNS Server services. To continue without installing DNS Server services, click Yes. Keep in mind that you'll then need to manually configure the required DNS settings, including SRV and A resource records.

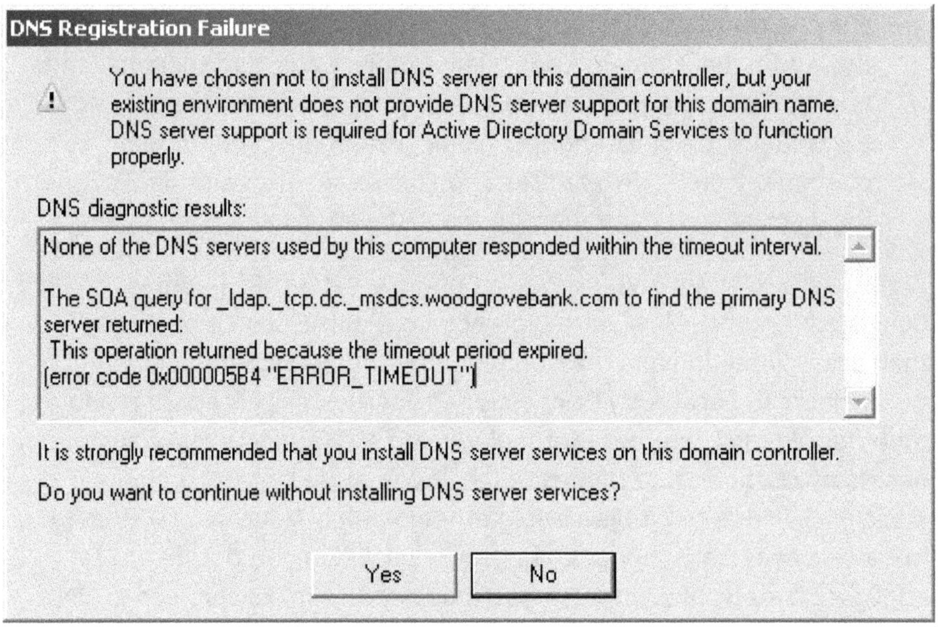

DNS Registration Failure

⚠ You have chosen not to install DNS server on this domain controller, but your existing environment does not provide DNS server support for this domain name. DNS server support is required for Active Directory Domain Services to function properly.

DNS diagnostic results:

None of the DNS servers used by this computer responded within the timeout interval.

The SOA query for _ldap._tcp.dc._msdcs.woodgrovebank.com to find the primary DNS server returned:
 This operation returned because the timeout period expired.
(error code 0x000005B4 "ERROR_TIMEOUT")

It is strongly recommended that you install DNS server services on this domain controller.

Do you want to continue without installing DNS server services?

[Yes] [No]

FIGURE 2-7 Determine whether the DNS Server service should be available.

12. On the Location For Database, Log Files, And SYSVOL page, select a location to store the Active Directory database folder, log folder, and SYSVOL, as shown in Figure 2-8, and then click Next. The default location for the database and log folders is a subfolder of %SystemRoot%\NTDS. The default location for the SYSVOL folder is %SystemRoot%\Sysvol. You'll get better performance if the database and log folders are on two separate volumes, each on a separate disk. Placement of the SYSVOL is less critical, and you can accept the default in most cases. Although you can change the storage locations later, the process is lengthy and complex.

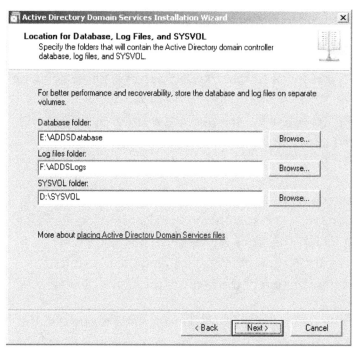

FIGURE 2-8 Configure storage locations for Active Directory data.

> **Note**   Your organization should have a specific plan in place for sizing the server hardware and designating Active Directory storage locations. You'll want to ensure the server you use is powerful enough to handle authentication, replication, and other directory duties. The server's hard disk configuration should be optimized for storage of Active Directory data. Each storage volume should have at least 20 percent free storage space at all times. You may also want to use a redundant array of independent disks (RAID) to protect against disk failure.

13. On the Directory Services Restore Mode Administrator Password page, type and confirm the password that should be used when you want to start the computer in Directory Services Restore mode. Be sure to track this password carefully. This special password is used only in Restore mode and is different from the Administrator account password. Click Next.

14. On the Summary page, review the installation options. If desired, click Export Settings to save these settings to an answer file that you can

use to perform unattended installation of other domain controllers. When you click Next again, the wizard will use the options you've selected to install and configure Active Directory. This process can take several minutes. If you specified that the DNS Server service should be installed, the server will also be configured as a DNS Server at this time.

15. When the wizard finishes configuring Active Directory, click Finish. You are then prompted to restart the computer. Click Restart Now to reboot.

After installing Active Directory, you should verify the installation. Start by examining the installation log, which is stored in the Dcpromo.log file in the %SystemRoot%\Debug folder. The log is very detailed and takes you through every step of the installation process, including the creation of directory partitions and the securing of the Registry for Active Directory.

Next, check the DNS configuration in the DNS console. DNS is updated to add SRV and A records for the server. Because you created a new domain, DNS is updated to include a Forward Lookup Zone for the domain. You may also need to add a Reverse Lookup Zone for the domain.

Check for updates in Active Directory Users And Computers. Because you created a new domain, the following containers are created and populated as appropriate:

- Builtin contains the built-in accounts for administration, including Administrators and Account Operators.
- Computers contains computer accounts for the domain.
- Domain Controllers contains the domain controller accounts and should have an account for the domain controller you installed.
- ForeignSecurityPrincipals is a container for security principals from other domain trees.
- Users is the default container for user accounts in the domain.

On a Full Server or Core Server installation of Windows Server, you can add a new forest using an unattended installation or the command line. You must be logged on as the local Administrator for the computer and also must ensure the Administrator password isn't blank. If the password is blank, you can set the password to a desired value by entering **net user Administrator /passwordreq:yes** at a command prompt and then entering a password when prompted.

With the unattended method of installation, you must first prepare an answer file that contains the desired configuration values. You can create an answer file for installing a new forest by completing the following steps:

1. Open Notepad or any other text editor.

2. If you want to enter comments into the answer file, start each comment line with a semicolon (;). A line that begins with a semicolon (;) is interpreted as a comment.

> **Tip** You can tell Dcpromo not to apply an option by preceding an option with a semicolon and a space. In answer files, you'll often see options that are commented out in this way. Commenting out an option is an easy way to not apply an option while ensuring you can easily apply the option later.

3. On the first line, type **[DCINSTALL]**, and then press Enter.

4. Type the following entries, one entry on each line:

```
ReplicaOrNewDomain=Domain
NewDomain=Forest
NewDomainDNSName=FullyQualifiedDNSName
ForestLevel=ForestFunctionalLevel
DomainNetBiosName=NetBiosName
DomainLevel=DomainFunctionalLevel
InstallDNS=Yes
ConfirmGc=Yes
CreateDNSDelegation=No
DatabasePath="LocalDatabasePath"
LogPath="LocalLogPath"
SYSVOLPath="LocalSysVolPath"
SafeModeAdminPassword=
RebootOnCompletion=Yes
```

> **Note** Values you must specify are shown in bold. SafeModeAdminPassword sets the Directory Services Restore mode password in the answer file. If you don't want to include the password,

you enter a blank value. However, you will need to use the /SafeModeAdminPassword command-line parameter to provide the password later when you run Dcpromo to initiate the unattended installation.

Tip   Table 2-1 details how each parameter is used. In this example, by setting InstallDNS to *yes*, you ensure the DNS Server service is installed. You set ReplicaOrNewDomain to domain because you are installing a new domain rather than an additional *domain* controller. You set NewDomain to *forest* because you are creating a new forest. Be sure to set ForestLevel and DomainLevel to a value that supports the operating systems you plan to use. For example, you could specify *ForestLevel=2* to set the forest functional level to Windows Server 2003.

The following is a complete example:

```
; New forest promotion
[DCInstall]
ReplicaOrNewDomain=Domain
NewDomain=Forest
NewDomainDNSName=reagentpress.com
ForestLevel=0
DomainNetbiosName=REAGENTPRESS
DomainLevel=0
InstallDNS=Yes
ConfirmGc=Yes
CreateDNSDelegation=No
DatabasePath="D:\Windows\NTDS"
LogPath="D:\Windows\NTDS"
SYSVOLPath="D:\Windows\SYSVOL"

; Set SafeModeAdminPassword later
SafeModeAdminPassword=

; Run-time flags (optional)
RebootOnCompletion=Yes
```

5. Save the answer file as a .txt file and then copy the file to a location accessible from the server you want to promote.

6. After you create the answer file, you can start the unattended installation by entering the following at a command prompt:

```
dcpromo /unattend:"PathToAnswerFile"
```

where *PathToAnswerFile* is the full file path to the answer file, such as: dcpromo /unattend:"C:\data\imaginedlforest.txt"

At the command line, you can create the first domain controller in a new forest using the following command:

```
dcpromo /unattend
/ReplicaOrNewDomain:Domain
/NewDomain:Forest
/NewDomainDNSName:FullyQualifiedDNSName
/ForestLevel:ForestFunctionalLevel
/DomainNetBiosName:NetBiosName
/DomainLevel:DomainFunctionalLevel
/InstallDNS:Yes
/ConfirmGc:Yes
/CreateDNSDelegation:No
/DatabasePath:"LocalDatabasePath"
/LogPath:"LocalLogPath"
/SYSVOLPath:"LocalSysVolPath"
/SafeModeAdminPassword:"Password"
/RebootOnCompletion:Yes
```

For example:

```
dcpromo /unattend
/ReplicaOrNewDomain:Domain
/NewDomain:Forest
/NewDomainDNSName:reagentpress.com
/ForestLevel:0
/DomainNetbiosName:REAGENTPRESS
/DomainLevel:0
/InstallDNS:Yes
/ConfirmGc:Yes
/CreateDNSDelegation:No
/DatabasePath:"D:\Windows\NTDS"
/LogPath:"D:\Windows\NTDS"
/SYSVOLPath:"D:\Windows\SYSVOL"
/SafeModeAdminPassword:"FuzzyBunny007!!!"
/RebootOnCompletion:Yes
```

When the unattended installation or command-line execution completes, Dcpromo exits with a return code. A return code of 1 to 10 indicates success.

A return code of 11 to 100 indicates failure. Note the related error text and take appropriate corrective action as necessary.

Table 2-1 summarizes all the available parameters for unattended and command-line installations of Active Directory Domain Services. Default permitted values are shown in bold where applicable. You can refer to this table whenever you are installing forests, domain trees, child domains, or domain controllers.

TABLE 2-1 Parameters for Unattended and Command-Line Installations

/AllowDomainReinstall	Specifies whether an existing domain is re-created. Permitted values: Yes | **No**
/AllowDomainControllerReinstall	Specifies whether to continue installing this domain controller despite the fact that an active domain controller account with the same name is detected. Specify Yes only if you are sure that the account is no longer in use. Permitted values: Yes | **No**
/ApplicationPartitionsToReplicate	Specifies application partitions to be replicated in the format of "partition1" "partition2". If * is specified, all application partitions will be replicated. Use space-separated (or comma-and-space-separated) distinguished names, with the entire string enclosed in quotation marks. Permitted values: "p1 p2 ...pN"
/ChildName	Specifies the single-label DNS name of the child domain. Permitted values: ChildName
/ConfirmGc	Specifies whether the domain controller is a global catalog server. The default is Yes unless you are creating the first domain controller in a new child domain or new domain tree. Permitted values: **Yes** | No

/CreateDNSDelegation	Specifies whether to create a DNS delegation that references this new DNS server. Valid for Active Directory–integrated DNS only. The default value is computed automatically based on the environment. Permitted values: Yes | No
/CriticalReplicationOnly	Specifies whether the promotion operation performs only critical replication before reboot, and then continues, skipping the noncritical (and potentially lengthy) portion of replication. The noncritical replication happens after the role installation finishes and the computer restarts. Permitted values: Yes | **No**
/DatabasePath	Specifies the fully qualified, non-UNC path to a directory on a fixed disk of the local computer that contains the domain database. For example, C:\Windows\NTDS. The default value is %SystemRoot%\NTDS. Permitted values: LocalDBPath
/DCAccountName	Specifies the name of the DC account that you are creating. Permitted values: DCName
/DelegatedAdmin	Specifies the name of the user or group that will install and administer an RODC. If no value is specified, only members of the Domain Admins group or Enterprise Admins group can install and administer an RODC. Permitted values: User or group
/DNSDelegationPassword	Specifies the password for the user name (the account credentials) that is used to create or remove the DNS delegation. Specify * to prompt the user to enter credentials. Permitted values: Password | *
/DNSDelegationUserName	Specifies the user name to be used when the DNS delegation is created or removed. If you do not specify a value, the account credentials that you specify for the AD DS installation or removal are used for the DNS delegation. Permitted values: AdminAccount

/DNSOnNetwork	Specifies whether DNS service is available on the network. This is used only when the network adapter for this computer is not configured with the name of a DNS server for name resolution. Specifying No indicates that the DNS server will be installed on this machine for name resolution. Otherwise, the network adapter must be configured with a DNS server name first. Permitted values: **Yes** | No
/DomainLevel	Specifies the domain functional level when a new domain is created in an existing forest, as follows: 0 = Windows 2000 native, 2 = Windows Server 2003, 3 = Windows Server 2008 and 4 = Windows Server 2008 R2. The default value is based on levels existing in the forest. Permitted values: 0 | 2 | 3 | 4
/DomainNetBiosName	Assigns a NetBIOS name to the new domain. The default value is the leftmost label of the DNS name. Permitted values: NetBiosName
/ForestLevel	Specifies the forest functional level when a new domain is created in a new forest, as follows: 0 = Windows 2000 native, 2 = Windows Server 2003, 3 = Windows Server 2008 and 4 = Windows Server 2008 R2. Permitted values: **0** | 2 | 3 | 4
/InstallDNS	Specifies whether DNS is configured for a new domain if Dcpromo detects that the DNS dynamic update protocol is not available, or if Dcpromo detects an insufficient number of DNS servers for an existing domain. The default value is computed based on environment. Permitted values: Yes | No
/LogPath	Specifies the fully qualified, non-UNC path to a directory on a fixed disk of the local computer that contains the domain log files; for example, C:\Windows\NTDS. The default value is %SystemRoot%\NTDS. Permitted values: LocalLogPath

/NewDomain	Specifies the type of new domain: forest for the root domain of a new forest, tree for the root domain of a new tree in an existing forest, or child for a child domain in an existing forest. The type of new domain must be specified when AD DS is installed on a Windows server core installation. Permitted values: **Forest** | Tree | Child
/NewDomainDNSName	Specifies a fully qualified domain name (FQDN) for the new domain. Permitted values: FQDNOfNewD
/ParentDomainDNSName	Specifies the FQDN of an existing parent domain during the installation of a child domain. Permitted values: FQDNOfParentD
/Password	Specifies the password corresponding to the user name (account credentials) that is used to promote the domain controller. Specify * to prompt the user to enter credentials. Permitted values: Password | *
/PasswordReplicationAllowed	Specifies the names of computer and user accounts whose passwords can be replicated to the RODC you are installing. Specify NONE if you want to keep the value empty. By default, no user credentials will be cached on this RODC. To specify more than one security principal, add the entry multiple times. Permitted values: SecPr | NONE
/PasswordReplicationDenied	Specifies the names of user, group, and computer accounts whose passwords are not to be replicated to the RODC you are installing. Specify NONE if you do not want to deny the replication of credentials of any users or computers. To specify more than one security principal, add the entry multiple times. Permitted values: SecPr | NONE
/RebootOnCompletion	Specifies whether to restart the computer upon completion, regardless of success. Permitted values: **Yes** | No

/ReplicaDomainDNSName	Specifies the FQDN of the domain in which you want to promote an additional domain controller. Permitted values: DCDomain
/ReplicaOrNewDomain	Specifies how to install the domain controller: Replica means as an additional domain controller in an existing domain. ReadOnlyReplica means as an RODC in an existing domain. Domain means as the first domain controller in a new domain. Permitted values: **Replica** | ReadOnlyReplica | Domain
/ReplicationSourceDC	Sets the FQDN of the partner domain controller from which AD DS data is replicated to create the new domain controller. Permitted values: SourceDC
/ReplicationSourcePath	Sets the location of the installation media that will be used to install a new domain controller. Permitted values: FolderPath
/SafeModeAdminPassword	Sets the password for the administrator account to use when starting the computer in safe mode or a variant of safe mode, such as Directory Service Restore mode. You cannot specify a blank password. Permitted values: Password | NONE
/SiteName	Sets the name of an existing site where you can place the new domain controller. For a new forest, the default is Default-First-Site-Name. For all other writable domain controller installations, the default is the site that is associated with the subnet that includes the IP address of this server. If no such site exists, the default is the site of the replication source domain controller. For an RODC installation, you must specify the site name where the RODC will be installed. Permitted values: SiteName

/SkipAutoConfigDNS	Skips automatic configuration of client settings, forwarders, and root hints for DNS. The switch is in effect only if the DNS Server service is already installed on the server. Otherwise, this switch is ignored. If you use this switch, ensure that zones are created and properly configured before you install AD DS, or the domain controller will not operate correctly. This switch does not skip automatic creation of the DNS delegation in the parent DNS zone. To control DNS delegation creation, use the /CreateDNSDelegation switch.
/Syskey	Specifies the system key for the media from which you replicate the data. Permitted values: NONE | SystemKey
/SysVolPath	Specifies the fully qualified, non-UNC path to a directory on a fixed disk of the local computer; for example, C:\Windows\SYSVOL. The default value is %SystemRoot%\sysvol. Permitted values: FolderPath
/TransferIMRoleIfNeeded	Specifies whether to transfer the infrastructure master role to this domain controller, in case it is currently hosted on a global catalog server and you do not plan to make this domain controller a global catalog server. Choose Yes to transfer the infrastructure master role to this domain controller in case this is needed. If you choose Yes, be sure to specify /ConfirmGC:No. Permitted values: Yes | **No**
/UserDomain	Specifies the name of the domain for the administrative account used to promote the domain controller. This should be the same as the domain of the new domain controller. Permitted values: DomainOfAdminAccount

/UserName	Specifies the administrative account in the domain of the new domain controller that will be used for promoting the domain controller. You should specify the account credentials in the Domain\UserName format, such as IMAGINEDL\WilliamS.. Permitted values: AccountInDCDomain

Creating New Domain Trees

To create a new domain tree in an existing forest, you will be required to provide the credentials for an account that is a member of the Enterprise Admins group in the forest of which the domain will be a part. You can create a new domain tree by installing a domain controller in the desired namespace with these steps:

1. Start the Active Directory Domain Services Installation Wizard by clicking Start, typing **dcpromo** in the Search box, and pressing Enter. Before the wizard starts, it checks to ensure the AD DS binaries are installed. If you haven't installed the AD DS binaries, the wizard installs them. After installing the AD DS binaries as necessary, the wizard displays an introductory page.

2. On the initial wizard page, select the Use Advanced Mode Installation check box before clicking Next to continue. If you don't use advanced installation mode, you can create new child domains in an existing forest but cannot create a new domain tree in an existing forest. Advanced installation mode also lets you select the NetBIOS name of the domain.

3. If the Operating System Compatibility page is displayed, review the warning about the default security settings for domain controllers and then click Next.

4. On the Choose A Deployment Configuration page, select Existing Forest, select Create A New Domain In An Existing Forest, and then select Create A New Domain Tree Root Instead Of A New Child Domain, as shown in Figure 2-9. You choose this option to establish a new domain tree that is separate from any existing trees in the existing Active Directory forest. By selecting this option, you specify that there

isn't an existing parent domain with which you want to associate the new domain. For example, you should select this option if the reagentpress.com domain already exists and you want to establish the imaginedlands.com domain in a new tree in the existing forest.

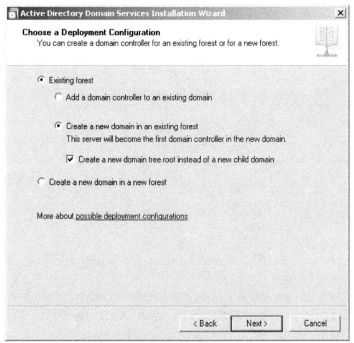

Figure 2-9   Create a new domain tree.

5.   When you click Next, you see the Network Credentials page, shown in Figure 2-10. In the field provided, enter the full DNS name of any domain in the forest where you plan to install the domain controller and establish the new domain tree. Preferably, this should be the name of the forest root domain, such as imaginedlands.com. If you are logged on to a domain in this forest and the account is a member of the Enterprise Admins group, you can use your current logged-on credentials to perform the installation. Otherwise, select Alternate Credentials, click Set, enter the user name and password for an account that is a member of the Enterprise Admins group, and then click Next.

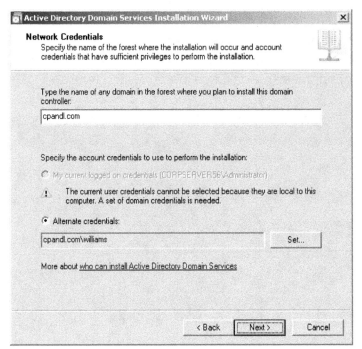

FIGURE 2-10 Identify a current domain in the forest and set credentials.

6. When you click Next, the wizard will check the forest configuration and attempt to contact a domain controller in the previously specified domain. If an authentication error occurs, you may have specified an invalid account or account password in the previous step and will need to go back and correct the credential settings. If a configuration error occurs, you'll see an error similar to the one shown in Figure 2-11 and will need to make configuration changes before continuing. Start by checking the TCP/IP configuration of the server you are trying to promote. At a minimum, the server should have a valid IPv4 address and a preferred DNS server. If these settings are correct, you'll need to examine the _ldap SRV records for the _tcp zone on the authoritative DNS server. Ensure these records and the corresponding A records are properly configured.

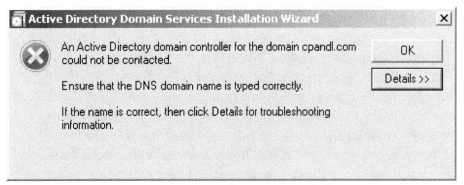

FIGURE 2-11 Review any warnings and correct issues before continuing.

7. Next, the wizard will enumerate domains in the forest and display the Name The New Domain Tree Root page shown in Figure 2-12. Enter the full DNS name for the new domain that will be the base of the new domain tree and then click Next. The domain name you use should not be a subdomain of an existing parent domain in any tree of the forest.

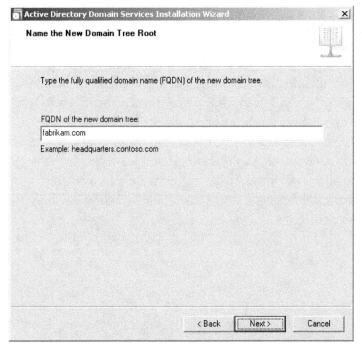

FIGURE 2-12 Specify the new domain at the base of the new domain tree.

8. The wizard will then attempt to validate the domain name. If there is an existing domain in the forest with this name, you will see an error

message and will need to provide a different domain name. If there isn't an existing domain in the forest with this name, the wizard will attempt to register the name. To do this, the wizard requires that the user credentials you elected to use or provided previously are a member of the Enterprise Admins group. If they aren't, the installation may fail, and you would then need to repeat this procedure in its entirety. Therefore, if you see a warning about the user credentials, click No to return to the Name The New Domain Tree Root page and then click Back so you can provide new credentials on the Network Credentials page.

9. Once the wizard validates the domain name, it uses the name to generate a default NetBIOS name. If you are using advanced installation mode or the wizard has detected a conflict, you will be able to accept the wizard-generated name or enter a new NetBIOS name of up to 15 characters. Then click Next to continue.

10. On the Set Domain Functional Level page, select the domain functional level that accommodates the domain controllers that you plan to install in the domain, and then click Next.

11. When you click Next, the wizard determines the available Active Directory sites. On the Select A Site page, you'll see a list of available sites, as shown in Figure 2-13. If there is a site that corresponds to the IP address of the server you are promoting, select the Use The Site That Corresponds To The IP Address Of This Computer check box to place the new domain controller in this site. If you want to place the new domain controller in a different site or there isn't an available subnet for the current IP address, select the site in which you want to locate the domain controller.

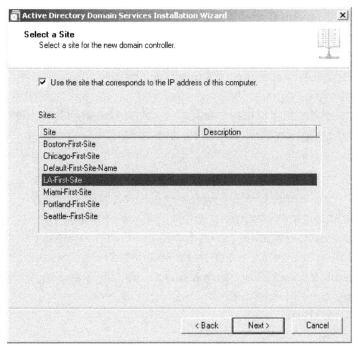

FIGURE 2-13 Place the domain controller in the appropriate site.

12. When you click Next, the wizard examines the DNS configuration and attempts to determine whether any authoritative DNS servers are available and then displays the Additional Domain Controller Options page. The DNS Server option is selected by default so that the domain controller can function as a DNS server. A DNS zone and a delegation for that zone will be automatically created for this domain. The Global Catalog option is not selected by default. If you select the Global Catalog option, keep in mind that because this is the first domain controller in a new domain tree, it will also host the domainwide operations master roles for the new domain, including the infrastructure master role. Hosting the infrastructure master role on a global catalog server in a child domain can cause problems unless all of the domain controllers in the domain are global catalog servers.

13. The rest of the installation proceeds as previously discussed. Continue with steps 10 to 15 and the postinstallation checks discussed in the previous section, "Creating New Forests." Note that if you selected Use Advanced Mode Installation, the Source Domain Controller page is displayed. You use the options on this page to specify the domain

controller from which to replicate the configuration and schema directory partitions. If you select Let The Wizard Choose An Appropriate Domain Controller, the first writable domain controller in the forest that responds to the wizard's query will be used for replication. To specify a domain controller from which to replicate the configuration and schema directory partitions, select Use This Specific Domain Controller and then click the name of the domain controller. Click Next.

14. Additionally, after installing AD DS, you need to configure DNS so that name resolution works appropriately with any existing domains. To enable name resolution for computers within the new domain, you typically need to create secondary zones for all existing domains in the new domain and then set up zone transfers. To enable name resolution into the new domain from existing domains, you typically need to create a secondary zone in existing domains for the new domain and then set up zone transfers.

On a Full Server or Core Server installation of Windows Server, you can add a new domain tree using an unattended installation or the command line. You must be logged on as the Enterprise Admins group in the forest.

With the unattended method of installation, you must first prepare an answer file that contains the desired configuration values. You can create an answer file for installing a new domain tree by completing the following steps:

1. Open Notepad or any other text editor.

2. On the first line, type **[DCINSTALL]**, and then press Enter.

3. Type the following entries, one entry on each line:

```
ReplicaOrNewDomain=Domain
NewDomain=Tree
NewDomainDNSName=FQDNOfNewDomain
DomainNetbiosName=NetBiosName
DomainLevel=DomainFunctionalLevel
SiteName=SiteName
InstallDNS=Yes
ConfirmGc=Yes
CreateDNSDelegation=Yes
```

```
UserDomain=DomainOfAdminAccount
UserName=AdminAccountInParentDomain
Password=*
ReplicationSourceDC=SourceDC
DatabasePath="LocalDatabasePath"
LogPath="LocalLogPath"
SYSVOLPath="LocalSysVolPath"
SafeModeAdminPassword=
RebootOnCompletion=Yes
```

> **Note**   Values you must specify are shown in bold. You can set Password to * if you do not want to include it in the answer file. When you run Dcpromo to initiate the unattended installation, you will be prompted for the password.
>
> **Tip**   By setting CreateDNSDelegation=Yes, you ensure DNS settings for the domain are configured. You set ReplicaOrNewDomain to Domain because you are installing a new domain rather than an additional domain controller. You set NewDomain to Tree because you are creating a new domain tree.

4. If the account that is being used to install AD DS is different from the account in the parent domain that has the privileges that are required to create a DNS delegation, you must specify the account that can create the DNS delegation by entering these additional parameters:

```
DNSDelegationUserName=DelegationAdminAccount
DNSDelegationPassword="Password"
```

5. Save the answer file as a .txt file and then copy the file to a location accessible from the server you want to promote.

   The following is a complete example:

```
; New Domain Tree
[DCInstall]
ReplicaOrNewDomain=Domain
NewDomain=Tree
NewDomainDNSName=fabrikam.com
DomainNetbiosName=FABRIKAM
DomainLevel=2
SiteName=LA-First-Site
InstallDNS=Yes
ConfirmGc=Yes
CreateDNSDelegation=No
```

```
UserDomain=imaginedlands.com
UserName=imaginedlands.com\williams
Password=*
ReplicationSourceDC=CorpServer65.imaginedlands.com
DatabasePath="D:\Windows\NTDS"
LogPath="D:\Windows\NTDS"
SYSVOLPath="D:\Windows\SYSVOL"

; Set SafeModeAdminPassword later
SafeModeAdminPassword=

; Run-time flags (optional)
RebootOnCompletion=Yes
```

6. After you create the answer file, you can start the unattended installation by entering the following at a command prompt:

```
dcpromo /unattend:"PathToAnswerFile"
```

where *PathToAnswerFile* is the full file path to the answer file, such as C:\data\newtree.txt.

At the command line, you can create the first domain controller in a new domain tree by using the following command:

```
dcpromo /unattend
/ReplicaOrNewDomain:Domain
/NewDomain:Tree
/NewDomainDNSName:FQDNOfNewDomain
/DomainNetbiosName:NetBiosName
/DomainLevel:DomainFunctionalLevel
/SiteName:SiteName
/InstallDNS:Yes
/ConfirmGc:Yes
/CreateDNSDelegation:Yes
/UserDomain:DomainOfAdminAccount
/UserName:AdminAccountInParentDomain
/Password:"Password"
/ReplicationSourceDC:SourceDC
/DatabasePath:"LocalDatabasePath"
/LogPath:"LocalLogPath"
/SYSVOLPath:"LocalSysVolPath"
/SafeModeAdminPassword:"Password"
/RebootOnCompletion:Yes
```

If the account that is being used to install AD DS is different from the account in the parent domain that has the privileges that are required to create a DNS delegation, you must specify the account that can create the DNS delegation by entering these additional parameters:

```
/DNSDelegationUserName:DelegationAdminAccount
/DNSDelegationPassword:"Password"
```

When the unattended installation or command-line execution completes, Dcpromo exits with a return code. A return code of 1 to 10 indicates success. A return code of 11 to 100 indicates failure. Note the related error text and take appropriate corrective action as necessary.

Creating New Child Domains

To create a new child domain in an existing forest, you will be required to provide the credentials for an account that is a member of the Enterprise Admins group in the forest of which the domain will be a part. You can create a new child domain by installing a domain controller in the desired namespace by using these steps:

1. Start the Active Directory Domain Services Installation Wizard by clicking Start, typing **dcpromo** in the Search box, and pressing Enter. Before the wizard starts, it checks to ensure the AD DS binaries are installed. If you haven't installed the AD DS binaries, the wizard installs them. After installing the AD DS binaries as necessary, the wizard displays an introductory page.

2. By default, the wizard uses Basic Installation mode. If you want to set the NetBIOS name of the domain, select Use Advanced Mode Installation before clicking Next to continue.

3. If the Operating System Compatibility page is displayed, review the warning about the default security settings for domain controllers and then click Next.

4. On the Choose A Deployment Configuration page, select Existing Forest and then select Create A New Domain In An Existing Forest, as shown in Figure 2-14. This establishes the first domain controller in a

domain that is a child domain of an existing domain. By selecting this option, you are specifying that the necessary parent domain already exists. For example, you would select this option if the parent domain reagentpress.com had already been created and you wanted to create the sales.reagentpress.com domain as a child of this domain.

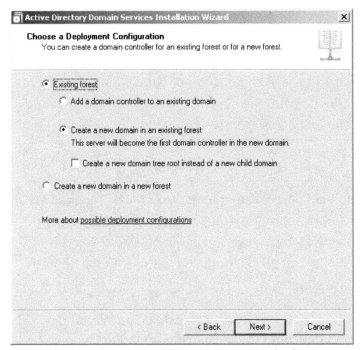

FIGURE 2-14 Create an additional domain in the forest.

5. When you click Next, you see the Network Credentials page. In the field provided, enter the full DNS name of any domain in the forest where you plan to install the domain controller and establish the new domain tree. Preferably, this should be the name of the forest root domain, such as imaginedlands.com. If you are logged on to a domain in this forest and the account is a member of the Enterprise Admins group, you can use your current logged-on credentials to perform the installation. Otherwise, select Alternate Credentials, click Set, enter the user name and password for an account that is a member of the Enterprise Admins group, and then click Next.

6. When you click Next, the wizard will check the forest configuration and attempt to contact a domain controller in the previously specified

domain. If an authentication error occurs, you may have specified an invalid account or account password in the previous step and will need to go back and correct the credential settings. If a configuration error occurs, you'll see an error and will need to make configuration changes before continuing. Start by checking the TCP/IP configuration of the server you are trying to promote. At a minimum, the server should have a valid IPv4 address and a preferred DNS server. If these settings are correct, you'll need to examine the _ldap SRV records for the _tcp zone on the authoritative DNS server. Ensure these records and the corresponding A records are properly configured.

7. On the Name The New Domain page, shown in Figure 2-15, enter the full DNS name for the parent domain, such as **imaginedlands.com**, in the field provided, or click Browse to search for an existing domain to use. In the next field, enter the single-name component of the child domain, such as **sales**. Before you click Next to continue, ensure the fully qualified domain name (FQDN) of the new child domain is correct.

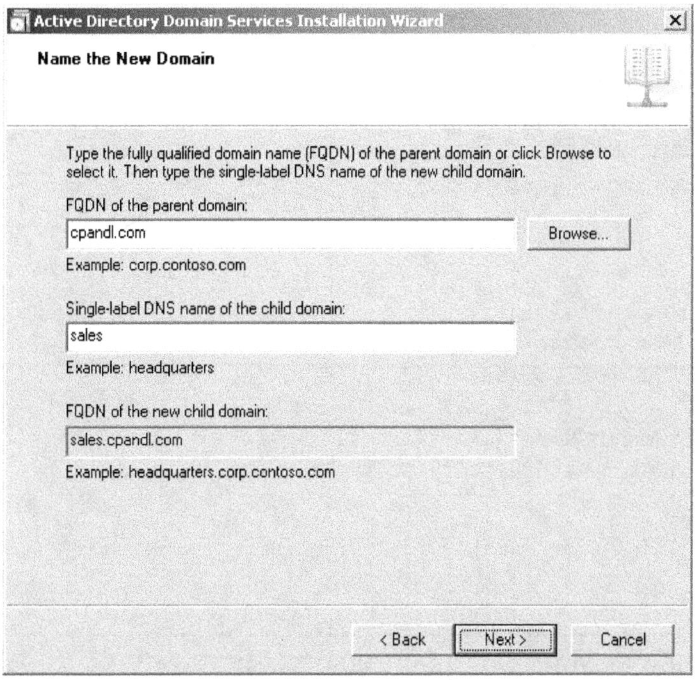

FIGURE 2-15 Set the full name of the child domain.

8. The rest of the installation proceeds as previously discussed. Continue with steps 8 through 14 and the postinstallation checks discussed previously in "Creating New Domain Trees."

On a Full Server or Core Server installation of Windows Server, you can add a new child domain by using an unattended installation or the command line. You must be logged on as the Enterprise Admins group in the forest.

With the unattended method of installation, you must first prepare an answer file that contains the desired configuration values. You can create an answer file for installing a new child domain by completing the following steps:

1. Open Notepad or any other text editor.
2. On the first line, type **[DCINSTALL]**, and then press Enter.
3. Type the following entries, one entry on each line:

```
ReplicaOrNewDomain=Domain
NewDomain=Child
ParentDomainDNSName=FQDNOfParentDomain
ChildName=SingleLableNameOfNewDomain
DomainNetbiosName=NetBiosName
DomainLevel=DomainFunctionalLevel
SiteName=SiteName
InstallDNS=Yes
ConfirmGc=Yes
CreateDNSDelegation=Yes
UserDomain=DomainOfAdminAccount
UserName=AdminAccountInParentDomain
Password=*
ReplicationSourceDC=SourceDCName
DatabasePath="LocalDatabasePath"
LogPath="LocalLogPath"
SYSVOLPath="LocalSysVolPath"
SafeModeAdminPassword=
RebootOnCompletion=Yes
```

> **Tip** You set ReplicaOrNewDomain to Domain because you are installing a new domain rather than an additional domain controller. You set NewDomain to Child because you are creating a new child domain. You set ChildName to the single-label name of the new child

domain, such **as sales**. You set NewDomainDNSName to the fully qualified domain name, such as **sales.imaginedlands.com**.

4. If the account that is being used to install AD DS is different from the account in the parent domain that has the privileges that are required to create a DNS delegation, you must specify the account that can create the DNS delegation by entering these additional parameters:

```
DNSDelegationUserName=DelegationAdminAccount
DNSDelegationPassword="Password"
```

5. Save the answer file as a .txt file and then copy the file to a location accessible from the server you want to promote.

The following is an example of a completed answer file:

```
; New child domain promotion
[DCInstall]
ReplicaOrNewDomain=Domain
NewDomain=Child
ParentDomainDNSName=imaginedlands.com
ChildName=sales
DomainNetbiosName=SALES
DomainLevel=2
SiteName=LA-First-Site
InstallDNS=Yes
ConfirmGc=Yes
CreateDNSDelegation=Yes
DNSDelegationUserName=imaginedlands.com\williams
DNSDelegationPassword=*
UserDomain=imaginedlands.com
UserName=imaginedlands.com\williams
Password=*
ReplicationSourceDC=CorpServer65.imaginedlands.com
DatabasePath="D:\Windows\NTDS"
LogPath="D:\Windows\NTDS"
SYSVOLPath="D:\Windows\SYSVOL"

; Set SafeModeAdminPassword later
SafeModeAdminPassword=

; Run-time flags (optional)
RebootOnCompletion=Yes
```

6. After you create the answer file, you can start the unattended installation by entering the following at a command prompt:

```
dcpromo /unattend:"PathToAnswerFile"
```

where *PathToAnswerFile* is the full file path to the answer file, such as C:\data\newchild.txt.

At the command line, you can create the child domain by using the following command:

```
dcpromo /unattend
/ReplicaOrNewDomain=Domain
/NewDomain=Child
/ParentDomainDNSName=FQDNOfParentDomain
/ChildName=SingleLableNameOfNewDomain
/DomainNetbiosName=NetBiosName
/DomainLevel=DomainFunctionalLevel
/SiteName=SiteName
/InstallDNS=Yes
/ConfirmGc=Yes
/CreateDNSDelegation=Yes
/UserDomain=DomainOfAdminAccount
/UserName=AdminAccountInParentDomain
/Password="Password"
/ReplicationSourceDC=SourceDCName
/DatabasePath="LocalDatabasePath"
/LogPath="LocalLogPath"
/SYSVOLPath="LocalSysVolPath"
/SafeModeAdminPassword="Password"
/RebootOnCompletion=Yes
```

If the account that is being used to install AD DS is different from the account in the parent domain that has the privileges that are required to create a DNS delegation, you must specify the account that can create the DNS delegation by entering these additional parameters:

```
/DNSDelegationUserName:DelegationAdminAccount
/DNSDelegationPassword:"Password"
```

When the unattended installation or command-line execution completes, Dcpromo exits with a return code. A return code of 1 to 10 indicates success. A return code of 11 to 100 indicates failure. Note any related error text and take appropriate corrective action as necessary.

Chapter 3. Deploying Writable Domain Controllers

In this chapter, I provide tips and techniques for adding and removing writable domain controllers. After setting up the initial domain controller in a domain, you deploy additional domain controllers to increase fault tolerance and improve operational efficiency. Just as you establish a server as a domain controller by installing Active Directory Domain Services (AD DS), you decommission a domain controller by removing AD DS. The decommissioned domain controller can then be taken out of service, or it can act as a server.

Preparing to Deploy or Decommission Domain Controllers

Before deploying or decommissioning domain controllers, you should create a plan that lists any prerequisites, necessary postmodification changes, and overall impact on your network. Create your plan by reviewing "Preparing for Active Directory Installation" in Chapter 2, "Installing New Forests, Domain Trees, and Child Domains."

Domain controllers host the Active Directory database and handle related operations. Active Directory uses a multimaster replication model that creates a distributed environment where no single domain controller is authoritative with regard to logon and authentication requests. This model allows any domain controller to be used for logon and authentication. It also allows you to make changes to standard directory information without regard to which domain controller you use.

Domain controllers also can have special roles as operations masters and global catalog servers. As discussed in Chapter 5, "Managing Operations Masters," operations masters perform tasks that can be performed only by a single authoritative domain controller. Global catalog servers store partial replicas of data from all domains in a forest to facilitate directory searches for resources in other domains and to determine membership in universal groups.

When you establish the first domain controller in a forest, the domain controller hosts the forestwide and domainwide operations master roles and also acts as the global catalog server for the domain. When you establish the first domain controller in a domain, the domain controller hosts the domainwide operations master roles and also acts as the global catalog server for the domain.

Every domain in the enterprise should have at least two domain controllers. If a domain has only one domain controller, you could lose the entire domain and all related accounts if disaster strikes. Although you may be able to recover the domain from a backup, you will have significant problems until the restore is completed. For example, users may not be able to log on to the domain or obtain authenticated access to domain resources.

Every site should have at least one domain controller. If a domain controller is not available in a site, computers in the site will perform logon and authentication activities with domain controllers in another site, which could significantly affect response times.

Every site should have a global catalog server. If a global catalog server is not available in a site, computers in the site will query a global catalog server in another site when searching for resources in other domains in the forest. Global catalog servers are also used during logon and authentication because they store universal group membership information for all domains in the forest. If a global catalog server isn't available in the site and the universal group membership has not been previously cached, the domain controller responding to a user's logon or authentication request will need to obtain the required information from a global catalog server in another site.

Adding Writable Domain Controllers

You establish a server as a domain controller by installing the necessary binaries for the Active Directory Domain Services (AD DS) and then configuring the services using the Active Directory Domain Services Installation Wizard (Dcpromo.exe). If you are deploying Windows Server 2008 or Windows Server 2008 R2 for the first time in an existing forest, you must prepare Active Directory as discussed in "Deploying Windows Server 2008 and R2" in Chapter 2.

Installing Additional Writable Domain Controllers

Any computer running Windows Server can act as a domain controller. Essentially, domain controllers are database servers with extensive directory, application, and replication features. Because of this, the hardware you choose for the domain controllers should be fairly robust. You'll want to look carefully at the server's processor, memory, and hard disk configuration.

In many cases, you'll want to install domain controllers on hardware with multiple, fast processors. This will help ensure the domain controller can efficiently handle replication requests and topology generation. When you install the second domain controller in a forest, the *Knowledge Consistency Checker (KCC)* begins running on every domain controller. Not only does the KCC generate replication topology, it also dynamically handles changes and failures within the topology. By default, the KCC recalculates the replication topology every 15 minutes. As the complexity of the replication topology increases, so does processing power required for this calculation. You'll need to monitor processor usage and upgrade as necessary.

In addition to running standard processes, domain controllers must run processes related to storage engine operations, knowledge consistency checking, replication, and garbage collection. Most domain controllers should have at least 2 gigabytes (GB) of RAM as a recommended starting point for full server installations and 1 GB of RAM for core server installations. You'll need to monitor memory usage and upgrade as necessary.

With regard to hard disks, you'll want to closely examine fault tolerance and storage capacity needs. Domain controllers should use fault-tolerant drives to protect against hardware failure of the system volume and any other volumes used by Active Directory. I recommend using a redundant array of independent disks (RAID), RAID 1 for system volumes and RAID 5 for data. Hardware RAID is preferable to software RAID. Storage capacity needs depend on the number of objects related to users, computers, groups, and resources that are stored in the Active Directory database. Each storage volume should have ample free disk space at all times to ensure proper operational efficiency.

When you add a domain controller to an existing domain, you should consider whether you want to perform an installation from media rather than creating the domain controller from scratch. With either technique, you will need to log on to the local machine using either the local Administrator account or an account that has administrator privileges on the local machine. Then start the installation. You also will be required to provide the credentials for an account that is a member of the Domain Admins group in the domain of which the domain controller will be a part. Because you will be given the opportunity to join the domain controller to the domain if necessary, it is not necessary for the server to be a member of the domain.

Adding Writable Domain Controllers Using Replication

You can add a writable domain controller to an existing domain by completing the following steps:

1. Check the TCP/IP configuration of the server. The server must have a valid IP address and must have properly configured DNS settings.

   > **Note**   Domain controllers that also act as DNS servers should not have dynamic IP addresses, to ensure reliable DNS operations. Otherwise, the server can have a static IP address or a dynamic IP address assigned by a DHCP server.

2. Install the Active Directory binaries by entering the following command at an elevated command prompt: **servermanagercmd –install adds-domain-controller**. This installs the AD DS binaries, which enables the Active Directory Domain Services role on the server.

3. Before starting an Active Directory installation, you should examine local accounts to determine whether you need to take special steps to preserve any local accounts. You should also check for encrypted files and folders using the EFSInfo utility. At a command prompt, enter **efsinfo /s:*DriveDesignator* /i | find ": Encrypted"** where *DriveDesignator* is the drive designator of the volume to search, such as C:.

> **Caution** Domain controllers do not have local accounts or separate cryptographic keys. Making a server a domain controller deletes all local accounts and all certificates and cryptographic keys from the server. Any encrypted data on the server, including data stored using the Encrypting File System (EFS), must be decrypted before Active Directory is installed, or it will be permanently inaccessible.

4. Start the Active Directory Domain Services Installation Wizard by clicking Start, typing **dcpromo** in the Search box, and pressing Enter.

5. By default, the wizard uses Basic Installation mode. If you want to install from media as discussed in "Adding Writable Domain Controllers Using Installation Media," later in this chapter, or choose the source domain controller for replication, select the Use Advanced Installation Mode check box before clicking Next to continue.

6. If the Operating System Compatibility page is displayed, review the warning about the default security settings for domain controllers and then click Next.

7. On the Choose A Deployment Configuration page, as in Figure 3-1, select Existing Forest and then select Add A Domain Controller To An Existing Domain. By choosing this option, you specify that you are adding a domain controller to an existing domain in the Active Directory forest.

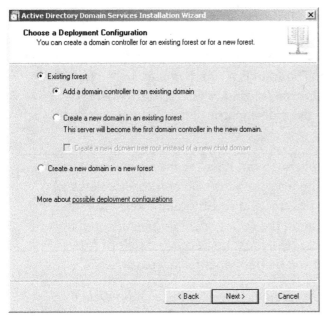

FIGURE 3-1 Specify that you want to add a domain controller to the domain.

8. When you click Next, you see the Network Credentials page, shown in Figure 3-2. In the field provided, enter the full DNS name of any domain in the forest where you plan to install the domain controller. Preferably, this should be the name of the forest root domain, such as imaginedlands.com. If you are logged on to a domain in this forest and have the appropriate permissions, you can use your current logged-on credentials to perform the installation. Otherwise, select Alternate Credentials, click Set, enter the user name and password for an enterprise administrator account in the previously specified domain, and then click OK.

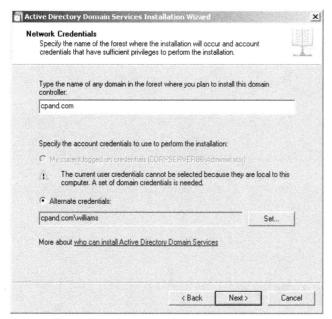

FIGURE 3-2 Set the network credentials.

9. When you click Next, the wizard validates the domain name you
    provided and then lists all domains in the related forest. On the Select
    A Domain page, shown in Figure 3-3, select the domain to which the
    domain controller will be added and then click Next.

10. When you click Next, the wizard determines the available Active
    Directory sites. On the Select A Site page, you'll see a list of available
    sites. If there is a site that corresponds to the IP address of the server
    you are promoting, select the Use The Site That Corresponds To The IP
    Address check box to place the new domain controller in this site. If
    you want to place the new domain controller in a different site or there
    isn't an available subnet for the current IP address, select the site in
    which you want to locate the domain controller.

FIGURE 3-3 Select the target domain.

11. When you click Next, the wizard examines the DNS configuration and attempts to determine whether any authoritative DNS servers are available. It then displays the Additional Domain Controller Options page, shown in Figure 3-4. As permitted, select additional installation options for the domain controller and then click Next.

12. If you choose to let the wizard install the DNS Server service, note the following:

   a. The DNS Server service will be installed, and the domain controller will also act as a DNS server. A primary DNS zone will be created as an Active Directory–integrated zone with the same name as the new domain you are setting up. The wizard will also update the server's TCP/IP configuration so that its primary DNS server is set to itself.

   b. During installation of the operating system, Windows Setup installs and configures IPv4 and IPv6 if networking components were detected. If you've configured dynamic IPv4, IPv6, or both addresses, you'll see a warning. Click Yes to ignore the warning and continue.

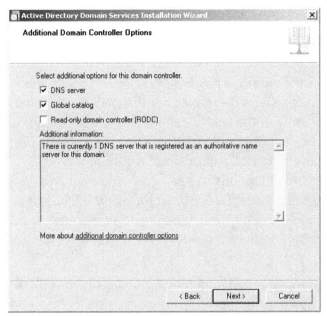

FIGURE 3-4 Specify the additional installation options.

c. If you want to modify the TCP/IP configuration, click No to return to the Additional Domain Controller Options page and then make the appropriate changes to the system configuration before clicking Next to continue. If you configure a static IPv4 address but do not configure a static IPv6 address, you'll also see the warning. To ignore the warning and continue with the installation, click Yes.

> **Note** At a minimum, you should configure a static IPv4 address before continuing. Click Start, type **ncpa.cpl** in the Search box, and then press Enter. In Network Connections, double-click Local Area Connection. In Local Area Connection Properties, click Properties and then double-click Internet Protocol Version 4 (TCP/IPv4), make any necessary changes, and then click OK. If you also want to configure a static IPv6 address, double-click Internet Protocol Version 6 (TCP/IPv6), make any necessary changes, and then click OK. If you decide not to configure a static IPv6 address, you may need to make changes to DNS records later if your organization starts using IPv6 addresses.

d. The wizard next attempts to register a delegation for the DNS server with an authoritative parent zone. If you are integrating with an existing DNS infrastructure, you should manually create a delegation to the DNS server and then click Yes to continue. Otherwise, you can ignore this warning and click Yes to continue.

13. If you choose to not let the wizard install the DNS Server service, the wizard next attempts to register a delegation for the DNS server with an authoritative parent zone. If the wizard cannot create a delegation for the DNS server, it displays a warning message to indicate that you must create the delegation manually. Click No to return to the Additional Domain Controller Options page so you can select and install DNS Server services. To continue without installing DNS Server services, click Yes. Keep in mind that you'll then need to manually configure the required DNS settings, including SRV and A resource records.

14. If you selected Use Advanced Installation Mode, the Install From Media page is displayed, as shown in Figure 3-5. You can provide the location of installation media to be used to create the domain controller and configure AD DS, or you can have all of the replication done over the network. Even if you install from media, some data will be replicated over the network from a source domain controller. For more information about installing from media, see "Adding Writable Domain Controllers Using Installation Media."

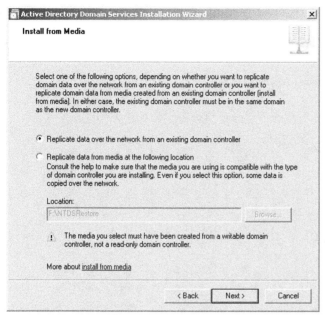

FIGURE 3-5 Set the installation mode.

15. If you selected Use Advanced Installation Mode, the Source Domain Controller page is displayed. Select Any Writable Domain Controller or select This Specific Domain Controller to specify a source domain controller for replication. Then click Next. If you choose to install from media, only changes since the media was created will be replicated from this source domain controller. If you choose not to install from media, all data will be replicated from this source domain controller.

16. On the Location For Database, Log Files, And SYSVOL page, shown in Figure 3-6, select a location to store the Active Directory database folder, log folder, and SYSVOL folder. The default location for the database and log folders is a subfolder of %SystemRoot%\NTDS. The default location for the SYSVOL folder is %SystemRoot%\Sysvol. You'll get better performance if the database folder and log folder are on two separate volumes, each on a separate disk. Placement of the SYSVOL is less critical, and you can accept the default in most cases. Although you can change the storage locations later, the process is lengthy and complex.

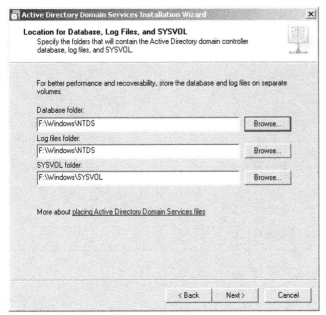

FIGURE 3-6 Configure storage locations.

> **Note** Your organization should have a specific plan in place for sizing the server hardware and designating Active Directory storage locations. You'll want to ensure the server you use is powerful enough to handle authentication, replication, and other directory duties. The server's hard disk configuration should be optimized for storage of Active Directory data. Each storage volume should have at least 20 percent free storage space at all times. You may also want to use a redundant array of independent disks (RAID) to protect against disk failure.

17. Click Next. On the Directory Services Restore Mode Administrator Password page, enter and confirm the password that should be used when you want to start the computer in Directory Services Restore Mode. Be sure to track this password carefully. This special password is used only in Restore mode and is different from the Administrator account password. The password complexity and length must comply with the domain security policy.

18. Click Next. On the Summary page, review the installation options. If desired, click Export Settings to save these settings to an answer file that you can use to perform unattended installation of other domain

controllers. When you click Next again, the wizard will use the options you've selected to install and configure Active Directory. This process can take several minutes. If you specified that the DNS Server service should be installed, the server will also be configured as a DNS server at this time.

19. When the wizard finishes configuring Active Directory, click Finish. You are then prompted to restart the computer. Click Restart Now to reboot.

After installing Active Directory, you should verify the installation. Start by examining the installation log, which is stored in the Dcpromo.log file in the %SystemRoot%\Debug folder. The log is very detailed and takes you through every step of the installation process, including the creation of directory partitions and the securing of the Registry for Active Directory.

Next, check the DNS configuration in the DNS console. DNS is updated to add SRV and A records for the server. Because you created a new domain, DNS is updated to include a forward lookup zone for the domain. You may also need to add a reverse lookup zone for the domain.

Check for updates in Active Directory Users and Computers. The Domain Controllers OU should have an account for the domain controller you installed.

Adding Writable Domain Controllers Using Installation Media

Performing an Active Directory installation from media allows the Active Directory Domain Services Installation Wizard to get the initial data for the Configuration, Schema, and Domain directory partitions, and optionally the SYSVOL, from the backup media rather than through a full synchronization over the network. In this way, you establish a domain controller using a media backup of another domain controller rather than using replication over the network. Although not designed to be used to restore failed domain controllers, this technique does help you rapidly establish additional domain controllers by reducing the amount of network traffic generated, accelerating the process of installing an additional domain controller, and getting the directory partition data synchronized.

You can use a 32-bit domain controller to generate installation media for a 64-bit domain controller, and vice versa. When installing Active Directory using a media backup, you'll want to follow these guidelines:

- Use the most recent media backup to reduce the number of updates that must be replicated.
- Use a backup of a domain controller running the same operating system in the same domain in which the new domain controller is being created.
- Copy the backup to a local drive on the server you are configuring. You cannot use backup media from Universal Naming Convention (UNC) paths or mapped drives.
- Don't use backup media that is older than the tombstone lifetime of the domain. The default value is 60 days. If you try to use backup media older than the tombstone lifetime, the Active Directory installation will fail.

You can create installation media by completing the following steps:

1. Log on to a domain controller. On a writable domain controller, the account you use must be a member of the Administrators, Server Operators, Domain Admins, or Enterprise Admins group. On a read-only domain controller, a delegated user can create the installation media for another read-only domain controller.

2. Click Start, right-click Command Prompt, and then click Run As Administrator to open an elevated command prompt. At the command prompt, enter **ntdsutil**. This starts the Directory Services Management tool.

3. At the ntdsutil prompt, enter **activate instance ntds**. This sets Active Directory as the directory service instance to work with.

4. Enter **ifm** to access the install from media prompt. Then enter one of the following commands, where *FolderPath* is the full path to the folder in which to store the Active Directory backup media files:

- **Create Full *FolderPath*** Creates a full writable installation media backup of Active Directory. You can use the media to install a writable domain controller or a read-only domain controller.
- **Create RODC *FolderPath*** Creates a read-only installation media backup of Active Directory. You can use the media to install a read-only domain controller. The backup media does not contain security credentials, such as passwords.

5. Ntdsutil creates snapshots of Active Directory partitions. When it finishes creating the snapshots, Ntdsutil mounts the snapshots as necessary and then defragments the media backup of the Active Directory database. The progress of the defragmentation is shown by percent complete.

6. Next, Ntdsutil copies registry data related to Active Directory. When it finishes this process, Ntdsutil unmounts any snapshots it was working with. The backup process should complete successfully. If it doesn't, note and resolve any issues that prevented successful creation of the backup media, such as the target disk running out of space or insufficient permissions to copy to the folder path.

7. Enter **quit** at the ifm prompt and then enter **quit** at the ntdsutil prompt.

8. Copy the backup media to a local drive on the server for which you are installing Active Directory.

9. On the server you want to make a domain controller, start the Active Directory Domain Services Installation Wizard in Advanced Installation mode. Follow all the same steps you would if you were adding a domain controller to the domain without media. After you select additional domain controller installation options and get past any DNS prompts, you see the Install From Media page. On this page, select Replicate From Media Stored At The Following Location, and then enter the location of the backup media files or click Browse to find the backup media files.

10. You can now complete the rest of the installation as discussed in the section titled "Adding Writable Domain Controllers Using Replication" earlier in this chapter. Continue with the rest of the steps and perform the postinstallation checks as well.

> **Real World**   Objects that were modified, added, or deleted since the installation media was created must be replicated. If the installation media was created recently, the amount of replication that is required should be considerably less than the amount of replication required otherwise.
>
> The only data that must be fully replicated from another domain controller is the SYSVOL data. Although you can run Ntdsutil with an option to include the SYSVOL folder in the installation media, the SYSVOL folder from the installation media cannot be used because SYSVOL must be absent when the Active Directory Domain Services server role starts on your server.

Adding Writable Domain Controllers Using Answer Files or the Command Line

On a Full Server or Core Server installation of Windows Server, you can add domain controllers using an unattended installation or the command line. You must be logged on as the Domain Admins group in the domain.

With the unattended method of installation, you must first prepare an answer file that contains the desired configuration values. You can create the required answer file by completing the following steps:

1. Open Notepad or any other text editor.
2. On the first line, type **[DCINSTALL]**, and then press Enter.
3. Type the following entries, one entry on each line.

```
ReplicaOrNewDomain=Replica
ReplicaDomainDNSName=FQDNOfDCDomain
SiteName=SiteName
InstallDNS=Yes
ConfirmGc=Yes
CreateDNSDelegation=Yes
UserDomain=DomainOfAdminAccount
```

```
UserName=AdminAccountInDomainOfDC
Password=*
ReplicationSourceDC=SoureDCName
DatabasePath="LocalDatabasePath"
LogPath="LocalLogPath"
SYSVOLPath="LocalSysVolPath"
SafeModeAdminPassword=
RebootOnCompletion=Yes
```

> **Note** Values you must specify are shown in bold. You can set Password to * if you do not want to include it in the answer file. When you run Dcpromo to initiate the unattended installation, you will be prompted for the password.
>
> **Tip** SafeModeAdminPassword sets the Directory Services Restore Mode password in the answer file. If you don't want to include the password, you can omit the password. However, you will need to use the /SafeModeAdminPassword command-line parameter to provide the password later when you run Dcpromo to initiate the unattended installation.

4. If you want to configure the domain controller as a DNS server, add the following command.

```
InstallDNS=yes
```

5. If you want to configure the domain controller as a global catalog server, add the following command.

```
ConfirmGC=yes
```

6. If you are installing from media, you can refer to the location where you stored the installation media by using the following command.

```
ReplicationSourcePath=FolderPathToMedia
```

7. Save the answer file as a .txt file and then copy the file to a location accessible from the server you want to promote.

   The following is a complete example.

```
; Replica DC promotion
[DCInstall]
ReplicaOrNewDomain=Replica
ReplicaDomainDNSName=imaginedlands.com
SiteName=LA-First-Site
InstallDNS=Yes
ConfirmGc=Yes
```

```
CreateDNSDelegation=No
UserDomain=imaginedlands.com
UserName=imaginedlands.com\williams
Password=*
ReplicationSourceDC=CorpServer65.imaginedlands.com
DatabasePath="D:\Windows\NTDS"
LogPath="D:\Windows\NTDS"
SYSVOLPath="D:\Windows\SYSVOL"

; Set SafeModeAdminPassword later
SafeModeAdminPassword=

; Run-time flags (optional)
RebootOnCompletion=Yes
```

8. After you create the answer file, you can start the unattended installation by entering the following at a command prompt:

```
dcpromo /unattend:"PathToAnswerFile"
```

where *PathToAnswerFile* is the full file path to the answer file, such as C:\data\newdc.txt.

At the command line, you can add a domain controller to a domain using the following command.

```
dcpromo /unattend
/ReplicaOrNewDomain:Replica
/ReplicaDomainDNSName:FQDNOfDCDomain
/SiteName:SiteName
/InstallDNS:Yes
/ConfirmGc:Yes
/CreateDNSDelegation:Yes
/UserDomain:DomainOfAdminAccount
/UserName:AdminAccountInDomainOfDC
/Password:"Password"
/ReplicationSourceDC:SoureDCName
/DatabasePath:"LocalDatabasePath"
/LogPath:"LocalLogPath"
/SYSVOLPath:"LocalSysVolPath"
/SafeModeAdminPassword:"Password"
/RebootOnCompletion:Yes
```

If you are installing from media, you can refer to the location where you stored the installation media by using the following command.

```
/ReplicationSourcePath:FolderPathtoMedia
```

When the unattended installation or command-line execution completes, Dcpromo exits with a return code. A return code of 1 to 10 indicates success. A return code of 11 to 100 indicates failure. Note any related error text and take appropriate corrective action as necessary.

Decommissioning Domain Controllers

When you no longer need a domain controller, you can decommission it and remove it from service. Running the Active Directory Domain Services Installation Wizard (Dcpromo.exe) on the domain controller allows you to remove Active Directory Domain Services and demote the domain controller to either a stand-alone server or a member server.

The process for removing an additional domain controller is different from the process for removing the last domain controller. If the domain controller is the last in the domain, it will become a stand-alone server in a workgroup. Otherwise, if other domain controllers remain in the domain, the domain controller will become a member server in the domain.

Preparing to Remove Domain Controllers

Before you demote a domain controller, you should determine the functions and roles the server has in the domains and plan accordingly. With regard to Active Directory Domain Services, the functions and roles to check for are as follows:

Global catalog server

- Don't accidentally remove the last global catalog server from a domain. If you remove the last global catalog server from a domain, you will cause serious problems. Users won't be able to log on to the domain, and directory search functions will be impaired. To avoid problems, ensure another global catalog server is available or designate a new one.

- Don't accidentally remove the last global catalog server from a site. If you remove the last global catalog server from a site, computers in the site will query a global catalog server in another site when searching for resources in other domains in the forest, and a domain controller responding to a user's logon or authentication request will need to obtain the required information from a global catalog server in another site. To avoid problems, ensure another global catalog server is available, designate a new one, or verify the affected site is connected to other sites with fast, reliable links.
- Determine whether a domain controller is acting as a global catalog server by entering the following at a command prompt: **dsquery server -domain *DomainName* | dsget server -isgc -dnsname** where *DomainName* is the name of the domain you want to examine. The resulting output lists all global catalog servers in the domain.

Bridgehead server

- Don't accidentally remove the last preferred bridgehead server from a site. If you remove the last preferred bridgehead server, intersite replication will stop until you change the preferred bridgehead server configuration options. You can avoid problems by (1) removing the preferred bridgehead server designation prior to demoting the domain controller and thereby allowing Active Directory to select the bridgehead servers to use, or (2) ensuring one or more additional preferred bridgehead servers are available.
- Determine whether a domain controller is acting as a bridgehead server by entering the following at a command prompt: **repadmin /bridgeheads site:*SiteName*** where *SiteName* is the name of the site, such as repadmin /bridgeheads site:Seattle-First-Site. The resulting output is a list of bridgehead servers in the specified site. If you omit the site:SiteName value, the details for the current site are returned.

Operations master

- Don't accidentally demote a domain controller holding a forestwide or domainwide operations master role. If you remove an operations master without first transferring the role, Active Directory will try to transfer the role as part of the demotion process, and the domain controller that ends up holding the role may not be the one you would have selected.
- Determine whether a domain controller is acting as an operations master by entering the following at a command prompt: **netdom query fsmo**. The resulting output lists the forestwide and domainwide operations master role holders.

Before you remove the last domain controller in a domain, you should examine domain accounts and look for encrypted files and folders. Because the deleted domain will no longer exist, its accounts and cryptographic keys will no longer be applicable, and this results in the deletion of all domain accounts and all certificates and cryptographic keys. You must decrypt any encrypted data on the server, including data stored using the Encrypting File System (EFS), before removing the last domain controller, or the data will be permanently inaccessible.

You can check for encrypted files and folders by using the EFSInfo utility. At a command prompt, enter **efsinfo /s:*DriveDesignator* /i | find ": Encrypted"** where *DriveDesignator* is the drive designator of the volume to search, such as C:.

The credentials you need to demote a domain controller depend on the domain controller's functions and roles. Keep the following in mind:

- To remove the last domain controller from a domain tree or child domain, you must use an account that is a member of the Enterprise Admins group or be able to provide credentials for an enterprise administrator account.

- To remove the last domain controller in a forest, you must log on to the domain as Administrator or use an account that is a member of the Domain Admins group.
- To remove other domain controllers, you must use an account that is a member of either the Enterprise Admins or Domain Admins group.

Removing Additional Domain Controllers

You can remove an additional domain controller from a domain by completing the following steps:

1. Start the Active Directory Domain Services Installation Wizard by clicking Start, typing **dcpromo** in the Search box, and pressing Enter.

2. When the wizard starts, it will confirm that the computer is a domain controller. You should see a message stating the server is already a domain controller and that by continuing you will remove Active Directory, as shown in Figure 3-7. Click Next.

FIGURE 3-7 Initiate Active Directory removal.

3. If the domain controller is a global catalog server, a message appears to warn you about ensuring other global catalog servers are available, as shown in Figure 3-8. Before you click OK to continue, you should ensure one or more global catalog servers are available, as discussed previously.

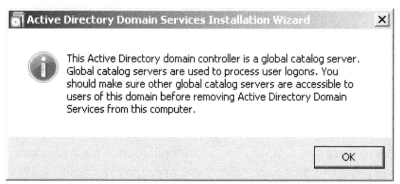

FIGURE 3-8   Ensure that you don't accidentally remove the last global catalog server.

4. On the Delete The Domain page, click Next without making a selection. If the domain controller is the last in the domain, you'll see a warning like the one shown in Figure 3-9. In this case, I recommend clicking No and then clicking Cancel, which will exit the wizard and allow you to perform any necessary preparatory tasks if you do indeed want to remove the last domain controller. When you are ready to proceed, you should perform the tasks discussed in "Removing the Last Domain Controller," later in this chapter.

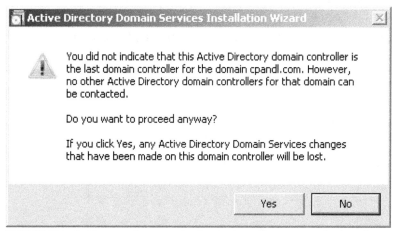

FIGURE 3-9   Ensure that you don't accidentally remove the last domain controller.

5. If the domain controller is the last DNS server for one or more Active Directory–integrated zones, a message appears to warn you that you may be unable to resolve DNS names in the applicable zones. Before continuing by clicking OK, you should ensure that you establish another DNS server for these zones.

6. If the domain controller has application directory partitions, the next page you will see is the Application Directory Partitions page, shown in Figure 3-10. You will need to do the following:

   a. If you want to retain any application directory partitions that are stored on the domain controller, you will need to use the application that created the partition to extract and save the partition data as appropriate. If the application does not provide such a tool, you can let the Active Directory Domain Services Installation Wizard remove the related directory partitions. When you are ready to continue with Active Directory removal, you can click Refresh to update the list and see any changes.

   b. Click Next. Confirm that you want to delete all application directory partitions on the domain controller by selecting the related option and then clicking Next. Keep in mind that deleting the last replica of an application partition will delete all data associated with that partition.

7. The wizard checks DNS to see if any active delegations for the server need to be removed. If the Remove DNS Delegation page is displayed, as shown in Figure 3-11, verify that the Delete The DNS Delegations Pointing To This Server check box is selected. Then click Next. If you don't remove the delegations at this time, you'll need to manually remove them later using the DNS console.

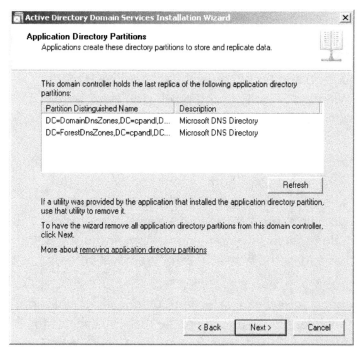

FIGURE 3-10 Ensure you don't accidentally remove the last replica.

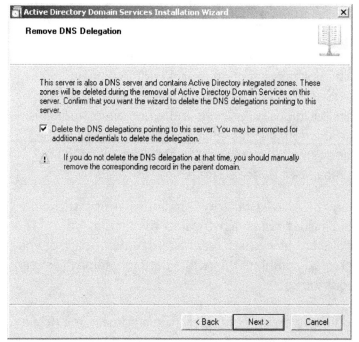

FIGURE 3-11 Verify that you want to remove DNS delegations.

8. If you are removing DNS delegations, the Active Directory Domain Services Installation Wizard then examines the DNS configuration, checking your credentials and attempting to contact a DNS server in the domain. If you need additional credentials to remove DNS delegations, the Windows Security dialog box is displayed. Enter administrative credentials for the server that hosts the DNS zone in which the domain controller is registered and then click OK.

9. On the Administrator Password page, you are prompted to enter and confirm the password for the local Administrator account on the server. You need to enter a password for the local Administrator account because domain controllers don't have local accounts but member or stand-alone servers do, so the local Administrator account will be re-created as part of the Active Directory removal process. Click Next.

10. On the Summary page, review your selections. Optionally, click Export Settings to save these settings to an answer file that you can use to perform unattended demotion of other domain controllers. When you click Next again, the wizard uses the options you've selected to demote the domain controller. This process can take several minutes.

Note If there are updates to other domains in the forest that have not been replicated, the domain controller replicates these updates, and then the wizard begins the demotion process. If the domain controller is also a DNS server, the DNS data in the ForestDnsZones and DomainDnsZones partitions is removed. If the domain controller is the last DNS server in the domain, this results in the last replica of the DNS information being removed from the domain. All associated DNS records are lost and may need to be re-created.

---

11. On the Completing The Active Directory Domain Services Installation Wizard page, click Finish. You can either select the Reboot On Completion check box to have the server restart automatically, or you can restart the server to complete the Active Directory removal when you are prompted to do so.

When removing an additional domain controller from a domain, the Active Directory Domain Services Installation Wizard does the following:

- Removes Active Directory and all related services from the server and makes it a member server in the domain
- Changes the computer account type and moves the computer account from the Domain Controllers container in Active Directory to the Computers container
- Transfers any operations master roles from the server to another domain controller in the domain
- Updates DNS to remove the domain controller SRV records
- Creates a local Security Accounts Manager (SAM) account database and a local Administrator account

> **Real World**   When you remove a domain controller, the related server object is removed from the domain directory partition automatically. However, the server object representing the retired domain controller in the configuration directory partition can have child objects and is therefore not removed automatically. For more information on these objects, refer to "Confirming Removal of Deleted Server Objects," later in this chapter.

Removing the Last Domain Controller

You can remove the last domain controller in a domain or forest by completing the following steps:

1. Start the Active Directory Domain Services Installation Wizard by clicking Start, typing **dcpromo** in the Search box, and pressing Enter.

2. When the wizard starts, click Next. If the domain controller is a global catalog server, a message appears to warn you about ensuring other global catalog servers are available. Click OK to continue.

3. On the Delete The Domain page, select Delete The Domain Because This Server Is The Last Domain Controller In The Domain check box, as shown in Figure 3-12. Click Next to continue. After you remove the last domain controller in a domain or forest, you can no longer access any directory data, Active Directory accounts, or encrypted data.

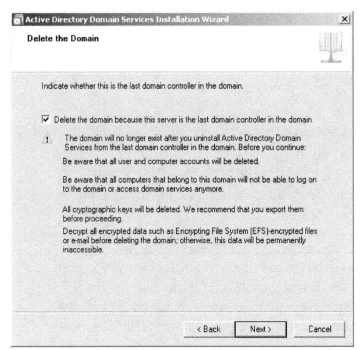

FIGURE 3-12   Verify that you want to delete the domain or forest.

4. The rest of the installation proceeds as previously discussed. Continue
    with steps 6 through 11 of the previous section, "Removing Additional
    Domain Controllers." Note the following:

▪ If you are removing the last domain controller from a domain, the
   wizard verifies that there are no child domains of the current domain
   before performing the removal operation. If child domains are found,
   removal of Active Directory fails, with an error telling you that you
   cannot remove Active Directory.

▪ When the domain being removed is a child domain, the wizard notifies
   a domain controller in the parent domain that the child domain is
   being removed. For a parent domain in its own tree, a domain
   controller in the forest root domain is notified. Either way, the domain
   object is tombstoned, and this change is then replicated to other
   domain controllers. The domain object and any related trust objects
   are also removed from the forest.

- As part of removing Active Directory from the last domain controller in a domain, all domain accounts, all certificates, and all cryptographic keys are removed from the server. The wizard creates a local SAM account database and a local Administrator account. It then changes the computer account type to a stand-alone server and puts the server in a new workgroup.

Removing Domain Controllers Using Answer Files or the Command Line

On a Full Server or Core Server installation of Windows Server, you can remove domain controllers using an unattended removal or the command line. You must be logged on as the Domain Admins group in the domain.

With the unattended removal method, you must first prepare an answer file that contains the desired removal values. You can create an answer file for removing a domain controller by completing the following steps:

1. Open Notepad or any other text editor.
2. On the first line, type **[DCINSTALL]**, and then press Enter.
3. Type the following entries, one entry on each line.

```
UserName=AdminAccountInDomainOfDC
UserDomain=DomainOfAdminAccount
Password="PasswordOfAdminAccount"
AdministratorPassword=NewLocalAdminPassword
RemoveApplicationPartitions=yes
RetainDCMetadata=No
RemoveDNSDelegation=yes
RebootOnCompletion=yes
```

4. If the account that is being used to remove AD DS is different from the account in the parent domain that has the privileges that are required to remove a DNS delegation, you must specify the account that can remove the DNS delegation by entering the following additional parameters.

```
DNSDelegationUserName=DelegationAdminAccount
DNSDelegationPassword="Password"
```

5. If the domain controller is the last DNS server for one or more Active Directory–integrated DNS zones that it hosts, Dcpromo will exit with an

error. You can force Dcpromo to proceed by entering the following additional parameter.

```
IgnoreIsLastDNSServerForZone=yes
```

6. If the domain controller is the last in the domain or forest, Dcpromo will exit with an error. You can force Dcpromo to proceed by entering the following additional parameter.

```
IsLastDCInDomain=yes
```

> **Note**   If there is actually another domain controller in the domain, Dcpromo will exit with a mismatch error. Typically, this is what you'd want to happen. However, you can force Dcpromo to continue with the removal as if this were the last domain controller by using IgnoreIsLastDCInDomainMismatch=Yes.

7. Save the answer file as a .txt file and then copy the file to a location accessible from the server you want to promote.

8. After you create the answer file, you can start the unattended removal by entering the following at a command prompt:

```
dcpromo /unattend:"PathToAnswerFile"
```

where *PathToAnswerFile* is the full file path to the answer file, such as C:\data\removedc.txt.

At the command line, you can remove a domain controller from a domain using the following command.

```
dcpromo /unattend
/UserName:AdminAccountInDomainOfDC
/UserDomain:DomainOfAdminAccount
/Password:"PasswordOfAdminAccount"
/AdministratorPassword:NewLocalAdminPassword
/RemoveApplicationPartitions:yes
/RetainDCMetadata:No
/RemoveDNSDelegation:yes
/RebootOnCompletion:yes
```

If the domain controller is the last DNS server for one or more Active Directory–integrated DNS zones that it hosts, Dcpromo will exit with an error. You can force Dcpromo to proceed using the following additional parameter.

```
/IgnoreIsLastDNSServerForZone:yes
```

If the domain controller is the last in the domain or forest, Dcpromo will exit with an error. You can force Dcpromo to proceed using the following additional parameter.

```
/IsLastDCInDomain:yes
```

When the unattended removal or command-line execution completes, Dcpromo exits with a return code. A return code of 1 to 10 indicates success. A return code of 11 to 100 indicates failure. Note any related error text and take appropriate corrective action as necessary.

Forcing the Removal of Domain Controllers

A domain controller must have connectivity to other domain controllers in the domain in order to demote the domain controller and successfully remove Active Directory Domain Services. If a domain controller has no connectivity to other domain controllers, the standard removal process will fail, and you will need to connect the domain controller to the domain and then restart the removal process. In a limited number of situations, however, you might not want or be able to connect the domain controller to the domain and instead might want to force the removal of the domain controller.

Forcing the removal of a domain controller is a three-part process. You must:

1. Restart the domain controller in Directory Services Restore Mode.
2. Perform the forced removal of the domain controller.
3. Clean up the Active Directory forest metadata.

These tasks are discussed in the sections that follow.

Restarting a Domain Controller in Directory Services Restore Mode

Before you can forcibly remove Active Directory Domain Services, you must restart the domain controller in Directory Services Restore Mode. Restarting in this mode takes the domain controller offline, meaning it functions as a member server, not as a domain controller. During installation of Active Directory Domain Services, you set the Administrator password for logging on to the server in Directory Services Restore Mode.

You can restart a domain controller in Directory Services Restore Mode manually by pressing the F8 key during domain controller startup. You must then log on by using the Directory Services Restore Mode password for the local Administrator account. A disadvantage of this technique is that if you accidentally restart the domain controller, you might forget to put it back into Directory Services Restore Mode.

To ensure the domain controller is in Directory Services Restore Mode until you specify otherwise, you can use the System Configuration utility or the Boot Configuration Data (BCD) editor to set a Directory Repair flag. Once this flag is set, the domain controller will always start in Directory Services Restore Mode, and you can be sure that you won't accidentally restart the domain controller in another mode.

To restart a domain controller in Directory Services Restore Mode using the System Configuration utility, complete the following steps:

1. On the Start menu, point to Administrative Tools, and then click System Configuration.
2. On the Boot tab, in Boot Options, select Safe Boot, and then click Active Directory Repair, as shown in Figure 3-13.
3. Click OK to exit the System Configuration utility and save your settings.
4. Restart the domain controller. The domain controller restarts in Directory Services Restore Mode.

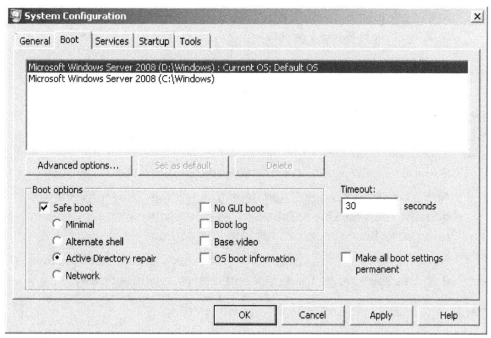

FIGURE 3-13 Change the boot options.

When you have finished performing procedures in Directory Services Restore Mode, restart the domain controller in normal mode by completing the following steps:

1. On the Start menu, point to Administrative Tools, and then click System Configuration.

2. On the General tab, in Startup Selection, click Normal Startup, and then click OK.

3. The domain controller restarts in normal mode.

To restart a domain controller in Directory Services Restore Mode using the BCD editor, complete the following steps:

1. Click Start, right-click Command Prompt, and then click Run As Administrator to open an elevated command prompt.

2. At the command prompt, enter the following command: **bcdedit /set safeboot disrepair**. This configures the boot process to start in Directory Services Restore Mode.

3. At the command prompt, enter the following command: **shutdown -t 0 -r**. This shuts down the server and restarts it without delay.

When you have finished performing procedures in Directory Services Restore Mode, restart the domain controller in normal mode by completing the following steps:

1. Click Start, right-click Command Prompt, and then click Run As Administrator to open an elevated command prompt.

2. At the command prompt, you need to enter the following command: **bcdedit /deletevalue safeboot**. This deletes the safeboot value and returns the boot process to the previous setting.

3. At the command prompt, enter the following command: **shutdown -t 0 -r**. This shuts down the server and restarts it without delay.

Performing Forced Removal of Domain Controllers

You can force the removal of a domain controller by completing the following steps:

1. Click Start, right-click Command Prompt, and then click Run As Administrator to open an elevated command prompt.

2. At the command prompt, enter the following command: **dcpromo /forceremoval**. This starts the Active Directory Domain Services Installation Wizard in Force Removal mode.

3. If the domain controller hosts any operations master roles, is a DNS server, or is a global catalog server, warnings similar to the one shown in Figure 3-14 are displayed to explain how the forced removal will affect the rest of the environment. After you review the recommendations and take action (if possible), click Yes to continue.

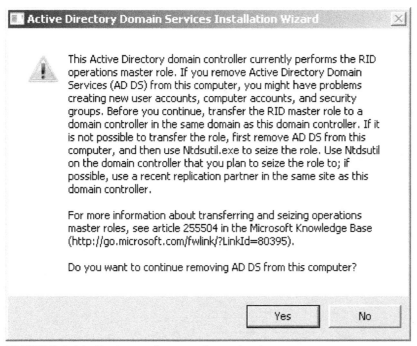

Active Directory Domain Services Installation Wizard

This Active Directory domain controller currently performs the RID operations master role. If you remove Active Directory Domain Services (AD DS) from this computer, you might have problems creating new user accounts, computer accounts, and security groups. Before you continue, transfer the RID master role to a domain controller in the same domain as this domain controller. If it is not possible to transfer the role, first remove AD DS from this computer, and then use Ntdsutil.exe to seize the role. Use Ntdsutil on the domain controller that you plan to seize the role to; if possible, use a recent replication partner in the same site as this domain controller.

For more information about transferring and seizing operations master roles, see article 255504 in the Microsoft Knowledge Base (http://go.microsoft.com/fwlink/?LinkId=80395).

Do you want to continue removing AD DS from this computer?

Yes   No

FIGURE 3-14 Review each removal warning in turn.

4. The Active Directory Domain Services Installation Wizard starts. On the Welcome page, click Next.

5. On the Force The Removal Of Active Directory Domain Services page, shown in Figure 3-15, review the information about forcing the removal of Active Directory Domain Services and the required metadata cleanup operations, and then click Next.

6. If the domain controller is a DNS server with zones integrated with Active Directory, you'll see a warning stating one or more Active Directory–integrated zones will be deleted. Before continuing by clicking OK, you should ensure that there is another DNS server for these zones. Also note that you'll need to manually remove DNS delegations pointing to this server.

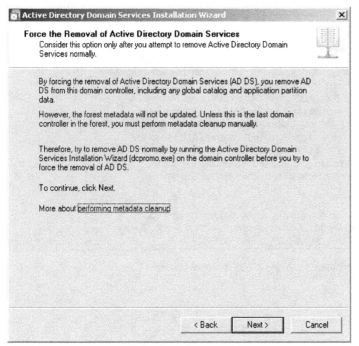

FIGURE 3-15 Review the forced removal warning.

7. On the Administrator Password page, you are prompted to enter and confirm the password for the local Administrator account on the server. You need to enter a password for the local Administrator account because domain controllers don't have local accounts, but member or stand-alone servers do, so the local Administrator account will be re-created as part of the Active Directory removal process. Click Next.

8. On the Summary page, review your selections. Optionally, click Export Settings to save these settings to an answer file that you can use to perform unattended forced removal of other domain controllers. When you click Next again, the wizard uses the options you've selected to forcibly remove Active Directory Domain Services. This process can take several minutes.

9. On the Completing The Active Directory Domain Services Installation Wizard page, click Finish. Do not select the Reboot On Completion check box. When you are prompted to restart the server, do not do so. Instead, you'll want to examine the server and perform any necessary

additional tasks. Then when you are finished, restart the server in normal mode using the appropriate technique discussed previously.

When forcibly removing a domain controller from a domain, the Active Directory Domain Services Installation Wizard does the following:

- Removes Active Directory and all related services from the server
- Changes the computer account type
- Creates a local Security Accounts Manager (SAM) account database and a local Administrator account

At the command line, you can force the removal of a domain controller from a domain using the following command:

```
dcpromo /unattend /forceremoval
/AdministratorPassword:NewLocalAdminPassword
/RemoveApplicationPartitions:yes
/RemoveDNSDelegation:yes
/RebootOnCompletion:yes
```

If the domain controller is an operations master, Dcpromo will exit with an error. You can force Dcpromo to proceed using the following additional parameter.

```
/DemoteFSMO:yes
```

This option should also suppress errors related to the domain controller being a global catalog server, a DNS server, or both.

When the command-line execution completes, Dcpromo exits with a return code. A return code of 1 to 10 indicates success. A return code of 11 to 100 indicates failure. Note the related error text and take appropriate corrective action as necessary.

Cleaning Up Metadata in the Active Directory Forest

When you force the removal of a disconnected domain controller, the Active Directory forest metadata is not updated automatically as it is when a domain controller is removed normally. Because of this, you must manually update the forest metadata after you remove the domain controller.

You perform metadata cleanup on a domain controller in the domain of the domain controller that you forcibly removed. During metadata cleanup, Active Directory automatically performs the following tasks:

- Removes data from the directory that identifies the retired domain controller to the replication system
- Removes any related File Replication Service (FRS) and Distributed File System (DFS) Replication connections
- Attempts to transfer or seize any operations master roles that the retired domain controller holds

Cleaning Up Server Metadata

On domain controllers that are running Windows Server 2008 or Windows Server 2008 R2, you can use Active Directory Users and Computers to clean up server metadata. Deleting the computer object in the Domain Controllers organizational unit (OU) initiates the cleanup process, and all related tasks are performed automatically. Using Active Directory Users and Computers, you can clean up metadata by completing the following steps:

1. Open Active Directory Users and Computers by clicking Start, clicking Administrative Tools, and then clicking Active Directory Users And Computers.

2. You must be connected to a domain controller in the domain of the domain controller that you forcibly removed. If you aren't or are unsure, right-click the Active Directory Users And Computers node and then click Change Domain Controller. Click the name of a domain controller in the appropriate domain, and then click OK.

3. Expand the domain of the domain controller that you forcibly removed, and then click Domain Controllers.

4. In the details pane, right-click the computer object of the retired domain controller, and then click Delete.

5. In the Active Directory Domain Services dialog box, click Yes to confirm that you want to delete the computer object.

6. In the Deleting Domain Controller dialog box, select This Domain Controller Is Permanently Offline And Can No Longer Be Demoted, and then click Delete.

7. If the domain controller was a global catalog server, in the Delete Domain Controller dialog box, click Yes to continue with the deletion.

8. If the domain controller currently holds one or more operations master roles, click OK to move the role or roles to the domain controller that is shown. Although you cannot change this domain controller at the present time, you can move the role once the metadata cleanup procedure is completed.

On domain controllers that are running Windows Server 2003 with Service Pack 1 (SP1), Windows Server 2003 with Service Pack 2 (SP2), Windows Server 2003 R2, Windows Server 2008 or Windows Server 2008 R2, you also can perform metadata cleanup by using the Ntdsutil command-line tool. Using Ntdsutil, you can clean up server metadata by completing the following steps:

1. Click Start, right-click Command Prompt, and then click Run As Administrator to open an elevated command prompt.

2. At the command prompt, enter the following command: **ntdsutil**.

3. At the ntdsutil prompt, enter the following command: **metadata cleanup**.

4. At the metadata cleanup prompt, enter the following command if you are logged on to the domain of the domain controller that you forcibly removed: **remove selected server *RetiredServer*** where *RetiredServer* is the distinguished name of the retired domain controller. Otherwise, enter the following command: **remove selected server *RetiredServer* on *TargetServer*** where *RetiredServer* is the distinguished name of the retired domain controller and where *TargetServer* is the DNS name of a domain controller in the domain of the domain controller that you forcibly removed.

> **Real World** This process initiates removal of objects that refer to the retired domain controller and then removes those objects from a specified server. Once the changes are replicated, the related objects will be removed throughout the Active Directory forest. You must identify the retired server by its distinguished name, such as "CN=CorpServer27,OU=Domain Controllers,DC=imaginedlands,DC=com". If you specify a target server, you must use the DNS name of the domain controller to which you want to connect, such as "CorpServer27.Imaginedlands.com". If you do not specify a target server, the objects are removed from the domain controller to which you are currently connected.

5. When prompted with the Server Remove Configuration dialog box, read the details provided. Click Yes to remove the server object and related metadata. Ntdsutil will then confirm that the server object and related metadata was removed successfully. If you receive an error message that indicates that the object cannot be found, the server object and related metadata might have been removed previously.

6. At the metadata cleanup prompt, enter the following command: **quit**.

7. At the ntdsutil prompt, enter the following command: **quit**.

Confirming Removal of Deleted Server Objects

When you remove a domain controller, the related server object is removed from the domain directory partition automatically. You can confirm this using Active Directory Users and Computers. However, the server object representing the retired domain controller in the configuration directory partition can have child objects and is therefore not removed automatically. You can confirm the status of the server object in the configuration directory partition by using Active Directory Sites And Services.

You can confirm removal of server objects for a retired domain controller by completing the following steps:

1. Open Active Directory Users and Computers by clicking Start, clicking Administrative Tools, and then clicking Active Directory Users And Computers.

2. Expand the domain of the domain controller that you forcibly removed, and then click Domain Controllers.

3. In the details pane, the computer object of the retired domain controller should not appear. If it does, follow the steps in "Cleaning Up Server Metadata," earlier in this chapter, to remove the object using Active Directory Users and Computers.

4. Open Active Directory Sites and Services by clicking Start, clicking Administrative Tools, and then clicking Active Directory Sites And Services.

5. Any domain controllers associated with a site are listed in the site's Servers node. Select the site that the retired domain controller was previously associated with and then expand the related Servers node.

6. Confirm that the server object for the retired domain controller does not contain an NTDS Settings object. If no child objects appear below the server object, you can delete the server object. Right-click the server object and then click Delete. When prompted to confirm, click Yes.

Real World Do not delete the server object if it has a child object. If an NTDS Settings object appears below the server object, either replication on the domain controller on which you are viewing the configuration container has not occurred or the domain controller was not properly decommissioned. If a child object other than NTDS Settings is listed, another application has published the object. You must contact the appropriate application administrator and determine the required actions to remove the child object.

Chapter 4. Deploying Read-Only Domain Controllers

When the domain and forest are operating at the Windows Server 2003 functional level or higher, Active Directory supports both writable and read-only domain controllers. Writable domain controllers are the primary type of domain controllers you will use throughout the enterprise. Read-only domain controllers (RODCs) host read-only replicas of a domain's Active Directory database and are designed to be placed in locations that require fast and reliable authentication services but aren't necessarily secure. As such, RODCs are ideally suited to the needs of branch offices where a domain controller's physical security cannot be guaranteed.

Before you deploy RODCs in an Active Directory forest, you must perform some preliminary tasks. These tasks include preparing the forest schema to use RODCs and ensuring your writable domain controllers are running the appropriate operating systems. Because RODCs are managed differently than writable domain controllers, there are some administrative tasks that apply only to RODCs. Therefore in addition to detailing how to add and remove RODCs, I discuss the unique tasks you'll use to maintain RODCs.

Preparing to Deploy Read-Only Domain Controllers

Only Windows Server 2008 and later releases of Windows Server can act as read-only domain controllers. Typically, you do not need to make any changes to client computers to allow them to use an RODC. Client computers running any current Windows and Windows Servers operating systems are supported for use with RODCs.

RODCs support the same features as writable domain controllers and can be used in both Core Server and Full Server installations. RODCs by default do not store passwords or credentials other than for their own computer accounts and the Kerberos Target (krbtgt) accounts. Instead, RODCs pull user and computer credentials from a writable domain controller running

Windows Server 2008 or later. You must explicitly allow any other credentials to be cached on an RODC by using Password Replication Policy.

> **Tip** After an RODC has cached the password for a user, it remains in the Active Directory database until the user changes the password or the Password Replication Policy for the RODC changes such that the user's password should no longer be cached. Accounts that will not have credentials cached on the RODC can still use the RODC for domain logon. The RODC retrieves the credentials from its writable domain controller replication partner. The credentials, however, will not be cached for subsequent logons using the RODC.

Except for passwords and designated, nonreplicated attributes, RODCs store the same objects and attributes as writable domain controllers. These objects and attributes are replicated to RODCs using unidirectional replication from a writable domain controller acting as a replication partner.

Although Active Directory clients and applications can access the directory to read data, the clients are not able to write changes directly to an RODC. Clients and applications that need to write changes are referred to a writable domain controller. This prevents changes made by malicious users at branch locations from corrupting the Active Directory forest.

RODCs can host a global catalog but cannot act as bridgehead servers or as operations master role holders. On an RODC, you can install the Domain Name System (DNS) Server service. If you do, the RODC receives a read-only replica of all application directory partitions that are used by DNS, including ForestDNSZones and DomainDNSZones. Clients and applications can then query DNS on the RODC for name resolution as they would query any other DNS server. As with Active Directory data, the DNS server on an RODC does not support direct updates. Clients and applications that need to make updates to DNS are referred to a writable DNS server.

Because no changes are written directly to RODCs, replication is unidirectional, and writable domain controllers acting as replication partners do not have to pull changes from RODCs. This reduces the workload of bridgehead servers and the scope of your replication monitoring efforts. RODCs reduce the administration burden on the enterprise by allowing any domain user to be delegated as a local administrator without granting any other rights in the domain. This creates a clear separation between domain administrators and delegated administrator users at branch offices.

RODCs are designed to be placed in sites that have no other domain controllers. Although you cannot place RODCs from the same domain in the same site, you can

- Place an RODC in the same site with writable domain controllers from the same domain.
- Place an RODC in the same site with writable domain controllers from different domains.
- Place RODCs from different domains in the same site.

RODCs can pull most directory information from domain controllers running Windows Server 2003. However, RODCs can pull updates of the domain partition only from a writable domain controller running Windows Server 2008 or later in the same domain.

You can install an RODC only in an existing domain. Before you install RODCs in any domain, you must ensure the following are true:

- Forest functional level is Windows Server 2003 or higher. This ensures that linked-value replication is available to help maintain replication consistency.
- Domain functional level is Windows Server 2003 or higher. This ensures that Kerberos-constrained delegation is available so that security calls can be impersonated under the context of the caller.
- The domain in which you are deploying the RODC includes domain controllers running Windows Server 2003 and domain controllers running Windows Server 2008 or later.
- At least one domain controller running Windows Server 2008 or later for the same domain must be located in the site closest to the site that

includes the RODC. To ensure the RODC can replicate all directory partitions, this domain controller must be a global catalog server.

- The primary domain controller (PDC) emulator operations master role holder for the domain is running Windows Server 2008 or later. You must ensure there is a bidirectional communications path open between the RODC and the PDC emulator.

Like writable domain controllers, RODCs have no local accounts or separate cryptographic keys. Making a server a domain controller deletes all local accounts and all certificates and cryptographic keys from the server. Any encrypted data on the server, including data stored using the Encrypting File System (EFS), must be decrypted before Active Directory is installed, or the data will be permanently inaccessible.

Because of this, you should examine local accounts to determine whether you need to take special steps to preserve any local accounts before you install Active Directory Domain Services. You should also check for encrypted files and folders by using the EFSInfo utility. At a command prompt, enter **efsinfo /s:DriveDesignator /i | find ": Encrypted"** where *DriveDesignator* is the drive designator of the volume to search, such as C:.

To run the DNS Server service on an RODC, another domain controller running Windows Server 2008 or later must be running in the domain and hosting the Active Directory–integrated DNS domain zone. An Active Directory–integrated DNS zone on an RODC is always a read-only copy of the zone file.

Finally, you must run the **adprep /rodcprep** command before installing any RODCs. This ensures RODCs can replicate DNS partitions. This is not required for new forests with only domain controllers that run Windows Server 2008 or later, or when you are not using Active Directory–integrated DNS in the existing forest.

Adding RODCs to Domains

When you install an RODC, you should use Advanced Installation mode. This mode allows you to configure Password Replication Policy, delegate administrative permissions, and install from media.

Password Replication Policy controls whether passwords are replicated to the RODC that you are installing. As discussed in "Setting Password Replication Policy" later in this chapter, you can configure denied accounts, for which passwords are never replicated, and allowed accounts, for which passwords are always replicated.

Through delegation of administrative permissions, you allow a specified user or group to act as the local administrator of the RODC while granting no other administrative permissions in the domain. For ease of administration, you should create a new group for this purpose before deploying an RODC. (For more information, see "Delegating Administrative Permissions" later in this chapter.)

When you install from media, the RODC gets its initial directory data from a local or shared folder rather than over the network. Performing an RODC installation from media reduces directory replication traffic over the network. You must create the media before installing the RODC. Follow the technique discussed in "Adding Writable Domain Controllers Using Installation Media" in Chapter 3, "Deploying Writable Domain Controllers."

You use the same technique as for writable domain controllers to create installation media for read-only domain controllers. In step 4, instead of entering **create full**, enter **create rodc**. Because you're creating installation media for an RODC, passwords are not included in the data.

You can add an RODC to a domain by using a nonstaged or staged installation. When you plan to deliver a ready-to-use RODC to a branch office or a single person is installing the RODC in the branch office, you'll typically want to use a nonstaged installation. With a nonstaged installation, an administrator with domainwide administrative credentials completes the entire installation process as with writable domain controllers.

Staged installations are completed in two stages. In stage one, an administrator with domainwide administrative credentials creates an account for the RODC in Active Directory. In stage two, a delegated user installs the RODC. When two different people are installing an RODC, you'll want to use a staged installation.

Adding RODCs Using Replication

After you complete any necessary preliminary tasks, you can add an RODC to a domain by using a nonstaged installation by completing the following steps:

1. Check the TCP/IP configuration of the server. The server must have a valid IP address and must have properly configured DNS settings. To ensure reliable DNS operations, domain controllers that also act as DNS servers should not have dynamic IP addresses. Otherwise, the server can have a static IP address or a dynamic IP address assigned by a DHCP server.

2. Install the Active Directory binaries by entering the following command at an elevated, administrator command prompt: **servermanagercmd – install adds-domain-controller**. This installs the AD DS binaries, which enables the Active Directory Domain Services role on the server.

3. Start the Active Directory Domain Services Installation Wizard by clicking Start, typing **dcpromo** in the Search box, and pressing Enter.

4. Select the Use Advanced Installation Mode check box before clicking Next to continue.

5. If the Operating System Compatibility page is displayed, review the warning about the default security settings for domain controllers and then click Next.

6. On the Choose A Deployment Configuration page, select Existing Forest and then select Add A Domain Controller To An Existing Domain, as shown in Figure 4-1. By choosing this option, you specify

that you are adding a domain controller to an existing domain in the Active Directory forest.

7. When you click Next, you see the Network Credentials page. In the field provided, enter the full DNS name of any domain in the forest where you plan to install the domain controller. Preferably, this should be the name of the forest root domain, such as imaginedlands.com. If you are logged on to a domain in this forest and have the appropriate permissions, you can use your current logged-on credentials to perform the installation. Otherwise, select Alternate Credentials, click Set, enter the user name and password for an enterprise administrator account in the previously specified domain, and then click OK.

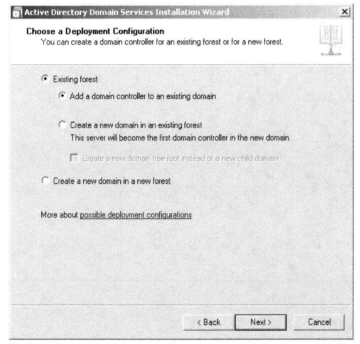

FIGURE 4-1 Specify that you want to add a domain controller to the domain.

8. When you click Next, the wizard validates the domain name you provide and then lists all domains in the related forest. On the Select A Domain page, select the domain to which the RODC will be added and then click Next.

9. When you click Next, the wizard determines the available Active Directory sites. On the Select A Site page, select the site in which you want to locate the RODC and then click Next.

10. When you click Next, the wizard examines the DNS configuration and attempts to determine whether any authoritative DNS servers are available. It then displays the Additional Domain Controller Options page. As shown in Figure 4-2, select the Read-Only Domain Controller (RODC) check box as an additional installation option for the domain controller. If you want the RODC to act as a read-only DNS server, select the DNS Server check box. If you want the RODC to act as a global catalog, select the Global Catalog check box. Click Next when you are ready to continue.

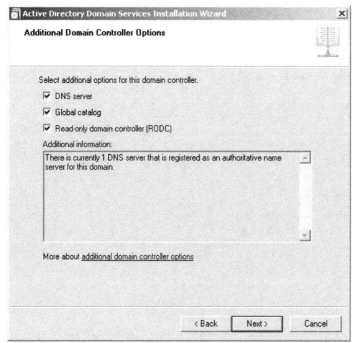

FIGURE 4-2 Select Read-Only Domain Controller (RODC) as an option.

11. If you choose to let the wizard install the DNS Server service, note the following:

    a. The DNS Server service will be installed, and the RODC will also act as a DNS server with a read-only replica of all application directory partitions that are used by DNS, including ForestDNSZones and

DomainDNSZones. The wizard will also update the server's TCP/IP configuration so that its DNS server is set to itself (using the local loopback addresses 127.0.0.1 for IPv4 and ::1 for IPv6). If you've already entered a primary DNS server, the alternate DNS server points to the server itself.

b. During installation of the operating system, Windows Setup installs and configures IPv4 and IPv6 if networking components were detected. If you've configured dynamic IPv4, IPv6, or both addresses, you'll see a warning. Click Yes to ignore the warning and continue.

c. If you want to modify the TCP/IP configuration, click No to return to the Additional Domain Controller Options page and then make the appropriate changes to the system configuration before clicking Next to continue. If you configure a static IPv4 address but do not configure a static IPv6 address, you'll also see the warning. To ignore the warning and continue with the installation, click Yes.

d. The wizard next attempts to register a delegation for the DNS server with an authoritative parent zone. If you are integrating with an existing DNS infrastructure, you should manually create a delegation to the DNS server and then click Yes to continue. Otherwise, you can ignore this warning and click Yes to continue.

12. If you choose to not let the wizard install the DNS Server service, the wizard next attempts to register a delegation for the DNS server with an authoritative parent zone. If the wizard cannot create a delegation for the DNS server, it displays a warning message to indicate that you must create the delegation manually. Click No to return to the Additional Domain Controller Options page so that you can select and install DNS Server services. To continue without installing DNS Server services, click Yes. Keep in mind that you'll then need to manually configure the required DNS settings, including SRV and A resource records.

13. On the Specify The Password Replication Policy page, shown in Figure 4-3, configure the initial Password Replication Policy for the RODC. By default, no account passwords are replicated to the RODC, and security-sensitive accounts (such as members of the Administrators, Account Operators, Server Operators and Backup Operators groups) are explicitly denied from ever having their passwords replicated to the

RODC. To add other accounts to the policy, click Add. If the accounts will be allowed to have their passwords replicated to the RODC, click Allow Passwords For The Account To Replicate To This RODC. If the accounts will be denied from having their passwords replicated to the RODC, click Deny Passwords For The Account From Replicating To This RODC. Then click OK. When you are done adding other accounts, click Next. (For more information, see "Setting Password Replication Policy" later in this chapter.)

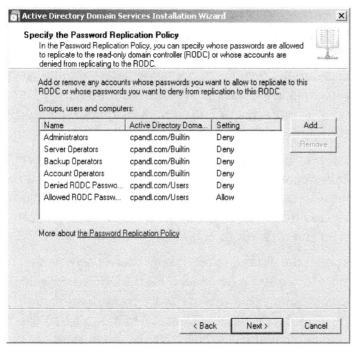

FIGURE 4-3 Configure the Password Replication Policy.

14. On the Delegation Of RODC Installation And Administration page, shown in Figure 4-4, you'll configure the initial delegation settings. Click Set, use the Select User Or Group dialog box to specify a delegated user or group, and then click OK. The delegated user or group will have local administrative permissions on the RODC. (For more information, see "Delegating Administrative Permissions" later in this chapter.) Click Next to continue.

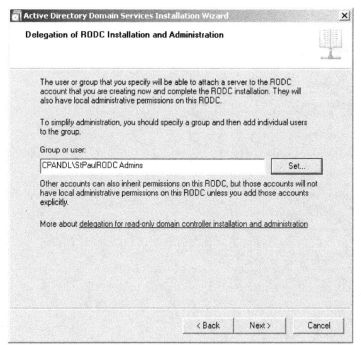

FIGURE 4-4 Specify the delegated administrative user or group.

15. On the Install From Media page, shown in Figure 4-5, you'll be able to specify whether you want to replicate over the network or use installation media. If you don't want to install from media, use the default selection to allow data to replicate over the network. If you want to install from media, select Replicate Data From Media At The Following Location and then enter the relevant folder path in the Location box. Alternatively, click Browse and then use the Browse For Folder dialog box to locate the folder to use. The media you specify must already be available. Click Next to continue.

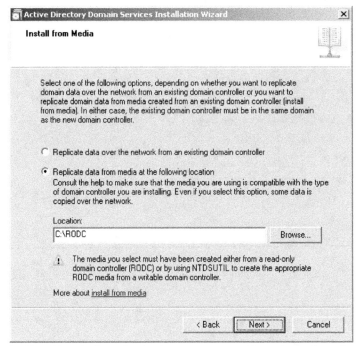

FIGURE 4-5 Specify whether you are installing through replication or by using media.

16. On the Source Domain Controller page, you can let the wizard choose
a replication partner for the installation of the RODC or select a desired
replication partner for the installation. When you install an RODC and
do not use installation media, all directory data is replicated from the
replication partner to the domain controller you are installing. Because
this can be a considerable amount of data, you typically want to ensure
that both domain controllers are located in the same site or connected
over reliable, high-speed networks. On the other hand, when you
install from media, the RODC replicates only the changes or the
missing data over the network from the replication partner. Click Next
to continue.

17. On the Location For Database, Log Files, And SYSVOL page, select a
location to store the Active Directory database folder, log folder, and
SYSVOL folder. The default location for the database and log folders is
a subfolder of %SystemRoot%\NTDS. The default location for the
SYSVOL folder is %SystemRoot%\Sysvol. You'll get better performance
if the database and log folders are on two separate volumes, each on a
separate disk. Placement of the SYSVOL folder is less critical, and you

can accept the default in most cases. Although you can change the storage locations later, the process is lengthy and complex.

18. Click Next. On the Directory Services Restore Mode Administrator Password page, enter and confirm the password that should be used when you want to start the computer in Directory Services Restore Mode. Be sure to track this password carefully. This special password is used only in Restore mode and is different from the Administrator account password. The password complexity and length must comply with the domain security policy.

19. Click Next. On the Summary page, review the installation options. If desired, click Export Settings to save these settings to an answer file that you can use to perform unattended installation of other domain controllers. When you click Next again, the wizard will use the options you've selected to install and configure Active Directory. If you specified that the DNS Server service should be installed, the server will also be configured as a DNS server at this time.

20. When the wizard finishes configuring Active Directory, click Finish. You are then prompted to restart the computer. Click Restart Now to reboot.

After installing Active Directory, you should verify the installation. Start by examining the installation log, which is stored in the Dcpromo.log file in the %SystemRoot%\Debug folder. The log is very detailed and takes you through every step of the installation process, including the creation of directory partitions and the securing of the Registry for Active Directory.

Next, check the DNS configuration in the DNS console. DNS is updated to add SRV and A records for the server. Because you created a new domain, DNS is updated to include a forward lookup zone for the domain. You may also need to add a reverse lookup zone for the domain.

Check for updates in Active Directory Users and Computers. The Domain Controllers OU should have an account for the domain controller you installed.

Adding RODCs Using Answer Files or the Command Line

On a Full Server or Core Server installation of Windows Server 2008 or later, you can add RODCs using an unattended installation or the command line. You must be logged on as the Domain Admins group in the domain.

With the unattended method of installation, you must first prepare an answer file that contains the desired configuration values. You can create the required answer file by completing the following steps:

1. Open Notepad or any other text editor.
2. On the first line, type **[DCINSTALL]** and then press Enter.
3. Type the following entries, one entry on each line.

```
ReplicaOrNewDomain=ReadOnlyReplica
ReplicaDomainDNSName=FQDNOfDCDomain
SiteName="SiteName"
CreateDNSDelegation=Yes
UserDomain=DomainOfAdminAccount
UserName=AdminAccountInDomainOfDC
Password=*
ReplicationSourceDC=SourceDCName
DatabasePath="LocalDatabasePath"
LogPath="LocalLogPath"
SYSVOLPath="LocalSysVolPath"
SafeModeAdminPassword=
RebootOnCompletion=Yes
```

> **Note** Values you must specify are shown in bold. The site name is mandatory for an RODC installation. You can set Password to * if you do not want to include it in the answer file. When you run Dcpromo to initiate the unattended installation, you will be prompted for the password.
>
> **Tip** SafeModeAdminPassword sets the Directory Services Restore Mode password in the answer file. If you don't want to include the password, you can omit this entry. However, you will need to use the /SafeModeAdminPassword command-line parameter to provide the password later when you run Dcpromo to initiate the unattended installation.

4. Define the RODC Password Replication Policy by specifying the denied and allowed users and groups. Insert one entry on each line, as shown in the following example.

```
DelegatedAdmin="RODCAdministrator"
PasswordReplicationDenied="BUILTIN\Administrators"
PasswordReplicationDenied="BUILTIN\Server Operators"
PasswordReplicationDenied="BUILTIN\Backup Operators"
PasswordReplicationDenied="BUILTIN\Account
  Operators"
PasswordReplicationDenied="DomainName\Denied RODC
  Password Replication Group"
PasswordReplicationAllowed="GroupName1"
PasswordReplicationAllowed="GroupName2"
 . . .
PasswordReplicationAllowed="GroupNameN"
PasswordReplicationAllowed="User_Name1"
PasswordReplicationAllowed="User_Name2"
 . . .
PasswordReplicationAllowed="User_NameN"
PasswordReplicationAllowed="Computer_Name1"
PasswordReplicationAllowed="Computer_Name2"
 . . .
PasswordReplicationAllowed="Computer_NameN"
```

> **Note** Users and groups that you specify for the PasswordReplicationAllowed and PasswordReplicationDenied parameters must already exist. The easiest way to specify users and groups is to use the DOMAIN\UserName format, such as IMAGINEDL\WilliamS. Other examples are shown in the previous listing.

5. If you want configure the domain controller as a DNS server, add the following command.

```
InstallDNS=Yes
```

6. If you want configure the domain controller as a global catalog server, add the following command.

```
ConfirmGC=Yes
```

7. If you are installing from media, you can refer to the location where you stored the installation media by using the following command.

```
ReplicationSourcePath=FolderPathToMedia
```

8. Save the answer file as a .txt file and then copy the file to a location accessible from the server you want to promote.

    The following is a complete example.

```
; Read-Only Replica DC promotion
[DCInstall]
; RODC Password Replication Policy
PasswordReplicationDenied="BUILTIN\Administrators"
PasswordReplicationDenied="BUILTIN\Server Operators"
PasswordReplicationDenied="BUILTIN\Backup Operators"
PasswordReplicationDenied="BUILTIN\Account
  Operators"
PasswordReplicationDenied="IMAGINEDL\Denied RODC
Password Replication Group"
PasswordReplicationAllowed="IMAGINEDL\Allowed RODC
  Password Replication Group"
DelegatedAdmin="IMAGINEDL\StPaulRODC Admins"

; RODC settings
ReplicaOrNewDomain=ReadOnlyReplica
ReplicaDomainDNSName=imaginedlands.com
SiteName=LA-First-Site
InstallDNS=Yes
ConfirmGc=Yes
CreateDNSDelegation=Yes
UserDomain=imaginedlands.com
UserName=imaginedlands.com\tonyg
Password=*
ReplicationSourceDC=CorpServer65.imaginedlands.com
DatabasePath="D:\Windows\NTDS"
LogPath="D:\Windows\NTDS"
SYSVOLPath="D:\Windows\SYSVOL"

; Set SafeModeAdminPassword later
SafeModeAdminPassword=

; Run-time flags (optional)
RebootOnCompletion=Yes
```

9. After you create the answer file, you can start the unattended installation by entering the following at a command prompt:

```
dcpromo /unattend:"PathToAnswerFile"
```

    where *PathToAnswerFile* is the full file path to the answer file, such as C:\Data\NewRodc.txt.

At the command line, you can add the RODC by using the following command.

```
dcpromo /unattend
/ReplicaOrNewDomain:ReadOnlyReplica
/ReplicaDomainDNSName:FQDNOfDCDomain
/SiteName:"SiteName"
/CreateDNSDelegation:No
/UserDomain:DomainOfAdminAccount
/UserName:AdminAccountInDomainOfDC
/Password:"Password"
/ReplicationSourceDC:SourceDCName
/DatabasePath:"LocalDatabasePath"
/LogPath:"LocalLogPath"
/SYSVOLPath:"LocalSysVolPath"
/SafeModeAdminPassword:"Password"
/RebootOnCompletion:Yes
/DelegatedAdmin:"RODCAdministrator"
/PasswordReplicationDenied:"BUILTIN\Administrators"
/PasswordReplicationDenied:"BUILTIN\Server
  Operators"
/PasswordReplicationDenied:"BUILTIN\Backup
  Operators"
/PasswordReplicationDenied:"BUILTIN\Account
  Operators"
/PasswordReplicationDenied:"DomainName\Denied RODC
  Password Replication Group"
/PasswordReplicationAllowed:"GroupName1"
/PasswordReplicationAllowed:"GroupName2"
. . .
/PasswordReplicationAllowed:"GroupNameN"
/PasswordReplicationAllowed:"User_Name1"
/PasswordReplicationAllowed:"User_Name2"
. . .
/PasswordReplicationAllowed:"User_NameN"
/PasswordReplicationAllowed:"Computer_Name1"
/PasswordReplicationAllowed:"Computer_Name2"
. . .
/PasswordReplicationAllowed:"Computer_NameN"
```

Note that the site name is mandatory for an RODC installation. If you are installing from media, you can refer to the location where you stored the installation media by using the following command.

```
/ReplicationSourcePath:FolderPathtoMedia
```

When the unattended installation or command-line execution completes, Dcpromo exits with a return code. A return code of 1 to 10 indicates success. A return code of 11 to 100 indicates failure. Note the related error text and take appropriate corrective action as necessary.

Using Staged Installations

Rather than having a single person deploy an RODC, you can perform a staged installation of an RODC that involves two people. In the first stage of the installation, an administrator with domainwide administrative permissions uses the Active Directory Domain Services Installation Wizard to create an account for the RODC in Active Directory and record all data about the RODC that will be stored in Active Directory, such as its domain controller account name and the site in which it will be placed. The administrator must be a member of the Domain Admins group for the domain in which the RODC will be deployed. The administrator can also specify which users or groups can complete the next stage of the installation.

The second stage of the installation can be performed in the branch office by any user who was delegated the right to complete the installation when the RODC account was created in Active Directory. The user does not need to be a member of any administrative groups in the domain. However, if the administrator who created the RODC account did not specify any delegate to complete the installation, only a member of the Domain Admins or Enterprise Admins group can complete the installation.

During the second stage, the delegated user uses the Active Directory Domain Services Installation Wizard to install Active Directory Domain Services on the server that will become the RODC and attaches the server to the domain account that was previously created for it. Data that resides locally, such as in the database, log files, and so on, is created on the RODC in this stage and can be replicated to the RODC from another domain controller over the network or from installation media.

The server that will become the RODC must not be joined to the domain before you try to attach it to the RODC account. As part of the installation, the wizard automatically detects whether the name of the server matches the names of any RODC accounts that have been created in advance for the domain. When it finds a matching account name, the wizard prompts the user to use that account to complete the RODC installation.

Stage 1: Creating the RODC Account and Preparing for Installation

You can create an RODC account and prepare for RODC installation by completing the following steps:

1. Open Active Directory Users and Computers by clicking Start, clicking Administrative Tools, and then clicking Active Directory Users And Computers.

2. Right-click the Domain Controllers organizational unit (OU) and then click Pre-Create Read-Only Domain Controller Account. This starts the Active Directory Domain Services Installation Wizard.

> **Tip** Instead of performing steps 1 and 2, you can run the Active Directory Domain Services Installation Wizard in RODC account creation mode directly. At a command prompt, enter the following command: **dcpromo.exe /CreateDCAccount**.

3. Select the Use Advanced Installation Mode check box before clicking Next to continue.

4. On the Operating System Compatibility page, review the warning about the default security settings for domain controllers and then click Next.

5. On the Network Credentials page, under Specify The Account Credentials To Use To Perform The Installation, click My Current Logged On Credentials or click Alternate Credentials, and then click Set. In the Windows Security dialog box, provide the user name and password for an account that can install the RODC account. To install the RODC account, you must be a member of the Enterprise Admins group or the Domain Admins group. When you are finished providing credentials, click Next.

6. On the Specify The Computer Name page, enter the computer name of the server that will be the RODC.

7. On the Select A Site page, you must specify the site for the RODC. Select a site from the list, or select the option to install the domain controller in the site that corresponds to the IP address of the computer on which you are running the wizard, and then click Next.

8. On the Additional Domain Controller Options page, select the Read-Only Domain Controller check box as an additional installation option for the domain controller. If you want the RODC to act as a read-only DNS server, select the DNS Server check box. If you want the RODC to act as a global catalog, select the Global Catalog check box. Click Next when you are ready to continue.

9. On the Specify The Password Replication Policy page, configure the initial Password Replication Policy for the RODC. By default, no account passwords are replicated to the RODC, and security-sensitive accounts (such as members of the Administrators, Account Operators, Server Operators, and Backup Operators groups) are explicitly denied from ever having their passwords replicated to the RODC. To add other accounts to the policy, click Add. If the accounts will be allowed to have their passwords replicated to the RODC, click Allow Passwords For The Account To Replicate To This RODC. If the accounts will be denied from having their passwords replicated to the RODC, click Deny Passwords For The Account From Replicating To This RODC. Then click OK. When you are done adding other accounts, click Next. (For more information, see "Setting Password Replication Policy" later in this chapter.)

10. On the Delegation Of RODC Installation And Administration page, enter the name of the user or the group that will attach the server to the RODC account that you are creating. You can enter the name of only one security principal. Click Set, use the Select User Or Group dialog box to specify the security principal, and then click OK. The delegated user or group also will have local administrative permissions on the RODC. (For more information, see "Delegating Administrative Permissions" later in this chapter.) Click Next to continue.

11. On the Summary page, review the installation options. If desired, click Export Settings to save these settings to an answer file that you can

use to create an RODC account and prepare for installation. When you click Next again, the wizard will use the options you've selected to create the RODC account and prepare Active Directory. When the wizard finishes configuring Active Directory, click Finish.

Stage 2: Attaching the RODC and Finalizing Installation

After you create the account for the RODC and prepare the installation, the user or group to whom you delegated installation and administration of the RODC can attach the RODC and complete the installation by running the Active Directory Domain Services Installation Wizard on the server that will become the RODC. The server must not be joined to the domain before the second stage.

To attach a server to an RODC account and complete the installation, complete the following steps:

1. Log on as the local administrator to the server that will become the RODC.

2. Open a command prompt by clicking Start and then clicking Command Prompt.

3. At the command prompt, enter the following command: **dcpromo /UseExistingAccount:Attach**. This command runs the Active Directory Domain Services Installation Wizard and starts the second stage of the RODC installation.

4. On the Network Credentials page, enter the name of any existing domain in the forest where you plan to install the RODC. Under Specify The Account Credentials To Use To Perform The Installation, click Alternate Credentials and then click Set. In the Windows Security dialog box, enter the user name and password for an account that was delegated the authority to install and administer the RODC. When you are finished providing credentials, click Next.

5. The wizard will automatically detect the name of the server and try to match it to an RODC account that has been precreated for it. On the Select Domain Controller Account page, confirm that the wizard has

found an existing RODC account that matches the name of the server, and then click Next.

6. On the Install From Media page, you'll be able to specify whether you want to replicate over the network or use installation media. If you don't want to install from media, use the default selection to allow data to replicate over the network. If you want to install from media, select Replicate Data From Media At The Following Location and then enter the folder path to use in the Location box. Alternatively, click Browse and then use the Browse For Folder dialog box to locate the folder to use. The media you specify must already be available. Click Next to continue.

7. On the Source Domain Controller page, you can let the wizard choose a replication partner for the installation of the RODC or select a desired replication partner for the installation. When you install an RODC and do not use installation media, all directory data is replicated from the replication partner to the domain controller you are installing. When you install from media, the RODC replicates only the changes or the missing data over the network from the replication partner. Click Next to continue.

8. On the Location For Database, Log Files, And SYSVOL page, select a location to store the Active Directory database folder, log folder, and SYSVOL folder. The default location for the database and log folders is a subfolder of %SystemRoot%\NTDS. The default location for the SYSVOL folder is %SystemRoot%\Sysvol. You'll get better performance if the database and log folders are on two separate volumes, each on a separate disk. Placement of the SYSVOL folder is less critical, and you can accept the default in most cases. Although you can change the storage locations later, the process is lengthy and complex.

9. Click Next. On the Directory Services Restore Mode Administrator Password page, enter and confirm the password that should be used when you want to start the computer in Directory Services Restore Mode. Be sure to track this password carefully. This special password is used only in Restore mode and is different from the Administrator account password. The password complexity and length must comply with the domain security policy.

10. Click Next. On the Summary page, review the installation options. If desired, click Export Settings to save these settings to an answer file that you can use to attach an RODC and finalize installation. When you click Next again, the wizard will use the options you've selected to install and configure Active Directory. If you specified that the DNS Server service should be installed, the server will also be configured as a DNS Server at this time.

11. When the wizard finishes configuring Active Directory, click Finish. You are then prompted to restart the computer. Click Restart Now to reboot.

Performing Staged Installations Using the Command Line or Answer Files

On a Full Server or Core Server installation of Windows Server 2008 or later, you can perform staged installations of RODCs using an unattended installation or the command line. As with GUI installation, you must first create an RODC account and prepare the installation. Then you must attach and finalize the RODC.

Performing Stage 1: Creating the RODC Account

You can create an answer file for creating the RODC account by completing the following steps:

1. Open Notepad or any other text editor.

2. On the first line, type **[DCINSTALL]** and then press Enter.

3. Type the following entries, one entry on each line.

```
ReplicaOrNewDomain=ReadOnlyReplica
ReplicaDomainDNSName=FQDNOfDCDomain
SiteName="SiteName"
CreateDNSDelegation=Yes
UserDomain=DomainOfAdminAccount
UserName=AdminAccountInDomainOfDC
Password="Password"
DCAccountName=RODCName
```

4. Define the RODC Password Replication Policy by specifying the denied and allowed users and groups. Insert one entry on each line, as shown in the following example.

```
DelegatedAdmin="RODCAdministrator"
PasswordReplicationDenied="BUILTIN\Administrators"
PasswordReplicationDenied="BUILTIN\Server Operators"
PasswordReplicationDenied="BUILTIN\Backup Operators"
PasswordReplicationDenied="BUILTIN\Account
  Operators"
PasswordReplicationDenied="DomainName\Denied RODC
  Password Replication Group"
PasswordReplicationAllowed="GroupName1"
PasswordReplicationAllowed="GroupName2"
.  .  .
PasswordReplicationAllowed="GroupNameN"
PasswordReplicationAllowed="User_Name1"
PasswordReplicationAllowed="User_Name2"
.  .  .
PasswordReplicationAllowed="User_NameN"
PasswordReplicationAllowed="Computer_Name1"
PasswordReplicationAllowed="Computer_Name2"
.  .  .
PasswordReplicationAllowed="Computer_NameN"
```

5. If you want to configure the domain controller as a DNS server, add the following command.

```
InstallDNS=Yes
```

6. If you want to configure the domain controller as a global catalog server, add the following command.

```
ConfirmGC=Yes
```

7. Save the answer file as a .txt file and then copy the file to a location accessible from the server you want to promote.

8. After you create the answer file, you can start the unattended installation by entering the following at a command prompt:

```
dcpromo /CreateDCAccount /unattend:"PathToAnswerFile"
```

where *PathToAnswerFile* is the full file path to the answer file, such as C:\Data\CreateRodcAccount.txt.

At the command line, you can create the RODC account using the following command.

```
dcpromo /unattend
/CreateDCAccount
/InstallDns:Yes
```

```
/confirmGC:Yes
/ReplicaOrNewDomain:ReadOnlyReplica
/ReplicaDomainDNSName:FQDNOfDCDomain
/SiteName:"SiteName"
/CreateDNSDelegation:Yes
/UserDomain:DomainOfAdminAccount
/UserName:AdminAccountInDomainOfDC
/Password:"Password"
/DCAccountName:RODCName
/DelegatedAdmin:"RODCAdministrator"
/PasswordReplicationDenied:"BUILTIN\Administrators"
/PasswordReplicationDenied:"BUILTIN\Server
  Operators"
/PasswordReplicationDenied:"BUILTIN\Backup
  Operators"
/PasswordReplicationDenied:"BUILTIN\Account
  Operators"
/PasswordReplicationDenied:"DomainName\Denied RODC
  Password Replication Group"
/PasswordReplicationAllowed:"GroupName1"
/PasswordReplicationAllowed:"GroupName2"
. . .
/PasswordReplicationAllowed:"GroupNameN"
/PasswordReplicationAllowed:"User_Name1"
/PasswordReplicationAllowed:"User_Name2"
. . .
/PasswordReplicationAllowed:"User_NameN"
/PasswordReplicationAllowed:"Computer_Name1"
/PasswordReplicationAllowed:"Computer_Name2"
. . .
/PasswordReplicationAllowed:"Computer_NameN"
. . .
```

If you are installing from media, you can refer to the location where you stored the installation media by using the following command.

```
/ReplicationSourcePath:FolderPathtoMedia
```

When the unattended installation or command-line execution completes, Dcpromo exits with a return code. A return code of 1 to 10 indicates success. A return code of 11 to 100 indicates failure. Note the related error text and take appropriate corrective action as necessary.

Performing Stage 2: Attaching the RODC

You can create an answer file for attaching and finalizing the RODC by completing the following steps:

1. Open Notepad or any other text editor.

2. On the first line, type **[DCINSTALL]** and then press Enter.

3. Type the following entries, one entry on each line.

```
ReplicaDomainDNSName=FQDNOfDCDomain
ReplicationSourceDC=SourceDCName
UserDomain=DomainOfDelegatedAdminAccount
UserName=DelegatedAdminAccountInDomainOfDC
Password=*
DatabasePath="LocalDatabasePath"
LogPath="LocalLogPath"
SYSVOLPath="LocalSysVolPath"
SafeModeAdminPassword=
RebootOnCompletion=yes
```

4. If you are installing from media, you can refer to the location where you stored the installation media by using the following command.

```
ReplicationSourcePath=FolderPathtoMedia
```

5. Save the answer file as a .txt file, and then copy the file to a location accessible from the server you want to promote.

6. After you create the answer file, you can start the unattended installation by entering the following at a command prompt:

```
dcpromo /UseExistingAccount:Attach /unattend:"PathToAnswerFile"
```

where *PathToAnswerFile* is the full file path to the answer file, such as C:\Data\AttachRodc.txt.

At the command line, you can attach the RODC by using the following command.

```
dcpromo /unattend
/UseExistingAccount:Attach
/ReplicaDomainDNSName:FQDNOfDCDomain
/ReplicationSourceDC:SourceDCName
/UserDomain:DomainOfDelegatedAdminAccount
/UserName:DelegatedAdminAccountInDomainOfDC
/Password:"Password"
```

```
/DatabasePath:"LocalDatabasePath"
/LogPath:"LocalLogPath"
/SYSVOLPath:"LocalSysVolPath"
/SafeModeAdminPassword:"Password"
/RebootOnCompletion:Yes
```

When the unattended installation or command-line execution completes, Dcpromo exits with a return code. A return code of 1 to 10 indicates success. A return code of 11 to 100 indicates failure. Note the related error text and take appropriate corrective action as necessary.

Decommissioning RODCs

In a domain, RODCs act as additional domain controllers. If you no longer need an RODC, you can remove it from the domain in the same way as you would remove an additional writable domain controller. (For more information, see "Removing Additional Domain Controllers" in Chapter 3.)

You can remove an RODC using unattended removal or the command line as well. Because you are working with an RODC, the process is simplified somewhat. You can create an answer file for removing an RODC by completing the following steps:

1. Open Notepad or any other text editor.
2. On the first line, type **[DCINSTALL]** and then press Enter.
3. Type the following entries, one entry on each line.

```
UserName=AdminAccountInDomainOfDC
UserDomain=DomainOfAdminAccount
Password="PasswordOfAdminAccount"
AdministratorPassword=NewLocalAdminPassword
RemoveApplicationPartitions=Yes
RetainDCMetadata=No
RebootOnCompletion=Yes
```

4. Save the answer file as a .txt file and then copy the file to a location accessible from the server you want to promote.
5. After you create the answer file, you can start the unattended removal by entering the following at a command prompt:

```
dcpromo /unattend:"PathToAnswerFile"
```

> where *PathToAnswerFile* is the full file path to the answer file, such as C:\Data\RemoveRodc.txt.

At the command line, you can remove an RODC by using the following command.

```
dcpromo /unattend
/UserName:AdminAccountInDomainOfDC
/UserDomain:DomainOfAdminAccount
/Password:"PasswordOfAdminAccount"
/AdministratorPassword:NewLocalAdminPassword
/RemoveApplicationPartitions:Yes
/RetainDCMetadata:No
/RebootOnCompletion:Yes
```

When the unattended removal or command-line execution completes, Dcpromo exits with a return code. A return code of 1 to 10 indicates success. A return code of 11 to 100 indicates failure. Note any related error text and take appropriate corrective action as necessary.

Setting Password Replication Policy

When you deploy an RODC, you must configure the Password Replication Policy on the writable domain controller that will be its replication partner. The Password Replication Policy acts as an access control list (ACL) and determines whether an RODC should be permitted to cache a password for a particular user or group. After the RODC receives an authenticated user or computer logon request, it refers to the Password Replication Policy to determine whether it should cache the password for the account.

Password Replication Policy Essentials

You can configure Password Replication Policy in several ways:

- Allow no accounts to be cached, for the strictest control, such as when the physical security of the RODC cannot be guaranteed.

- Allow few accounts to be cached, for strong control, such as when the physical security of the RODC is good but cannot be reasonably assured at all times.
- Allow many accounts to be cached, for less strict control, such as when the physical security of the RODC can be reasonably assured at all times.

> **Note** The fewer account passwords replicated to RODCs, the less risk that security could be breached in case an RODC is compromised. The more account passwords replicated to RODCs, the greater the risk involved in case an RODC is compromised.

Password Replication Policy is managed on a per-computer basis. The computer object for an RODC is updated to include the following multivalued directory attributes that contain security principals (users, computers, and groups):

- msDS-Reveal-OnDemandGroup, which defines the Allowed Accounts list
- msDS-NeverRevealGroup, which defines the Denied Accounts list
- msDS-RevealedUsers, which defines the Revealed Accounts list
- msDS-AuthenticatedToAccountList, which defines the Authenticated To list

When you are using Active Directory Users And Computers in Advanced mode (by selecting the Advanced option on the View menu), you can view these attributes and their values on the Attribute Editor tab of the RODC's Properties dialog box, as shown in Figure 4-6. The RODC uses these attributes together to determine whether an account password can be replicated and cached. The passwords for denied accounts are never replicated and cached.

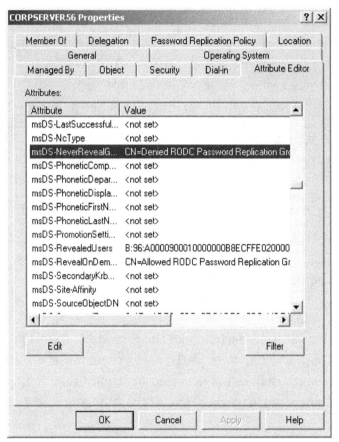

Figure 4-6 Review attributes related to Password Replication Policy.

Double-click an attribute to open an editor, which will list the attribute's current values. For example, the Denied Accounts list contains the security principals shown in Figure 4-7 by default. These security principals are Account Operators, Administrators, Backup Operators, Denied RODC Password Replication Group, and Server Operators.

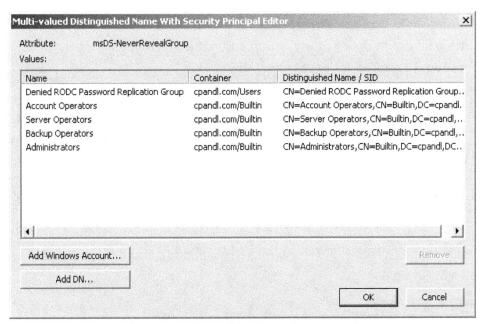

Figure 4-7   View the default members of the Denied Accounts list.

The passwords for allowed accounts can always be replicated and cached. Whether a password is cached doesn't depend on whether a user or computer has logged on to the domain via the RODC. At any time, an RODC can replicate the passwords for allowed accounts, and administrators can also prepopulate passwords for allowed accounts using Active Directory Users and Computers.

During an advanced installation of an RODC, you can configure the initial Password Replication Policy settings. When you install the first RODC in a domain by using either a nonstaged or a staged installation, the Active Directory Domain Services Installation Wizard creates domain group accounts that are required for RODCs to function. These groups are as follows:

- **Enterprise Read-Only Domain Controllers**   Every RODC in the Active Directory forest is a member of this group automatically. Membership in this group is required for proper operations.

- **Read-Only Domain Controllers**   Every RODC in the Active Directory domain is a member of this group automatically. Membership in this group is required for proper operations.
- **Allowed RODC Password Replication Group**   You can manage allowed accounts by using the Allowed RODC Password Replication Group. Passwords for members of this group are always replicated to RODCs.
- **Denied RODC Password Replication Group**   You can manage denied accounts using the Denied RODC Password Replication Group. Passwords for members of this group are never replicated to RODCs.

By default, the Denied RODC Password Replication Group has the members shown in Figure 4-8.

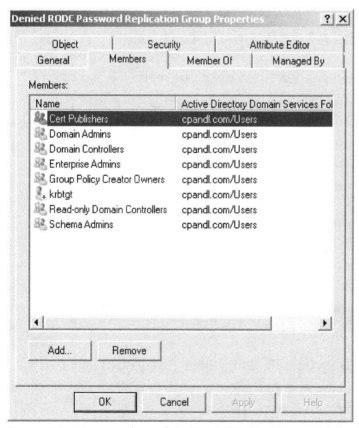

Figure 4-8   View members of the Denied RODC Password Replication Group.

By default, the Allowed RODC Password Replication Group has no members and is the only allowed account defined in Password Replication Policy.

Allowing and Denying Accounts

Each RODC has a separate Password Replication Policy. To manage the Password Replication Policy, you must be a member of the Domain Admins group. The easiest way to manage Password Replication Policy is to:

- Add accounts for which passwords should not be replicated to the Denied RODC Password Replication Group.
- Add accounts for which passwords should be replicated to the Allowed RODC Password Replication Group.

You can also edit Password Replication Policy settings directly. To edit the Password Replication Policy for an RODC, follow these steps:

1. After you open Active Directory Users and Computers, ensure that Active Directory Users and Computers points to a writable domain controller that is running Windows Server 2008 or later. Right-click the Active Directory Users And Computers node and then select Change Domain Controller. The domain controller to which you are connected should be a writable domain controller; that is, it should not list RODC under DC Type. If you are connected to an RODC, change to a writable domain controller. Click Cancel or OK as appropriate.

2. Expand the domain node and then select Domain Controllers. In the details pane, right-click the RODC computer account and then choose Properties.

3. On the Password Replication Policy tab, shown in Figure 4-9, you'll see the current settings for Password Replication Policy on the RODC.

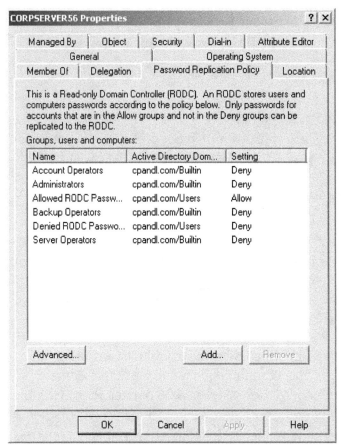

FIGURE 4-9 Review the Password Replication Policy settings.

4. Define allowed or removed accounts using the following techniques:

- To define an allowed account, click Add, select Allow Passwords For The Account To Replicate To This RODC, as shown in Figure 4-10, and then click OK. In the Select Users, Contacts, Computers, Or Groups dialog box, enter an account name and then click Check Names. If the account name is listed correctly, click OK to add it to the Password Replication Policy as an allowed account.

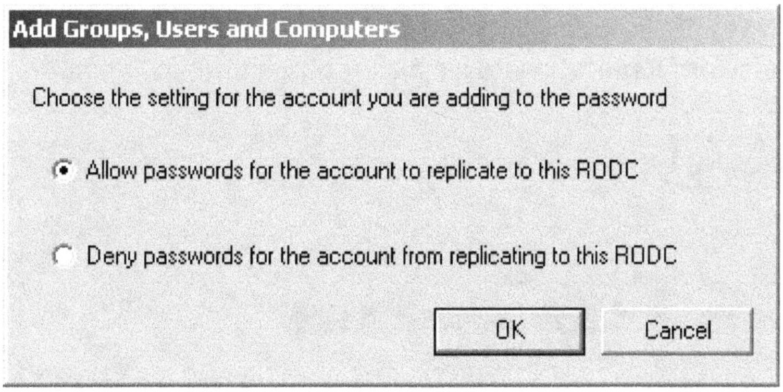

FIGURE 4-10 Define an allowed account.

- To define a denied account, click Add, select Deny Passwords For The Account To Replicate To This RODC, and then click OK. In the Select Users, Contacts, Computers, Or Groups dialog box, enter an account name and then click Check Names. If the account name is listed correctly, click OK to add it to the Password Replication Policy as a denied account.
- To remove an account from Password Replication Policy, select the account name in the Groups, Users And Computers list and then click Remove. When prompted to confirm, click Yes.

Managing Credentials on RODCs

You can review cached credentials or prepopulate credentials using the Advanced Password Replication Policy dialog box. When you are prepopulating user accounts, you should also consider prepopulating the passwords of computer accounts that the users will be using.

You can view and work with the Advanced Password Replication Policy dialog box by completing these steps:

1. In Active Directory Users and Computers, expand the domain node and then select Domain Controllers.
2. In the details pane, right-click the RODC computer account and then choose Properties.

3. On the Password Replication Policy tab, click Advanced to display the Advanced Password Replication Policy dialog box, shown in Figure 4-11.

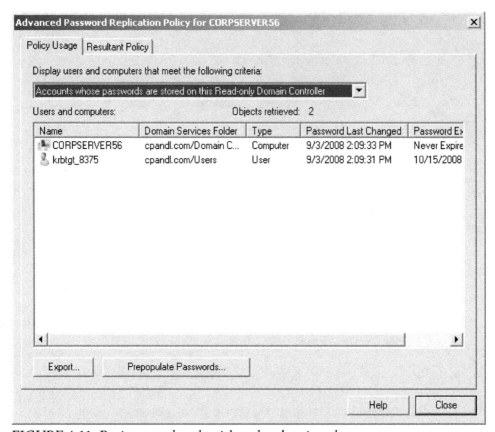

FIGURE 4-11 Review stored credentials and authenticated computers.

4. Review or manage cached credentials using the following techniques:

- Accounts for which passwords are stored on the RODC are displayed by default. To view accounts that have been authenticated to this RODC, on the Display Users And Computers list, select Accounts That Have Been Authenticated To This Read-Only Domain Controller.

- To prepopulate passwords for an account, click Prepopulate Passwords. In the Select Users Or Computers dialog box, enter an account name and then click Check Names. If the account name is listed correctly, click OK to add a request that its password be replicated to the RODC. When prompted to confirm, click Yes. The password is then prepopulated. Click OK.

Identifying Allowed or Denied Accounts

You can determine whether a user or computer account is allowed or restricted by using Resultant Set of Policy to examine all related group memberships and determine exactly what rules apply. To generate Resultant Set of Policy, follow these steps:

1. In Active Directory Users and Computers, expand the domain node and then select Domain Controllers.

2. In the details pane, right-click the RODC computer account and then choose Properties.

3. On the Password Replication Policy tab, click Advanced to display the Advanced Password Replication Policy dialog box.

4. On the Resultant Policy tab, click Add. In the Select Users Or Computers dialog box, enter an account name and then click Check Names. If the account name is listed correctly, click OK. Repeat for other accounts as necessary.

5. The Resultant Set of Policy for each account is displayed as shown in Figure 4-12. If the user or computer is restricted, the Resultant Setting is Deny. If the user or computer is permitted, the Resultant Setting is Allow.

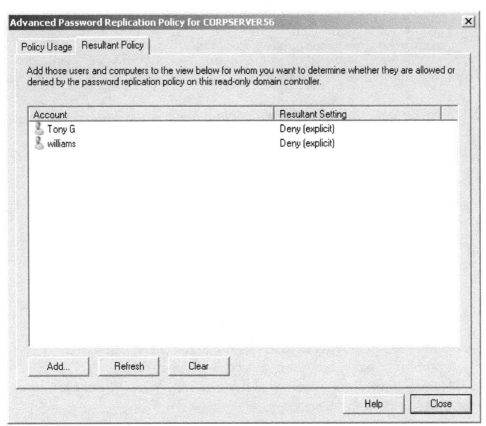

FIGURE 4-12 Determine whether a user or computer is allowed or denied according to the Password Replication Policy.

Resetting Credentials

In the event that an RODC is compromised or stolen, you can reset the passwords for all accounts for which credentials were cached on the RODC. To do this, complete the following steps:

1. After you open Active Directory Users and Computers, ensure that Active Directory Users And Computers points to a writable domain controller that is running Windows Server 2008 or later. Right-click the Active Directory Users And Computers node and then select Change Domain Controller. The domain controller to which you are connected should be a writable domain controller; that is, it should not list RODC

under DC Type. If you are connected to an RODC, change to a writable domain controller. Click Cancel or OK as appropriate.

2. Expand the domain node and then select Domain Controllers. In the details pane, right-click the RODC computer account and then choose Delete.

3. When prompted to confirm, click Yes.

4. When prompted again, specify that you want to reset all passwords for user accounts that were cached on this RODC.

5. Click Export to export the list of cached accounts to a file. The password for every user whose account is listed in this file has been reset.

Delegating Administrative Permissions

During configuration of an RODC, you have an opportunity to specify user or group accounts that should be delegated administrative permissions. After the initial configuration, you can add or remove administrative permissions by using Dsmgmt.

You can grant administrative permissions to an additional user by completing these steps:

1. Start an elevated, administrator command prompt by clicking Start, right-clicking Command Prompt, and then clicking Run As Administrator.

2. At the elevated command prompt, enter **dsmgmt**.

3. At the dsmgmt prompt, enter **local roles**.

4. At the local roles prompt, enter **show roles administrators** to list current administrators. In the default configuration, no users or groups are listed.

5. At the local roles prompt, enter **add _Domain\User_** administrator to grant administrative permissions, where _Domain_ is the domain in which the user account is located and _User_ is the account name, such as IMAGINEDL\WilliamS.

6. Confirm the addition by entering **show roles administrators**.

7. Enter **quit** twice to exit dsmgmt.

You can remove administrative permissions by following these steps:

1. At an elevated command prompt, enter **dsmgmt**.
2. At the dsmgmt prompt, enter **local roles**.
3. At the local roles prompt, enter **show roles administrators** to list current administrators. In the default configuration, no users or groups are listed.
4. At the local roles prompt, enter **remove *Domain\User* administrator** to remove administrative permissions for a specified user, where Domain is the domain in which the user account is located and User is the account name, such as IMAGINEDL\WilliamS.
5. Confirm the removal by entering **show roles administrators**.
6. Enter **quit** twice to exit dsmgmt.

Chapter 5. Configuring, Maintaining, and Troubleshooting Global Catalog Servers

Active Directory is a distributed directory service with a central repository at its core. In this repository are account and resource objects with a full complement of attributes. Active Directory stores directory data as replicas on multiple domain controllers and maintains consistency through replication. Domain controllers are the workhorses in this infrastructure. They store the domain data and provide the domainwide distribution of this data.

In addition to their standard roles, domain controllers can also act as global catalog servers. Global catalog servers provide the forestwide distribution of data in a multiple domain forest. Because global catalog servers have unique architecture and configuration requirements, the administrative tasks you use to manage and maintain them are different from those for standard domain controllers. In this chapter, I provide tips and techniques for configuring, maintaining, and troubleshooting global catalog servers.

Working with Global Catalog Servers

In an Active Directory forest with multiple domains, the global catalog provides a central repository of domain information for the forest by storing partial replicas of all domain directory partitions. In addition to its activities as a domain controller, a global catalog server supports the following special activities in the forest:

- Forestwide directory searches
- User logon and authentication
- Universal group membership caching and updates
- Global catalog advertisement and replication

Domain controllers acting as global catalog servers and hosting global catalogs distribute their partial replicas to all other global catalog servers in a forest. Because there is no single master, any global catalog server can process and then replicate changes to other global catalog servers. Because they store a partial attribute set for all objects in the forest as well as universal group membership information, global catalog servers enable forestwide search and authentication. When users or administrators search for resources in the Active Directory forest, a global catalog server processes the query in the global catalog and then returns the result. Without a global catalog, queries for forest resources would have to be made separately in every domain in the forest.

Real World Global catalog servers must either have replication partners for all domains in the forest or be able to replicate with another global catalog server. The replication topology for global catalogs is generated automatically by a built-in process called the Knowledge Consistency Checker (KCC). The KCC implements the replication topology required to distribute the contents of every directory partition to every global catalog server. The KCC also generates a cost matrix for locating the next-closest global catalog server according to site link cost settings. Global catalog servers register global catalog–specific service (SRV) resource records in DNS so that clients can locate them according to site. If no global catalog server is available in the user's logon site, a global catalog server is located in the next-closest site, according to the cost matrix generated by the KCC from site link cost settings.

During interactive user logon, the authenticating domain controller retrieves the security identifiers (SIDs) that the user's computer requires to build the user's access token. To retrieve the SIDs of all universal groups to which the user belongs, the authenticating domain controller must contact a global catalog server. If a global catalog server is not available in the site when a user logs on to a domain in which universal groups are available, the computer can use cached credentials to log the user on, but only if caching is enabled and if the user has previously logged on to the domain from the same computer. If the user has not previously logged on to the domain from the same computer, the computer cannot use cached credentials, and the user can log on to only the local computer.

> **Note** Because the global catalog stores the membership information for groups in the forest, access to a global catalog server is a requirement for authentication of noncached credentials in a forest with multiple domains. Before users can use cached credentials, you must enable universal group membership caching. When caching is enabled, domain controllers that are running Windows Server 2003 or later cache group memberships and keep the cache updated by contacting a global catalog server.

Additionally, if the user specifies a logon name in the form of a user principal name (UPN), and the authenticating domain controller has no knowledge of the account, the domain controller contacts a global catalog server to retrieve the domain of the user. The reason for this is that the DNS domain suffix associated with a UPN is not necessarily the user's domain, and the identity of the user's domain may need to be retrieved from a global catalog server. For example, if a user's account is located in ny.tech.imaginedlands.com and the user logs on as williams@imaginedlands.com, the domain name in the UPN suffix does not match the user's domain, and the authenticating domain controller must contact a global catalog server to retrieve the identity of the user's domain.

Regardless of whether a domain controller is a global catalog, the physical representation of Active Directory data is as a single database file (Ntds.dit). On a writable domain controller that is not a global catalog server, Ntds.dit contains a full, writable replica of every object in the domain directory partition for its own domain, plus a writable configuration directory partition. On a writable domain controller that is a global catalog server, Ntds.dit contains a full, writable replica of every object in the domain directory partition for its own domain; a partial read-only replica of every object in the domain directory partitions for all other domains in the forest; plus a writable configuration directory partition. In either case, if the domain controller is the schema operations master for the forest, it also has a writable schema directory partition. Otherwise, it has a read-only schema directory partition.

Deploying Global Catalog Servers

In an Active Directory forest with multiple domains, global catalog servers are an essential part of your Active Directory infrastructure. Before you deploy global catalog servers, you should carefully plan their placement. Afterward, as with any other critical server, you will need to manage and maintain the global catalog servers you've deployed to ensure they are configured properly and are performing as expected.

Adding Global Catalog Servers

The first domain controller installed in a domain is automatically designated as a global catalog server. When conditions in a site warrant adding a global catalog server, you can designate additional domain controllers to be global catalog servers as well. However, do not place the global catalog on a domain controller that hosts the infrastructure operations master role in the domain unless all domain controllers in the domain are global catalog servers or the forest has only one domain.

Generally speaking, each site in your organization should have a designated global catalog server. However, you might not want to add a global catalog to a site when the WAN links to the site cannot handle the related replication traffic. You might instead want to rely on universal group membership caching. For more information, see "Managing and Maintaining Universal Group Membership Caching" later in the chapter.

> **Real World**   In a large enterprise, you should carefully monitor the number of global catalog servers you've deployed and ensure that each additional global catalog is needed before you deploy it. The reason for this is that each time you add a global catalog, you increase the complexity of the replication topology. As you deploy an increasing number of global catalogs, the KCC requires more and more computational power to generate the related replication topology.

You configure a domain controller to act as a global catalog server by using Active Directory Sites And Services to set the Global Catalog Server option for the domain controller you want to be a global catalog server. The account you use must be a member of the Domain Admins group in the domain for which you are configuring the global catalog server. Follow these steps to establish a domain controller as a global catalog server:

1. Start Active Directory Sites And Services from the Administrative Tools menu.

2. Expand the site you want to work with, such as Default-First-Site-Name, expand the related Servers node, and then select the server you want to designate as a global catalog, as shown in Figure 5-1.

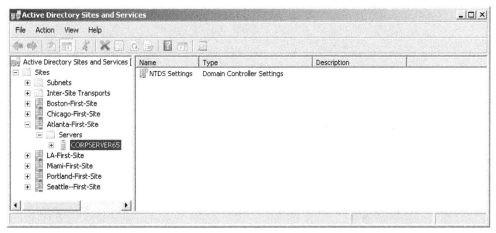

FIGURE 5-1 Select the domain controller you want to establish as a global catalog server.

3. In the right pane, right-click NTDS Settings and then select Properties. This displays the NTDS Settings Properties dialog box.

4. If you want the selected server to be a global catalog server, select the Global Catalog check box, as shown in Figure 5-2. When you click OK, Active Directory immediately designates the domain controller as a global catalog server.

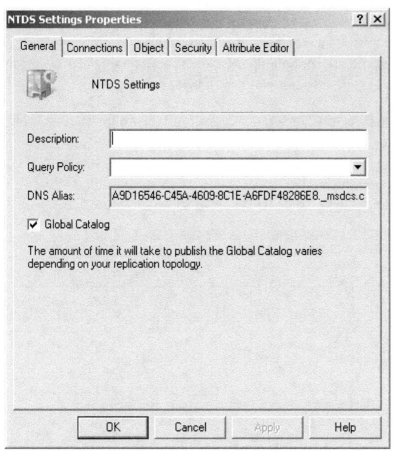

FIGURE 5-2 Designate the server as a global catalog server.

Monitoring and Verifying Global Catalog Promotion

When you designate a new global catalog server, the server will request a copy of the global catalog from an existing global catalog server in the domain. Through replication, a partial replica of each domain directory partition, other than the domain for which the domain controller is authoritative, is then copied to the domain controller. This replication occurs immediately within a site or at the next scheduled replication interval when Active Directory is replicating between sites. The time it takes to replicate the global catalog depends on the size of the catalog and the site configuration. Generally, the larger and more extensive the Active Directory environment, the longer it takes to complete the global catalog promotion process.

Note When you add a global catalog server to a site, the Knowledge Consistency Checker (KCC) updates the replication topology and then initiates replication. Replication of partial domain directory partitions that are available within the site begins immediately. Replication of partial domain directory partitions that are available only from other sites begins at the next scheduled replication interval. When you add subsequent global catalog servers to the same site, the existing global catalog server in the site can act as the replication partner for all domain directory partitions that will be replicated, and this reduces the replication burden across site links.

Tip Microsoft Exchange Server is tightly integrated with Active Directory. Exchange Server stores schema data, configuration data, domain data, and application data in the directory. It also uses Active Directory replication topology to determine how to route messages within the organization. To learn more about Exchange Server and Active Directory, please refer to William Stanek's Pocket Consultants for Microsoft Exchange Server.

You can monitor inbound replication progress to track progress. Follow these steps:

1. Start an elevated, administrator command prompt by clicking Start, right-clicking Command Prompt, and then clicking Run As Administrator.

2. At the command prompt, enter the following command: **dcdiag /s:ServerName /v | find "%",** where *ServerName* specifies the name of the global catalog server that you want to monitor, and */v | find "%"* finds the percentage of replication.

3. Repeat as necessary to track progress. If the test shows no output, replication has completed.

Using an elevated, administrator command prompt, you can verify successful replication by entering **repadmin /showrepl**. If you are not running Repadmin on the domain controller whose replication you are checking, you can specify a destination domain controller in the command. For example, if you want to check DomainController17, you enter the following command.

```
repadmin /showrepl DomainController17
```

As shown in Sample 5-1, Repadmin lists inbound neighbors for the current or specified domain controller. These inbound neighbors identify the distinguished name of each directory partition for which inbound directory replication has been attempted, the site and name of the source domain controller, and whether replication succeeded.

SAMPLE 5-1. Confirming replication with neighbors.

```
LA-First-Site\CORPSERVER56
DSA Options: IS_GC DISABLE_OUTBOUND_REPL IS_RODC
Site Options: (none)
DSA object GUID: a465bbc1-c3d9-46ec-96fc
DSA invocationID: c045996c-b163-45b7-80d3


==== INBOUND NEIGHBORS ======================================

DC=imaginedlands,DC=com
  Atlanta-First-Site\CORPSERVER65 via RPC
  DSA object GUID: a9d16546-c45a-4609-8c1e
  Last attempt @ 2008-09-06 11:56:16 was successful.

CN=Configuration,DC=imaginedlands,DC=com
  Atlanta-First-Site\CORPSERVER65 via RPC
  DSA object GUID: a9d16546-c45a-4609-8c1e
 Last attempt @ 2008-09-06 11:56:16 was successful.

CN=Schema,CN=Configuration,DC=imaginedlands,DC=com
  Atlanta-First-Site\CORPSERVER65 via RPC
  DSA object GUID: a9d16546-c45a-4609-8c1e
  Last attempt @ 2008-09-06 11:56:16 was successful.

DC=DomainDnsZones,DC=imaginedlands,DC=com
  Atlanta-First-Site\CORPSERVER65 via RPC
  DSA object GUID: a9d16546-c45a-4609-8c1e
  Last attempt @ 2008-09-06 11:56:16 was successful.

DC=ForestDnsZones,DC=imaginedlands,DC=com
  Atlanta-First-Site\CORPSERVER65 via RPC
  DSA object GUID: a9d16546-c45a-4609-8c1e
  Last attempt @ 2008-09-06 11:56:16 was successful.
```

The example shows the replication status for five directory partitions:

- **DC=imaginedlands,DC=com** A domain partition
- **CN=Configuration,DC=imaginedlands,DC=com** The forestwide Configuration partition
- CN=Schema,CN=Configuration,DC=imaginedlands,DC=com The forestwide Schema partition
- **DC=DomainDnsZones,DC=imaginedlands,DC=com** The DNS application partition for domain-level zones
- **DC=ForestDnsZones,DC=imaginedlands,DC=com** The DNS application partition for forest-level zones

Several conditions must be met before the global catalog server is locatable by clients. These conditions are referred to as *readiness levels*. The lowest readiness level is 0. Newly designated global catalog servers begin at level 0 and progress to level 6 as they successfully complete replication of partial domain partitions. By default, domain controllers running Windows Server 2008 or later require all readiness levels to be reached before a global catalog is ready for use.

At level 6, all partial directory partitions have been successfully replicated to the global catalog server, and the global catalog is ready to be used. The Net Logon service on the global catalog server then registers DNS service (SRV) resource records that identify the domain controller as a global catalog server in the site and in the forest. At this point, the global catalog server begins accepting queries on ports 3268 and 3269.

When a global catalog server has satisfied all replication requirements, the global catalog is ready to serve clients, and the isGlobalCatalogReady rootDSE attribute is set to True. Therefore, you can verify global catalog readiness by checking this attribute's current value in the directory. Follow these steps:

1. Start Ldp.exe by clicking Start, typing **Ldp** in the Search box, and then pressing Enter.

2. Connect to the target server whose global catalog readiness you want to verify. On the Connection menu, click Connect. In the Connect

dialog box, shown in Figure 5-3, enter the domain name or the fully qualified name of the server whose global catalog readiness you want to verify. In the Port box, enter 389 if this isn't already the default value. If the Connectionless check box is selected, clear it, and then click OK.

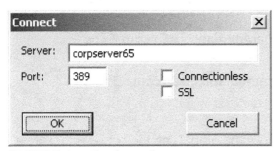

FIGURE 5-3 Configure the server connection.

3. Ldp will then establish a connection to the server, retrieve the base directory service information, and then write related information in the details pane, as shown in Figure 5-4. In the details pane, verify that the isGlobalCatalogReady attribute has a value of True. If it does, the global catalog server is ready.

4. On the Connection menu, click Disconnect to disconnect from the domain controller.

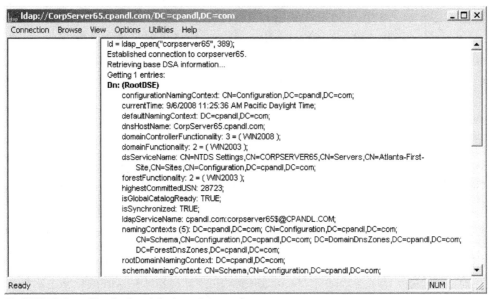

FIGURE 5-4 Check the global catalog readiness status.

Another way to verify global catalog readiness is to use Nltest. At a command prompt, enter the following command: **nltest /server:*ServerName* /dsgetdc:*DomainName***, where *ServerName* specifies the name of the domain controller that you have designated as a global catalog server, and *DomainName* specifies the name of the domain to which the server belongs. In the following example, you examine CorpServer65 in the cs.imaginedlands.com domain.

```
nltest /server:corpserver65 /dsgetdc:imaginedlands.com
```

The output will look similar to the following.

```
           DC: \\CORPSERVER65.cs.imaginedlands.com
      Address: \\192.168.1.200
     Dom Guid:
     Dom Name: cs.imaginedlands.com
  Forest Name: imaginedlands.com
 Dc Site Name: LA-First-Site
Our Site Name: LA-First-Site
        Flags: PDC GC DS LDAP KDC TIMESERV GTIMESERV WRITABLE
DNS_FOREST CLOSE_SITE FULL_SECRET
The command completed successfully
```

In the Flags line of the output, if *GC* appears, as shown in the previous sample output, the global catalog server has satisfied its replication requirements and is ready to be used.

You can verify that a server is advertised as a global catalog server by checking for a related SRV resource record in Domain Name System (DNS). To verify global catalog DNS registrations, follow these steps:

1. Click Start, point to Administrative Tools, and then click DNS.
2. Connect to a domain controller in the forest root domain. Right-click DNS, click Connect To DNS Server, and then click The Following Computer. Enter the name of the domain controller in the forest root domain and then click OK.
3. Expand Forward Lookup Zones and then expand the forest root domain.

4. Click the _tcp container.

5. The records that begin with _gc are global catalog service (SRV) resource records. In the details pane, look for a _gc SRV record that has the name of the global catalog server. An example is shown in Figure 5-5.

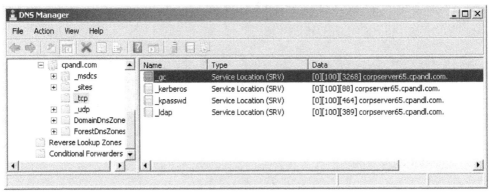

FIGURE 5-5 Identify the global catalog SRV resource records.

> **Note** The data field lists three values and the name of the server to which the resource record belongs. Respectively, these values are the priority, weight, and port number assigned to the resource record.

6. Double-click the global catalog SRV resource record. The record should be configured similarly to what is shown in Figure 5-6. The values assigned to the record are used as follows:

- **Domain** Specifies the fully qualified domain name for the domain to which the resource record applies.
- **Service** Specifies the universal symbolic name of the TCP/IP service to be served by the record. Here, _gc indicates the related record is for global catalog services.
- **Protocol** Specifies the transport protocol to be used by the TCP/IP service. Here, the transport protocol is TCP.

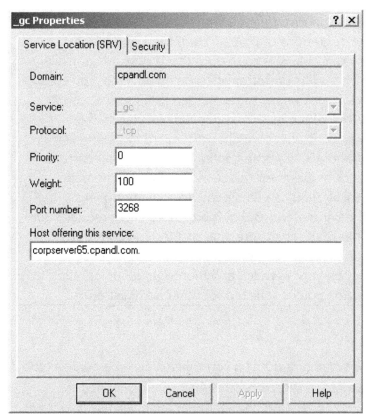

FIGURE 5-6 Verify the global catalog SRV resource record.

- **Priority**   Specifies the relative priority of the host with respect to other hosts in the domain that offer the same service. The highest priority goes to a host that has a value of 0. If two or more hosts have the same priority, weighting can be used to determine which host is used.
- **Weight**   Specifies the relative weighting of a host and is used to load-balance services. If two or more hosts of a service have the same priority, the weighting can set a preference for one host over another. Hosts with higher weights should be used first.
- **Port Number**   Specifies the TCP/IP port on the host that offers the service. The default TCP port for global catalog servers is 3268.
- **Host Offering This Service**   Identifies the host server by its fully qualified domain name.

> **Real World** As an administrator, you typically will have responsibility for ensuring proper operations of domain controllers and global catalog servers on a daily basis. If you notice that a domain controller is getting overloaded and its performance is being affected, you could use the priority and weight values to reconfigure DNS so that some tasks are performed by other, less-used domain controllers. By adjusting the domain controller's weight with regard to a particular service, such as LDAP or GC, you can configure the domain controller to receive fewer client requests for this service than other domain controllers. Alternatively, you can adjust the domain controller's priority in the DNS environment so that it processes client requests for a service only if other DNS servers are unavailable. However, don't modify service locator records without careful planning with regard to the potential impact on your network and thorough documentation to detail the configuration you've selected for other administrators.

Identifying Global Catalog Servers

One way to determine whether a domain controller is designated as a global catalog server is to use Active Directory Sites And Services. In Active Directory Sites And Services, expand the Sites container, expand the site of the domain controller that you want to check, expand the Servers container, and then expand the Server object. Right-click the NTDS Settings object and then click Properties. On the General tab, if the Global Catalog box is selected, the domain controller is designated as a global catalog server.

Another way to determine whether a domain controller is designated as a global catalog server is to use the DSQUERY command-line tool. Using this tool, you can locate the global catalog servers in your logon domain by entering **dsquery server -isgc**. The resulting output is a list of distinguished names for global catalogs, such as

```
"CN=CentraDC16,CN=Servers,CN=LA-First-
Site,CN=Sites,CN=Configuration,DC=
imaginedlands,DC=com"
```
```
"CN=CentraDC23,CN=Servers,CN=LA-First-
Site,CN=Sites,CN=Configuration,DC=
imaginedlands,DC=com"
```

Here, CentralDC16 and CentralDC23 are global catalog servers in your logon domain.

With the -Domain parameter, you can use DSQUERY SERVER to locate global catalog servers in a specific domain. For example, if you want to locate global catalog servers in the cs.reagentpress.com domain, you enter

```
dsquery server -domain cs.reagentpress.com -isgc
```

With the -Site parameter, you can use DSQUERY SERVER to locate global catalog servers in a specific site. For example, if you want to locate a global catalog server in the NY-First-Site site, you enter

```
dsquery server -site NY-First-Site -isgc
```

> **Tip** Being able to search site by site is important because you typically want at least one global catalog server per site. If you search a site and don't find a global catalog, server you may want to add one.

You can search the entire forest as well by entering

```
dsquery server -forest -isgc
```

Restoring Global Catalog Servers

Restoring a global catalog server from a backup can result in lingering objects, which in turn can cause replication inconsistencies. When restoring a global catalog server from backup, keep in mind that a restored global catalog server contains not only restored data from its domain but also some data from all other domains in the forest. Because of this, restoring a global catalog server can possibly reintroduce previously deleted objects, and these lingering objects can cause replication inconsistencies.

You can reduce the number of possible inconsistencies by restoring domain controllers and global catalogs from backups that were made at the same time or as close in time as possible. In this way, there will be less discrepancy between the authoritative domains and their partial replicas in the restored global catalogs.

If lingering objects are reintroduced, you can forcibly remove them by running the Repadmin /removelingeringobjects command. However, this approach should be a last resort. Rather than forcibly removing the lingering objects, you should wait for them to be removed through the normal replication update process.

Removing Global Catalog Servers

You might decide to remove the global catalog from a domain controller if universal group membership caching is adequate to satisfy logon requirements in a site where WAN link speeds are not adequate to handle the replication required to maintain global catalogs. If you no longer want a domain controller to act as a global catalog server, you can remove the global catalog by following these steps:

1. Start Active Directory Sites And Services from the Administrative Tools menu.

2. Expand the site you want to work with, such as Default-First-Site-Name, expand the related Servers node, and then select the server from which you want to remove the global catalog.

3. In the right pane, right-click NTDS Settings and then select Properties. This displays the NTDS Settings Properties dialog box. Clear the Global Catalog check box.

4. When you click OK, Active Directory immediately removes the domain controller's designation as a global catalog server. The Net Logon service immediately deregisters the SRV resource records that advertised the global catalog server in DNS. The domain controller also stops accepting LDAP requests over ports 3268 and 3269.

When you remove a global catalog from a domain controller, the global catalog removal is not immediate. Instead, global catalog directory partitions are removed gradually in the background. The KCC begins removing the read-only replicas one at a time using an asynchronous process that removes objects gradually until no read-only objects remain.

Once the work is scheduled, the KCC tracks the progress of replica removal, continuing to remove objects until either a replica is gone or a higher-priority replication operation is in the queue. Because read-only replica removal receives the lowest possible priority, any other replication work will interrupt it. Thus, removal work is preempted for the other work and then resumed later.

In the Directory Service log, you'll see related events that record when removal of a partial replica is starting, resuming, and finishing. Event ID 1744 states that the local domain controller is no longer a global catalog server. Event ID 1659 states that removal of a directory partition from the local database has been resumed, including the approximate number of objects remaining to be removed and the number of link values of attributes remaining to be removed. Event ID 1660 states that a specified directory partition has been removed from the domain controller.

You can verify that the global catalog has been removed from a domain controller by using Event Viewer. When the global catalog has been removed successfully, the Knowledge Consistency Checker (KCC) logs Event ID 1268 in the Directory Service log. In an extended Active Directory environment, it can take hours or days to fully remove a global catalog.

Controlling SRV Record Registration

DC Locator and GC Locator DNS SRV resource records are registered dynamically by the Net Logon service and are used to locate domain controllers and global catalog servers. In Group Policy, the following policies can be used to control exactly how registration and deregistration of SRV records works:

- **Automated Site Coverage By The DC Locator DNS SRV Records** Determines whether domain controllers will dynamically register site-specific DC Locator SRV resource records for the closest sites where no domain controller for the same domain exists (or where no global catalog server for the same forest exists).

- **Sites Covered By The GC Locator DNS SRV Records**   Specifies the sites for which the global catalog servers should register site-specific GC Locator SRV resource records in DNS. These records are registered in addition to the site-specific SRV resource records registered for the site where the global catalog server resides or for the sites without a global catalog server in the same forest for which this global catalog server is the closest global catalog server.

If a policy is not configured, it is not applied to any domain controller or global catalog servers, and domain controllers and global catalog servers use their local configuration. If a policy is enabled, its settings are used instead of a global catalog server's local configuration.

Managing and Maintaining Universal Group Membership Caching

Universal group membership caching enables domain controllers to cache group membership information after retrieving it the first time rather than having to retrieve group membership information each time a user logs on. On domain controllers that are running Windows Server 2003 or later, the universal group membership caching feature is available by default and can be enabled on a per-site basis as needed. Although universal group membership caching is the name of the feature, this name is somewhat of a misnomer because, technically speaking, both security identifiers (SIDs) for global groups and universal groups can be cached.

Universal Group Membership Caching Essentials

Universal security groups can contain security principals from other domains. During interactive user logon, the authenticating domain controller retrieves the SIDs that the user's computer requires to build the user's access token. To retrieve the SIDs of all universal groups to which the user belongs, the authenticating domain controller must contact a global catalog server. If a global catalog server is not available in the site when a user logs on to a domain in which universal groups are available, the computer will use cached credentials to log the user on if the user has previously logged on to the domain from the same workstation. If the user has not previously logged on to the domain from the same computer, the user can log on to only the local computer.

Universal group memberships are cached primarily because they can contain individual user accounts and global groups from any domain in the forest and because they can be added to access control lists in any domain in the forest. Therefore, a user who is logging on might have a membership in a universal group that exists in a different domain and might have permissions on objects in this domain by virtue of membership in a universal group that exists in a different domain.

In contrast, a domain controller can always determine a user's membership in all domain local and global groups that are required for authorization in its own domain. Whereas domain local groups can have members from other domains, you can add domain local groups to access control lists only in the domain in which they are created. Whereas you can add global groups to access control lists in any domain, global groups can contain only accounts from the domain in which they are created. That said, global groups can be members of universal groups that exist in different domains, and being a member of a global group that is itself a member of a universal group can give the user access to resources other than those allowed by membership in the global group alone.

During the logon process, the authenticating domain controller retrieves a list of global group SIDs from the user's domain and then passes the list of global group SIDs to the nearest global catalog server. The global catalog server enumerates the member attribute of all universal groups in the forest, adds all universal groups that contain the user's SID as well as all universal groups that contain the SID of any of the global groups in the user's SID list, and then returns the list to the domain controller. The authenticating domain controller caches the global group SIDs and the universal group SIDs that it retrieves from the global catalog servers and then sends the list of SIDs to the user's computer, along with domain local group SIDs from the user's domain. The user's local computer completes the authentication process by creating the access token for the user and adding the returned SIDs to the access token. The access token is static until the user logs off and logs on again.

> **Real World**   Domain controllers cache group membership for both user accounts and computer accounts. Although the term *cache* seems to imply storage in memory, cached memberships actually are stored in a nonvolatile Active Directory value. Therefore, cached memberships are not lost as a result of a restart or power outage.

Enabling Universal Group Membership Caching

In a domain with domain controllers running Windows Server 2003 or later, you can use the Active Directory Sites And Services tool to configure universal group membership caching. You enable caching on a per-site basis by completing these steps:

1. Start Active Directory Sites And Services from the Administrative Tools menu.

2. Select the site in which you want to enable universal group membership caching, as shown in Figure 5-7.

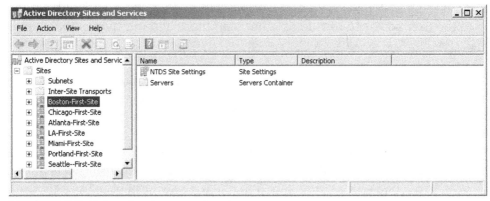

FIGURE 5-7   Select the site to configure.

3. In the right pane, right-click NTDS Site Settings and then select Properties. This displays the NTDS Site Settings Properties dialog box, shown in Figure 5-8.

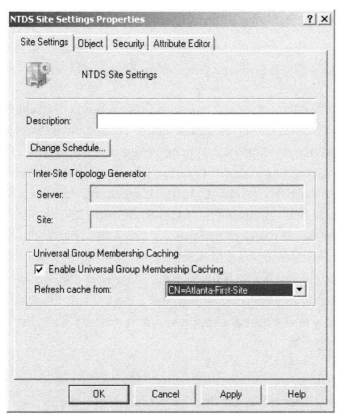

FIGURE 5-8 Configure universal group membership caching.

4. To enable universal group membership caching for the site, select the Enable Universal Group Membership Caching check box.

5. If the directory has multiple sites, you can replicate existing universal group membership information from a specific site's cache by selecting the site on the Refresh Cache From list. With this option, universal group membership information doesn't need to be generated and then replicated; it is simply replicated from the other site's cache. If you specify a site, ensure that it has a working global catalog server.

6. If the directory has only one site or you would rather get the information from a global catalog server in the nearest site, accept the default setting <Default>. With this option, universal group membership information is generated and then replicated if no other global catalog servers are available.

7. When you finish configuring universal group membership caching, click OK.

Monitoring and Troubleshooting Universal Group Membership Caching

When universal membership caching is enabled for a site, domain controllers in the site that are running Windows Server 2003 or later cache universal group membership and, as appropriate, global group membership for first-time logons. They keep the cache updated thereafter. When you configure caching, you can specify the site from which to retrieve group membership information that has already been cached. The msDS-Preferred-GC-Site attribute stores the distinguished name of the specified site and controls this setting. If no site is specified, the closest-site mechanism uses the cost setting on the site link to determine which site has the least-cost connection to contact a global catalog server. Keep in mind that if a user has not logged on to the domain previously and a global catalog server is not available, the user can log on to only the local computer.

Whereas Active Directory Sites And Services lists only sites with domain controllers, Active Directory does not check for the presence of a global catalog server in the preferred site you designate. Therefore, it is possible to designate a refresh site that does not contain a global catalog server. In this case, or in any case where a refresh site is designated but a global catalog server does not respond, the authenticating domain controller uses the site link cost matrix to determine which global catalog server can be contacted and logs event ID 1668 in the Directory Service event log. This event indicates that the group membership cache refresh task did not locate a global catalog in a preferred site, but it was able to find a global catalog in another available site. The event lists the named preferred site and the actual site that was used.

After a user or computer has logged on in a site that uses universal group membership caching, the group cache for the account on the authenticating domain controller is immediately populated. However, it can take up to eight hours for other domain controllers in the same site to populate the group cache for this account. During this time, if the account is authenticated by a domain controller that has not populated the account's group cache, a global catalog server must be contacted before the logon can proceed. After eight hours, all domain controllers that are running Windows Server 2003 or later in the site can process all subsequent logons by using the cached membership.

Keep in mind that by default, domain controllers update the membership cache for accounts in a site every eight hours. As a result, changes to the global group or universal group membership of an account can take up to eight hours to be reflected on domain controllers in a site where universal group membership caching is enabled. Further, although there is no limit to the number of accounts that can be cached, a maximum of 500 account caches can be updated during any single cache refresh. Finally, even though the cache refresh is not a replication event, the process uses the site link schedule, and a closed site link schedule postpones the cache refresh until the schedule opens.

You can restart Active Directory Domain Services on the domain controllers in a site to reset the cache refresh interval and trigger a cache refresh. Or you can refresh cached memberships on individual domain controllers by using Ldp.exe to modify the updateCachedMemberships attribute on the rootDSE and set a value of 1. Adding a value of 1 to this attribute instructs the local domain controller to refresh cached memberships. If the site link schedule allows replication at the time you modify the attribute, this update occurs right away.

To modify the updateCachedMemberships attribute, complete the following steps:

1. Start Ldp.exe on a server other than the one you want to configure by clicking Start, typing **Ldp** in the Search box, and then pressing Enter.
2. Connect to the target domain controller where you want to reset the cache. On the Connection menu, click Connect. In the Connect dialog box, shown in Figure 5-9, enter the domain name or the fully qualified

name of the server whose global catalog readiness you want to verify. In the Port box, enter **389** if this isn't already the default value. If the Connectionless check box is selected, clear it and then click OK.

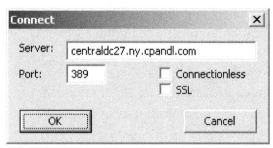

FIGURE 5-9 Connect to the domain controller where the cache reset is to be performed.

3. When you first connect to a domain controller with Ldp, the default location is rootDSE. You can view the attributes for rootDSE in the details pane. However, you do not have a binding connection to the domain controller, and operational attributes are not listed. To bind to the target domain controller so you can make changes, you must provide authenticated credentials. On the Connection menu, click Bind. In the Bind dialog box, select Bind As Currently Logged On User, if you currently are logged on using an account that is a member of Domain Admins or Enterprise Admins, and then click OK. Otherwise, select Bind With Credentials, provide the required credentials as shown in Figure 5-10, and then click OK.

FIGURE 5-10 Establish an authenticated bind to the domain controller.

4. On the Browse menu, click Modify. In the Modify dialog box, shown in Figure 5-11, in the Edit Entry Attribute box, enter **updateCachedMemberships**. In the Values box, enter **1**.

5. Ensure the operation is set as Add. Do not enter a value in the DN box.

6. Click Enter and then click Run. Click Close. If the operation was successful, Ldp will report "Modified" in the output. Otherwise, Ldp will report an error such as "Insufficient Access Rights" or "Unwilling To Perform".

Note You might receive an insufficient access rights error when you are logged on locally to the target domain controller rather than connecting remotely. In this case, repeat this procedure, beginning with step 1, from another server. If you receive an unwilling to perform error, repeat steps 4 to 6 and ensure you are entering the correct attribute name.

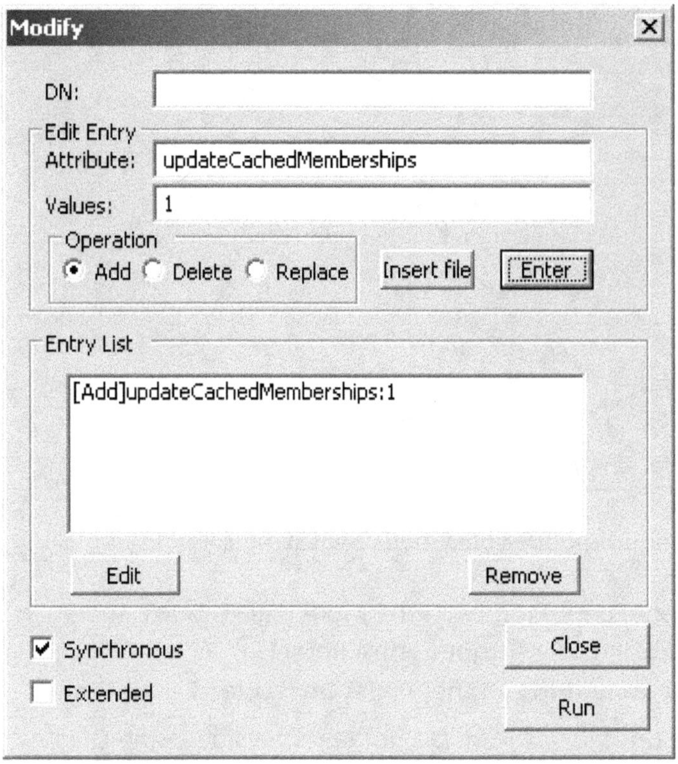

FIGURE 5-11 Reset the universal group membership cache.

Managing and Maintaining Replication Attributes

Global catalog servers maintain a partial read-only replica of every object in the domain directory partitions for all other domains in the forest. The attributes that are replicated are set when you establish a global catalog and can be modified as necessary to customize the way global catalogs are used on your network.

Understanding Global Catalog Search and the Partial Attribute Set

Clients use Lightweight Directory Access Protocol (LDAP) to query, create, update, and delete information that is stored in Active Directory. The default TCP port 389 is used for all domain-level read and write operations. When client queries target configuration, application, schema, and the local domain directory partitions, the clients make the queries through this port. LDAP can also run over User Datagram Protocol (UDP), such as for the domain controller locator process or to query the rootDSE.

Global catalog clients can use LDAP to query Active Directory over a TCP connection through the default TCP port 3268. If security using Secure Sockets Layer (SSL) is implemented, the server listens on TCP port 3269 as well. These ports are used for all global catalog search operations. When client queries target the global catalog directory partitions, including the local domain or other domain partitions in the forest, the clients make the queries over one of these ports.

Domain controllers use the replication (REPL) protocol not only for replication but also to contact the global catalog server when retrieving universal group membership information and when updating the group membership cache when universal group membership caching is enabled.

The set of attributes marked for inclusion in the global catalog is referred to as the partial attribute set (PAS). An attribute is marked for inclusion in the PAS as part of its schema definition. If an object's isMemberOfPartialAttributeSet attribute is set to True, the attribute is replicated to the global catalog.

The attributes that are replicated by default include those that Microsoft determined are most likely to be used in searches. As an administrator, you can specify additional attributes that should be replicated by editing the properties of an attribute in the Active Directory Schema snap-in, selecting the Replicate This Attribute To The Global Catalog check box, and clicking OK. This sets the value of the isMemberOfPartialAttributeSet attribute to True.

> **Note** When changes to the partial attribute set are made, domain controllers that are running Windows Server 2003 or later replicate only the updated attributes.

Designating Replication Attributes

The contents of the global catalog are determined by the attributes that are replicated for each object class. Schema administrators can configure additional attributes to be replicated, and the primary reason for this is to add attributes for which users routinely search. You shouldn't add attributes for which users search infrequently. You should rarely, if ever, remove attributes that are being replicated.

As a member of the Administrators, Domain Admins, or Enterprise Admins group, you can view Active Directory schema using the Active Directory Schema snap-in for the Microsoft Management Console (MMC). To change schema, you must be a member of the Schema Admins group.

The Active Directory Schema snap-in is not available by default. You must install this tool by registering its DLL. To do this, enter the following at an elevated command prompt.

```
regsvr32 schmmgmt.dll
```

Windows should confirm the registration by displaying a success message like the one shown in Figure 5-12. If you receive an error, ensure you entered the DLL name correctly and that you are using an elevated command prompt.

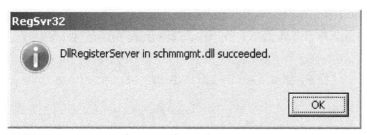

FIGURE 5-12 Windows confirms the registration.

After you install the required DLL, you can add the Active Directory Schema snap-in to a custom console by following these steps:

1. Open a blank MMC in Author mode. Click Start, type **mmc** in the Search box, and then press Enter.

2. In your MMC, choose Add/Remove Snap-In from the File menu in the main window. This displays the Add Or Remove Snap-Ins dialog box.

3. The Available Snap-Ins list shows all the snap-ins that are available. As shown in Figure 5-13, select Active Directory Schema and then click Add. The Active Directory Schema snap-in is added to the Selected Snap-Ins list.

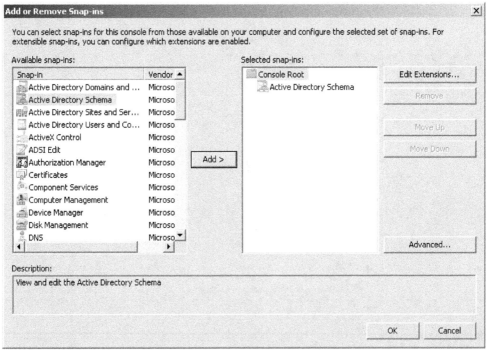

FIGURE 5-13 Select the Active Directory Schema snap-in.

4. Now close the Add Or Remove Snap-Ins dialog box by clicking OK, and return to the console you are creating. You can now use the Active Directory Schema snap-in to work with directory schema.

When you start the Active Directory Schema snap-in, it establishes a connection to the schema master for the forest. You can then view and edit the schema for the object whose attribute you want to replicate in the global catalog. Keep in mind that the snap-in doesn't check to ensure that you are a member of the Schema Admins group until you try to change attribute settings. If you try to change attribute settings and aren't a member of the Schema Admins group, the snap-in states that you have insufficient permissions.

You can change replication attributes by completing these steps:

1. In Active Directory Schema, expand the Active Directory Schema node and then select the Attributes node. A list of the attributes for all objects in the directory appears in the right pane, as shown in Figure 5-14.

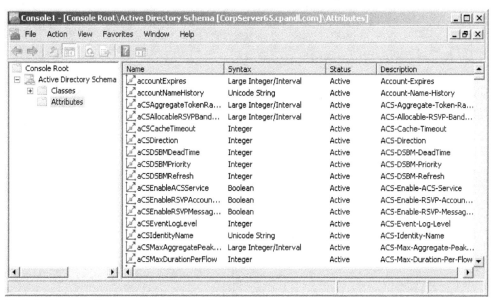

FIGURE 5-14 Display available attributes.

2. Double-click the attribute you want to replicate to the global catalog.

3. In the attribute's Properties dialog box, you can specify whether the attribute is replicated. To specify that the attribute should be replicated, select the Replicate This Attribute To The Global Catalog check box, as shown in Figure 5-15. To specify that the attribute should not be replicated, clear the Replicate This Attribute To The Global Catalog check box.

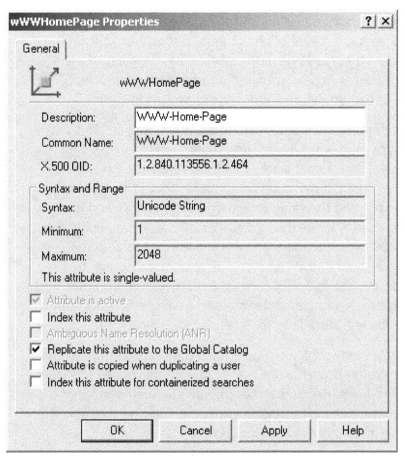

FIGURE 5-15 Select replication options.

4. If you are replicating the attribute and want the attribute to be indexed in the database for faster search and retrieval, select the Index This Attribute check box. Although indexing an attribute allows it to be found more quickly, each index you create slightly increases the size of the Active Directory database.

5. Click OK to apply the change.

Real World   Directory searches for attributes that are indexed are more efficient than searches for attributes that are not indexed. Attributes are indexed in the directory when you select and apply the Index This Attribute option. Applying this option adds the flag value 1 to the searchFlags property of the attribute. This tells Active Directory to dynamically build an index for the attribute, and a background thread on the directory server builds the index automatically. Conversely, clearing the Index This Attribute option and applying the change removes the flag value in the searchFlags property of the attribute. This causes Active Directory to remove the index, and a background thread on the directory server removes the index.

The values for indexed attributes are stored in a sorted list. This makes searching much more efficient because Active Directory needs to search only until it locates the area in the list where the value should be, based on the sort. If the value is not there, Active Directory can assume it will not find the value anywhere else in the list, and it can terminate the search. When attributes are not indexed, the entire list must be searched to determine whether a particular value actually exists. Thus, although Active Directory requires more storage to maintain indexed lists, indexing can make searching significantly more efficient. Conversely, nonindexed attributes are less efficient to search, but they require less storage to maintain.

Because of how indexing works, you should only index attributes that are frequently referenced. Ideally, the attributes you choose to index will be single-valued attributes rather than multivalued attributes. Although you can index multivalued attributes, building the related index requires more storage and updating to maintain.

While indexing an attribute improves the performance of queries run against the attribute, it doesn't enable containerized searches. To enable both indexing and containerized searches, you must first enable indexing by selecting and applying the Index This Attribute option. Then you must select and apply the Index This Attribute For Containerized Search option. Enabling both options in this way turns on the Index Over Container And Attribute flag in the searchFlags property of the attribute. Note that indexing the attribute for containerized searches will increase the size of the directory database and also might initially slow down processing.

When you encrypt entire volumes on a directory server with BitLocker Drive Encryption, you might find that Active Directory detects that a new index is needed for an encrypted VolumeGUID but is unable to create the index. This can occur because the volume is encrypted and the directory service is unable to set the required indexing flag. To resolve the issue, you typically would need to remove the containerized search option. For more information, see Microsoft Knowledge Base Article 932862 (*http://support.microsoft.com/kb/932862/en-us*).

Monitoring and Troubleshooting Replication Attributes

Every global catalog server in an Active Directory forest hosts a copy of every existing object in that forest. For objects of their own domain, global catalog servers store information related to all attributes that are associated with those objects. For objects in all other domains, global catalog servers store only information attributes that are marked for replication. As discussed previously, if you want to replicate an attribute, you do so by adding the attribute to the partial attribute set.

When you change the partial attribute set on the domain controller that has the schema operations master role, the writable schema directory partition replicates, using standard replication, to all domain controllers in the forest. Later, when a global catalog server attempts to synchronize its read-only directory partition from a source replication partner, the global catalog server receives the information that the replication attributes have been updated and initiates replication of only the attributes that were added to the partial attribute set. Because only the added attributes are replicated, there is limited network impact from the replication activity.

As discussed in Chapter 9, "Maintaining and Recovering Active Directory," you can use Repadmin to view the replication information on domain controllers. Using Repadmin, you can:

- View directory metadata.
- Determine the last successful replication of all directory partitions.
- Identify inbound and outbound replication partners.
- Identify domain controllers, global catalog servers, and bridgehead servers.
- Manage Active Directory replication topology.

- Force replication of an entire directory partition or of a single object.

To review the status of replication, enter **repadmin /showrepl** at an elevated command prompt.

For each directory partition that the global catalog server hosts, the global catalog server records related updates in the Directory Service log. Event ID 1704 states that in response to the addition of one or more attributes to the partial attribute set, the global catalog server has initiated replication of the partial attribute set for a specified directory partition from a specified domain controller. Event ID 1703 states that synchronization was initiated. Event ID 1702 states that synchronization of the partial attribute set was completed successfully. If these and other related events are not being recorded on a global catalog server, there is a problem.

Managing and Maintaining Name Suffixes

Active Directory uses name suffix routing for routing authentication between domains and across forests that are joined by forest trusts. Within forests, global catalog servers resolve names to enable cross-domain authentication. When a forest trust is created, all unique name suffixes are routed by default to enable authentication across forests.

Configuring User Principal Name Suffixes

Every user account has a user principal name (UPN), which consists of the User Logon Name joined with a UPN suffix by the at sign (@). The names of the current domain and the root domain are set as the default UPN suffix. You can specify an alternate UPN suffix to use to simplify logon or provide additional logon security. This name is used only within the forest and does not have to be a valid DNS name. For example, if the UPN suffix for a domain is it.seattle.imaginedlands.local, you could use an alternate UPN suffix to simplify this to imaginedlands.local. This would allow the user Williams to log on using williams@imaginedlands.local rather than williams@it.seattle.imaginedlands.local.

If you want alternate UPN suffixes to be available when you are creating accounts, you can add them to Active Directory by using Active Directory Domains and Trusts. When you add a UPN suffix, the suffix is available for all domains within the Active Directory forest.

You can add or remove UPN suffixes by completing the following steps:

1. Start Active Directory Domains and Trusts from the Administrative Tools menu.
2. Right-click the Active Directory Domains And Trusts node and then click Properties.
3. As shown in Figure 5-16, the UPN Suffixes tab of the properties dialog box will list all current UPN suffixes. To add a UPN suffix, enter the alternate suffix in the box provided and then click Add. To remove a UPN suffix, click the suffix in the list provided and then click Remove.
4. Click OK to apply your changes.

When you use UPN suffixes, you change the way authentication works. Because the domain of the user is not necessarily the same as the UPN suffix, the authenticating domain controller must determine whether the DNS name in the UPN suffix is the domain for which the domain controller is authoritative.

If the domain name in the UPN suffix matches the domain of the domain controller, the domain controller attempts to process the client authentication. Otherwise, the domain controller contacts a global catalog server.

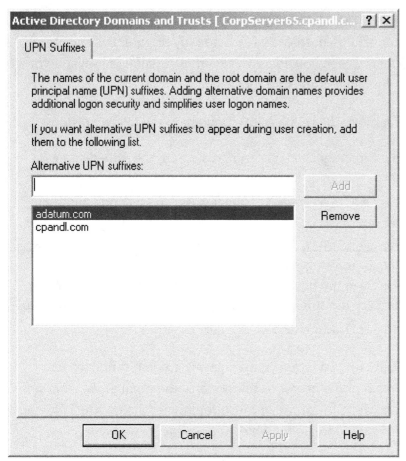

FIGURE 5-16 Review and modify UPN suffixes as necessary.

The global catalog server uses the userPrincipalName attribute of the user object to look up the distinguished name of the user object and returns this value to the authenticating domain controller. The authenticating domain controller extracts the domain name from the distinguished name of the user and returns this value to the client. The client then requests a domain controller for the user's domain.

Configuring Name Suffix Routing

When a forest trust is created, all unique name suffixes are routed by default. These include user principal name (UPN) suffixes and service principal name (SPN) suffixes as well as Domain Name System (DNS) forest or domain tree names that are not subordinate to any other name suffix. For example, the DNS forest name imaginedlands.com is a unique name suffix within the imaginedlands.com forest.

All names that are subordinate to unique name suffixes are routed implicitly. For example, if your forest uses imaginedlands.com as a unique name suffix, authentication requests for all child domains of imaginedlands.com will be routed because the child domains are part of the imaginedlands.com name suffix. If you want to exclude members of a child domain from authenticating in the specified forest, you can disable name suffix routing for that name. You can also disable routing for the forest name itself, if necessary.

You cannot enable a name suffix that is the same as another name in the routing list. If the conflict is with a local UPN name suffix, you must remove the local UPN name suffix from the list before you can enable the routing name. If the conflict is with a name that is claimed by another trust partner, you must disable the name in the other trust before it can be enabled for a particular trust.

If you want to prevent or allow authentication requests for all name suffixes that are identified by a forest trust (such as any request for a domain in the reagentpress.com forest) from being routed to a forest, you can disable routing for the forest name. You can enable or disable routing for a name suffix by using the Active Directory Domains and Trusts snap-in. Keep in mind that when you disable a name suffix, the DNS name and all child names of that name will be disabled.

To modify routing for a forest name suffix, follow these steps:

1. Start Active Directory Domains and Trusts from the Administrative Tools menu.
2. In the console tree, right-click the forest root domain for the forest trust that you want to manage, and then click Properties.
3. On the Trusts tab, under either Domains Trusted By This Domain (Outgoing Trusts) or Domains That Trust This Domain (Incoming

Trusts), click the forest trust that you want to administer, and then click Properties.

4. On the Name Suffix Routing tab, under Name Suffixes, do one of the following:

- To enable routing for a name suffix, click the suffix that you want to enable and then click Enable. If the Enable button is unavailable, the name suffix is already enabled.
- To disable routing for a name suffix, click the suffix that you want to disable and then click Disable. If the Disable button is unavailable, the name suffix is already disabled.

Another way to control name suffix routing is to enable or disable a name suffix that is subordinate to the name of a forest. For example, if the reagentpress.com forest trusts the imaginedlands.com forest and the imaginedlands.com forest includes the child domain sales.imaginedlands.com, you can enable or disable routing specifically for the child domain name suffix.

To modify routing for an existing subordinate name suffix, follow these steps:

1. Start Active Directory Domains and Trusts from the Administrative Tools menu.

2. In the console tree, right-click the forest root domain node for the forest trust that you want to administer, and then click Properties.

3. On the Trusts tab, under either Domains Trusted By This Domain (Outgoing Trusts) or Domains That Trust This Domain (Incoming Trusts), click the forest trust that you want to manage, and then click Properties.

4. On the Name Suffix Routing tab, under Name Suffixes, click the forest suffix whose subordinate name suffix you want to modify for routing and then click Edit.

5. In Existing Name Suffixes, click the suffix that you want to modify, and then click Enable or Disable.

You can exclude existing name suffixes from routing to a forest. When you exclude a name suffix, the DNS name and all child names of that name will be excluded. To exclude name suffixes from routing to a forest, follow these steps:

1. Start Active Directory Domains and Trusts from the Administrative Tools menu.

2. In the console tree, right-click the domain that you want to administer and then click Properties.

3. On the Trusts tab, under either Domains Trusted By This Domain (Outgoing Trusts) or Domains That Trust This Domain (Incoming Trusts), click the forest trust that you want to administer, and then click Properties.

4. On the Name Suffix Routing tab, under Name Suffixes, click the unique name suffix whose subordinate name suffix you want to exclude from routing, and then click Edit.

5. In Name Suffixes To Exclude From Routing, click Add, enter a DNS name suffix that is subordinate to the unique name suffix, and then click OK.

Chapter 6. Configuring, Maintaining, and Troubleshooting Operations Masters

Active Directory's multimaster replication model creates a distributed environment that allows any domain controller to be used for authentication and allows you to make changes to standard directory information without regard to which domain controller you use. The approach works well for most Active Directory operations—but not all.

Some Active Directory operations must be carefully controlled to maintain the integrity of the directory structure and data. These operations can be performed only by a single authoritative domain controller called an *operations master*. For example, you can make schema changes only on the domain controller serving as the schema master; if that server is unavailable, no changes can be made to the schema.

As an administrator, you have the responsibility to ensure that operations masters are always available and configured appropriately to handle their respective tasks. In this chapter, you will learn how operations masters are used as well as how to manage, maintain, and troubleshoot operations masters.

Operations Master Essentials

Operations masters keep the directory functioning properly by performing specific tasks that no other domain controllers are permitted to perform. A designated operations master has a flexible single-master operations (FSMO) role.

Introducing Operations Masters

As Table 6-1 depicts, there are five designated operations master roles, which can be organized into two broad categories. Forestwide roles are assigned on a per-forest basis. This means that there is only one schema master and only one domain naming master in an Active Directory forest. Domainwide roles are assigned on a per-domain basis. This means there is only one infrastructure master, PDC emulator, and relative ID master for each domain in an Active Directory forest.

TABLE 6-1 Available Operations Masters by Category

Forestwide	
	Domain naming master
	Schema master
Domainwide	
	Infrastructure master
	Primary domain controller (PDC) emulator
	Relative Identifier (RID) master

In an Active Directory forest, the domain naming master and schema master perform forest-level operations. The domain naming master controls domain creation and deletion, guaranteeing that each domain is unique within the forest. The schema master manages the schema and enforces schema consistency throughout the directory.

In an Active Directory domain, the infrastructure master, PDC emulator, and RID master perform domain-level operations. The infrastructure master handles user-to-group mappings, changes in group membership, and replication of those changes to other domain controllers. The PDC emulator is responsible for processing and replicating password changes and also must be available to reset and verify external trusts. The RID master manages the pool of relative identifiers (RIDs). RIDs are numeric strings used to construct security identifiers (SIDs) for security principals.

The first domain controller you install in the forest automatically receives the schema master and domain naming master roles. It also hosts the global catalog. Because the roles are compatible with the global catalog and moving the roles to other domain controllers does not improve performance, you can leave the roles on the initial domain controller. Note also that separating the roles creates additional administrative overhead when you must identify the operations masters and when you implement backup and restore procedures.

When you install the first domain controller in a new domain, it is assigned the three domain-level roles. Generally, you will want to keep the domain-level roles together unless the workload on your operations master justifies the additional management burden of separating the roles. For this reason, in nonforest root domains, you will probably want to leave the domain-level roles on the first domain controller (as long as you do not configure the domain controller as a global catalog server).

For the forest root domain, however, the first domain controller created in the domain hosts forest-level roles and all three domain-level roles, as well as the global catalog. However, the infrastructure master role is incompatible with the global catalog. Because of this, when you install the second domain controller in the forest root domain, the Active Directory Domain Services Installation Wizard prompts you to allow the wizard to transfer the infrastructure master role. If you transfer the role, you may also want to consider transferring the PDC emulator and RID master roles to the second domain controller after you install Active Directory Domain Services. This will keep the three domain-level roles together for easy administration.

Identifying Operations Masters

You can determine the current operations masters for your logon domain by entering the following at a command prompt.

```
netdom query fsmo
```

In the following example, the output lists each role owner by its fully qualified domain name.

```
Schema master              CentralDC17.imaginedlands.com
Domain naming master        CentralDC17.imaginedlands.com
PDC              CorpServer38.ny.imaginedlands.com
RID pool manager        CorpServer38.ny.imaginedlands.com
Infrastructure master      CorpServer15.ny.imaginedlands.com
```

From the output in this example, you can also determine that the forest root domain is imaginedlands.com and the current logon domain is ny.imaginedlands.com. If you want to determine the operations masters for a specific domain, use the following command.

```
netdom query fsmo /d:DomainName
```

Here, *DomainName* is the name of the domain, such as sales.imaginedlands.com.

Planning for Operations Masters

To perform their respective operations, the domain controllers that host operations master roles must be consistently available and must be located in highly available areas of your network. As you enlarge your Active Directory infrastructure by adding domains and sites, the careful placement of your operations masters becomes more and more important.

Improper placement of operations master role holders can:

- Prevent users and computers from maintaining their passwords.
- Prevent administrators from being able to add domains and new objects.
- Prevent administrators from making changes to schema.
- Prevent updated group membership information from being replicated.

As your Active Directory infrastructure changes, you must work to avoid the problems that are associated with improper operations master role placement, and you might need to reassign the roles to other domain controllers. As you design any forest or domain, consider how many domain controllers you need per domain and whether you need to change operations masters after you install new domain controllers.

Changing Operations Masters

Operations master roles can be changed in several ways. If the current operations master is online, you can perform a role transfer, gracefully shifting the role from one domain controller to another. If the current operations master has failed and will not be coming back online, you can seize the role and forcibly transfer it to another domain controller.

When you transfer a role, as discussed later in this chapter in "Working with Operations Masters," you move an operations master role from one domain controller to another. During the role transfer, the two domain controllers exchange any unreplicated information to ensure that no transactions are lost. If the two domain controllers are not direct replication partners, a substantial amount of information might have to be replicated before the domain controllers are completely synchronized with each other. If the two domain controllers are direct replication partners, there should be fewer outstanding transactions and the role transfer operation should complete faster. Once the transfer is complete, the previous role holder no longer attempts to perform as the operations master, and this eliminates the possibility of duplicate operations masters existing on the network.

Transferring a role is preferred to seizing a role. You reassign an operations master role by seizing it as a last restore. If you must seize a role, never reattach the previous role holder to the network without taking appropriate precautions to prevent the previous role holder from being active. Otherwise, reattaching the previous role holder to the network incorrectly can result in invalid data and corruption of data in the directory. For more information, see "Seizing Operations Master Roles" later in this chapter.

The reasons for transferring the operations master roles depend on several factors. First, you might want to transfer an operations master role to improve performance, as you might do when a server has too heavy a workload and you need to distribute some of the load. Second, you might need to transfer an operations master role if you plan to take the server with that role offline for maintenance or if the server fails. Keep in mind that although operations master roles can be placed on just about any writable domain controller, operations master roles cannot be placed on read-only domain controllers (RODCs).

When determining placement of operations masters, you should place the forestwide roles, schema master, and domain naming master on the same domain controller. There is very little overhead associated with these roles, so placement on the same server adds little load overall. However, it is important to safeguard this server because these are critical roles in the forest. In addition, the server acting as the domain naming master should also be a global catalog server.

You should place the relative ID master and PDC emulator roles on the same domain controller. The reason for this is that the PDC emulator uses more relative IDs than most other domain controllers. If the relative ID master and PDC emulator roles aren't on the same domain controller, the domain controllers on which they are placed should be in the same Active Directory site, and the domain controllers should have a reliable connection between them.

You should not place the infrastructure master on a domain controller that is also a global catalog server. The reason for this is a bit complicated, and there are some important exceptions to note. The infrastructure master is responsible for updating cross-domain group membership and determines whether its information is current or out of date by checking a global catalog and then replicating changes to other domain controllers as necessary. If the infrastructure master and the global catalog are on the same server, the infrastructure master doesn't see that changes have been made and thus doesn't replicate them.

The exceptions are for a single-domain forest or a multidomain forest where all domain controllers are global catalog servers. In the case of a single-domain forest, there are no cross-group references to update, so it doesn't matter where the infrastructure master is located. In the case of a multidomain forest where all domain controllers are global catalog servers, all the domain controllers know about all the objects in the forest already, so the infrastructure master doesn't really have to make updates.

Do not change the global catalog configuration of a domain controller that you intend to assume an operations master role. Modifying the global catalog configuration can cause changes within the directory that can take several days to complete, and the domain controller might be unavailable during that time.

Working with Operations Masters

The key to successful management of operations masters is in knowing what each operations master does and being able to readily diagnose problems that arise when an operations master isn't functioning properly. In addition to guidelines I provided previously for placing operations masters, you may want to consider transferring the three domain-level roles from the first domain controller that you installed in the forest root domain to an additional domain controller that has a high performance level. In all other domains, leave the domain-level roles on the first domain controller unless there is a compelling reason to move the roles. Finally, you should prepare additional domain controllers as standby operations masters and carefully monitor the workload of the busiest operations master—the PDC emulator.

Managing Domain Naming Masters

The domain naming master is responsible for adding and removing domains from the forest. Any time you create a domain, a remote procedure call (RPC) connection is made to the domain naming master, which assigns the domain a globally unique identifier (GUID). Any time you remove a domain, an RPC connection is made to the domain naming master and the previously assigned GUID reference is removed. If you cannot connect to the domain naming master when you are trying to add or remove a domain, you will not be able to create or remove the domain.

You can locate the domain naming master by following these steps:

1. Start Active Directory Domains And Trusts from the Administrative Tools menu.

2. Right-click the Active Directory Domains And Trusts node, and then select Operations Master.

   The Operations Master dialog box, shown in Figure 6-1, shows the current domain naming master.

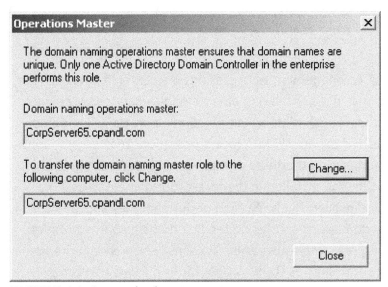

FIGURE 6-1 Locate the domain naming master.

You can transfer the domain naming master role to another server by following these steps:

1. Open Active Directory Domains And Trusts. Right-click the Active Directory Domains And Trusts node, and then select Change Active Directory Domain Controller.

2. In the Change Directory Server dialog box, select This Domain Controller. Enter the forest root domain name in the Look In This Domain field, and then press Tab.

3. Available domain controllers are listed by site, type, and operating system version. Select an available domain controller to which you want to transfer the domain naming master role, and then click OK.

4. Right-click the Active Directory Domains And Trusts node, and then select Operations Master. The name of the current domain naming master appears in the first text box. The domain controller to which you want to transfer the domain naming master role should appear in the second text box. If this is not the case, repeat this procedure, starting with step 1.

5. In the Change Operations Master dialog box, click Change, and then click Close. When prompted, click Yes to confirm you want to transfer the role.

6. When the transfer is complete, you'll see a message confirming this. Click OK. Click Close to close the Operations Master dialog box.

Managing Infrastructure Masters

The infrastructure master is responsible for updating objects for any attribute values with distinguished names that reference objects outside the current domain. These updates are particularly important for cross-domain group-to-security-principal references where the infrastructure master is responsible for ensuring that changes to the common name of security principal objects are correctly reflected in the group membership information for groups in other domains in the forest. The infrastructure master does this by comparing its directory data to that of a global catalog. If the data is outdated, it updates the data and replicates the changes to other domain controllers in the domain. If for some reason the infrastructure master is unavailable, group-to-security-principal references will not be updated, and cross-domain group membership may not accurately reflect the actual names of security principal objects.

To see how this process works, consider the following example:

1. A user in domain A is a member of a group in domain B. The user gets married, and her surname is changed in the first domain. This change affects name-related attributes of the related user object, including the

Full Name and Last Name, and also typically changes the DN attribute value of the user object. (The distinguished name (DN) is the value that is used in the member attribute of group objects.)

2. Because domain controllers in one domain do not replicate security principals to domain controllers in another domain, the second domain never receives the change. As a result, an out-of-date value on the member attribute of a group in another domain could result in denied privileges for the user whose name has changed.

3. To ensure consistency between domains, the infrastructure master monitors group memberships, looking for member attribute values that identify security principals from other domains. If it finds a cross-domain reference, it compares its stored distinguished name value with the distinguished name value in the originating domain to determine if the information has changed. If the distinguished name has changed, the infrastructure master performs an update and then replicates the change to other domain controllers in its domain.

Tip Except for the infrastructure master, you can assign operations master roles to any domain controller regardless of any other directory functions that the domain controller performs. Do not host the infrastructure master role on a domain controller that is also acting as a global catalog server unless all the domain controllers in the domain are global catalog servers or unless the forest has only one domain. If the domain controller that hosts the infrastructure master role is configured to be a global catalog server, you must transfer the infrastructure master role to another domain controller.

Real World The infrastructure master is incompatible with the global catalog, and it must not be placed on a global catalog server. However, if all the domain controllers in a domain are global catalog servers, the domain controller that hosts the infrastructure master role is inconsequential because global catalog servers replicate updated security principal information to all other global catalog servers. If the forest has only one domain, the infrastructure master role is inconsequential as well because security principals from other domains do not exist.

You can locate the infrastructure master by following these steps:

1. Start Active Directory Users And Computers from the Administrative Tools menu.

2. If the domain you want to work with isn't listed already, right-click the Active Directory Users And Computers node, and then select Change Domain. In the Change Domain dialog box, enter the DNS name of the domain you want to work with, such as **cs.imaginedlands.com**, and then click OK.

3. Right-click the domain you want to work with and then select Operations Masters.

4. The Operations Masters dialog box, shows the current infrastructure master on the Infrastructure tab. (See Figure 6-2.)

You can transfer the infrastructure master role to another server by following these steps:

1. Open Active Directory Users And Computers. If the domain you want to work with isn't listed already, right-click the Active Directory Users And Computers node, and then select Change Domain. In the Change Domain dialog box, enter the DNS name of the domain you want to work with, such as **cs.imaginedlands.com**, and then click OK.

2. Right-click the domain node, and then select Change Domain Controller. In the Change Directory Server dialog box, select This Domain Controller. Select an available domain controller to which you want to transfer the infrastructure master role, and then click OK.

3. Right-click the domain node again, and then select Operations Masters. In the Operations Masters dialog box, select the Infrastructure tab. The name of the current infrastructure master appears in the first text box. The domain controller to which you want to transfer the infrastructure master role should appear in the second text box. If this is not the case, repeat this procedure, starting with step 1.

4. Click Change, and then click Close. When prompted, click Yes to confirm you want to transfer the role.

5. When the transfer is complete, you'll see a message confirming this. Click OK. Click Close to close the Operations Masters dialog box.

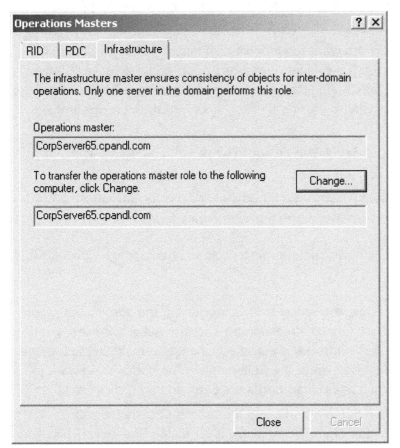

FIGURE 6-2 Locate the infrastructure master.

Managing PDC Emulators

When Active Directory was first released and Active Directory forests operated in Windows 2000 mixed mode, the PDC emulator operations master's primary job was to process all replication requests from Windows NT Server 4.0 backup domain controllers (BDCs). In a domain using the Windows 2000 native or higher functional level, a domain controller with the PDC emulator role is responsible for processing password changes. When a user changes a password, the change is first sent to the PDC emulator, which in turn replicates the change to all the other domain controllers in the domain. This makes the PDC emulator the definitive source for the latest password information whenever a logon attempt fails as a result of a bad password.

Every domain controller in a domain knows which server has the PDC emulator role. If a user tries to log on to the network but provides an incorrect password, the domain controller checks the PDC emulator to see if it has a recent password change for this account. If so, the domain controller retries the logon authentication on the PDC emulator. This approach is designed to ensure that if a user has recently changed a password, he is not denied logon with the new password.

As a result of this logon authentication activity, the PDC emulator operations master role has the highest impact on the performance of the domain controller that hosts that role out of all the operations master roles. Note that if an RODC is installed in the domain, the PDC emulator role must be placed on a domain controller that is running Windows Server 2008 or later. Additionally, note that the PDC emulator in the forest root domain is also the default Windows Time service (W32time) time source for the forest.

You can locate the PDC emulator by following these steps:

1. Open Active Directory Users And Computers from the Administrative Tools menu. If the domain you want to work with isn't listed already, right-click the Active Directory Users And Computers node, and then select Change Domain. In the Change Domain dialog box, enter the DNS name of the domain you want to work with, such as **cs.imaginedlands.com**, and then click OK.

2. Right-click the domain node and then select Operations Masters.

3. The Operations Masters dialog box shows the current PDC emulator on the PDC tab. (See Figure 6-3.)

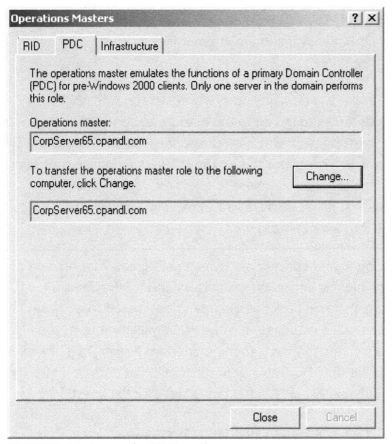

FIGURE 6-3 Locate the PDC emulator.

You can transfer the PDC emulator role to another server by following these
steps:

1. Open Active Directory Users And Computers. If the domain you want
    to work with isn't listed already, right-click the Active Directory Users
    And Computers node, and then select Change Domain. In the Change
    Domain dialog box, enter the DNS name of the domain, and then click
    OK.

2. Right-click the domain node, and then select Change Domain
    Controller. In the Change Directory Server dialog box, select This
    Domain Controller. Select an available domain controller to which you
    want to transfer the PDC emulator role, and then click OK.

3. Right-click the domain node again, and then select Operations Master. In the Operations Masters dialog box, select the PDC tab. The name of the current PDC emulator appears in the first text box. The domain controller to which you want to transfer the PDC emulator role should appear in the second text box. If this is not the case, repeat this procedure, starting with step 1.

4. Click Change, and then click Close. When prompted, click Yes to confirm you want to transfer the role.

5. When the transfer is complete, you'll see a message confirming this. Click OK. Click Close to close the Operations Masters dialog box.

Managing Relative ID Masters

The relative identifier (RID) master controls the creation of new security principals such as users, groups, and computers throughout its related domain. Every domain controller in a domain is issued a block of relative IDs by the RID master. These relative IDs are used to build the security IDs that uniquely identify security principals in the domain. The actual security ID generated by a domain controller consists of a domain identifier, which is the same for every object in a domain, and a unique relative ID that differentiates the object from any other objects in the domain.

The block of relative IDs issued to a domain controller is called an RID pool. Newly promoted domain controllers must acquire an RID pool before they can advertise their availability to Active Directory clients or share the SYSVOL. Existing domain controllers require additional RID allocations in order to continue creating security principals when their current RID pool becomes depleted. Since RIDs are 30 bits in length, a maximum of 1,073,741,824 (2^{30}) security principals can be created in an Active Directory domain. After the domainwide RID pool is used up, no new security principals can be created in the domain.

Typically, blocks of relative IDs are issued in lots of 500. A domain controller will start to request a new pool when 250 (50 percent of 500) RIDs have been used. It is the job of the RID master to issue blocks of RIDs, and it does so as long as it is running. If a domain controller cannot connect to the RID master and for any reason runs out of RIDs, no new objects can be created on the domain controller, and object creation will fail. Event 16645 and optionally event 16651 are logged in the Directory Service log on domain controllers that cannot acquire new RID pools. The message text for the respective events are:

- **Event 16645**   The maximum account identifier allocated to this domain controller has been assigned. The domain controller has failed to obtain a new identifier pool. A possible reason for this is that the domain controller has been unable to contact the master domain controller. Account creation on this controller will fail until a new pool has been allocated. There may be network or connectivity problems in the domain, or the master domain controller may be offline or missing from the domain. Verify that the master domain controller is running and connected to the domain.
- **Event 16651**   The request for a new account-identifier pool failed. The operation will be retried until the request succeeds. The error is %n " %1".

To resolve this problem, the RID master must be made available, or the RID master role must be transferred to another server.

> **Real World**   The RID Block Size setting in the registry can be used to increase the RID pool size. Increasing the RID pool size makes it possible for each domain controller to create a larger number of security principals without contacting the RID operations master. Although you only need to make the change on the RID master, you may want to configure the value on all domain controllers in case you later transfer the RID operations master role to another domain controller.
>
> The RID Block Size setting is used by the RID operations master to determine what size RID pool to return to a requesting domain controller. The RID Block Size setting has a REG_DWORD value and is located under

HKEY_LOCAL_MACHINE\SYSTEM\CurrentControlSet\Services\NTDS\RID Values.

Windows Server creates the RID Block Size setting automatically and its default value is 0. In this state, the internal default of 500 is used. Setting this value to less than 500 has no effect, and the default setting is still used. While no maximum block size is enforced, a value that is too large can have a severe adverse affect on the domain. Why? If you allocate RIDs in very large blocks, some domain controllers may run out of RIDs and may not be able to get new RIDs, while other domain controllers may have a large number of unused RIDs. Additionally, every time a domain controller is decommissioned through graceful or forceful demotion or because of a hardware failure, its RIDs are all lost. Similarly, every time a domain controller is restored from backup, its RIDs are all invalidated to help prevent more than one user account from being assigned the same RID.

You can locate the RID master by following these steps:

1. Start Active Directory Users And Computers from the Administrative Tools menu.

2. If the domain you want to work with isn't listed already, right-click the Active Directory Users And Computers node, and then select Change Domain. In the Change Domain dialog box, enter the DNS name of the domain you want to work with, such as **cs.imaginedlands.com**, and then click OK.

3. Right-click the domain you want to work with and then select Operations Masters.

4. The Operations Masters dialog box shows the current RID master on the RID tab. (See Figure 6-4.)

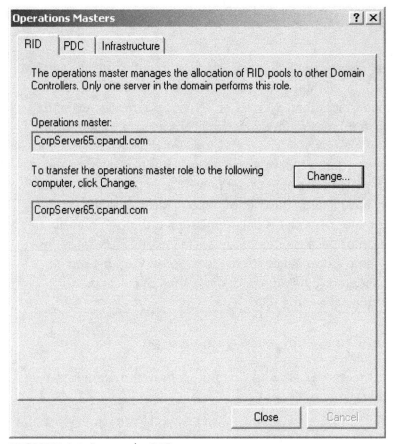

FIGURE 6-4 Locate the RID master.

You can transfer the RID master role to another server by following these steps:

1. Start Active Directory Users And Computers. If the domain you want to work with isn't listed already, right-click the Active Directory Users And Computers node, and then select Change Domain. In the Change Domain dialog box, enter the DNS name of the domain, and then click OK.

2. Right-click the domain node, and then select Change Domain Controller. In the Change Directory Server dialog box, select This Domain Controller. Select an available domain controller to which you want to transfer the RID master role, and then click OK.

3. Right-click the domain node again, and then select Operations Masters. In the Operations Masters dialog box, the RID tab is selected by default. The name of the current RID master appears in the first text box. The domain controller to which you want to transfer the RID master role should appear in the second text box. If this is not the case, repeat this procedure, starting with step 1.

4. Click Change, and then click Close. When prompted, click Yes to confirm you want to transfer the role.

5. When the transfer is complete, you'll see a message confirming this. Click OK. Click Close to close the Operations Masters dialog box.

Managing Schema Masters

The schema master is the only domain controller in the forest with a writable copy of the schema container. This means that it is the only domain controller in the forest on which you can make changes to the schema. You make changes to the schema using the Active Directory Schema snap-in. When you start the Active Directory Schema snap-in, it makes a direct connection to the schema master, allowing you to view the schema for the directory. To make changes to the schema, however, you must use an account that is a member of the Schema Admins group.

By default, the schema master is the first domain controller installed in the forest root domain. You can transfer this role using the Active Directory Schema snap-in or the NTDSUTIL command-line utility.

You can locate the schema master using the Active Directory Schema snap-in in a custom console. (For tips on registering and using this snap-in, see the section "Designating Replication Attributes" in Chapter 5, "Configuring, Maintaining, and Troubleshooting Global Catalog Servers.") After you open the snap-in, right-click the Active Directory Schema node, and then select Operations Master. The Change Schema Master dialog box, shown in Figure 6-5, shows the current schema master.

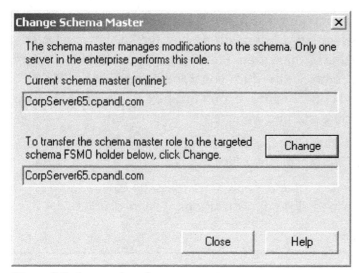

Figure 6-5   Locate the schema master.

You can transfer the schema master role to another server by following these steps:

1. Open the Active Directory Schema snap-in in a custom console. Right-click the Active Directory Schema node, and then select Change Active Directory Domain Controller.

2. In the Change Directory Server dialog box, select This Domain Controller. Enter the forest root domain name in the Look In This Domain field, and then press Tab.

3. Available domain controllers are listed by site, type, and operating system version. Select an available domain controller to which you want to transfer the schema master role, and then click OK.

4. Right-click the Active Directory Schema node, and then select Operations Master. In the Change Schema Master dialog box, the name of the current schema master appears in the first text box. The domain controller to which you want to transfer the schema master role should appear in the second text box. If this is not the case, repeat this procedure, starting with step 1.

5. Click Change, and then click Close. When prompted, click Yes to confirm you want to transfer the role.

6. When the transfer is complete, you'll see a message confirming this. Click OK. Click Close to close the Operations Master dialog box.

Maintaining Operations Masters

As an administrator, you'll perform a number of tasks to help maintain operations masters throughout the Active Directory forest. To help recover operations masters quickly, you may want to prepare standby operations masters. To ensure proper operations, you may need to reduce an operations master's workload. In the event of catastrophic failure, you may need to forcibly transfer an operations master role.

Preparing Standby Operations Masters

Operations master roles are critical to proper forest and domain function. When you install Active Directory and create the first domain controller in a new forest, all five roles are assigned to that domain controller. As you add domains, the first domain controller you install in a domain is automatically designated the RID master, infrastructure master, and PDC emulator roles for that domain.

If an operations master becomes inoperable or unreachable, the functions that the operations master performs will no longer be available, and this could cripple Active Directory. To ensure you are ready to handle the failure of an operations master, you can identify an additional domain controller as a standby operations master. A standby operations master is simply a domain controller that you identify to assume the operations master role if the role holder fails.

You will need to identify a standby for the forest roles in the forest root domain and a standby for the domain roles in each domain. The standby should be optimally connected to the current role holder, which ensures that role transfer can occur as quickly as possible and that there is minimal data loss in the event of an outage.

Other than ensuring a standby is available and optimally connected to the current operations master, you don't need to take any other special steps. That said, you can create a manual connection object between the standby domain controller and the operations master to ensure direct replication between the two operations masters. In this scenario, a manually created connection object is preferred to an automatically created one because Active Directory can alter automatically created connection objects at any time whereas manually created connections remain the same until you change them. Being directly connected helps reduce the chance of data loss in the event of a role seizure and in turn helps to reduce the chance of directory corruption.

> **Note** If you separate operations roles, you can still use a single standby operations master for a forest and a single operations master for a domain. However, you should ensure that the standby is a replication partner with all of the role holders.

Using an account that is a member of the Domain Admins or Enterprise Admins group, you can manually create a connection object on the operations master and standby by following these steps:

1. Start Active Directory Sites and Services from the Administrative Tools menu.

2. Expand the site name in which the current operations master role holder is located to display the related Servers folder.

3. Expand the related Servers folder to see a list of the servers in the selected site.

4. Create an inbound connection object from the standby server on the current operations master by doing the following:

   a. Expand the name of the operations master server on which you want to create the connection object to display its NTDS Settings object.

   b. Right-click NTDS Settings, click New, and then click Connection.

   c. In the Find Active Directory Domain Controllers dialog box, select the name of the standby server from which you want to create the connection object, and then click OK.

d. In the New Object-Connection dialog box, enter an appropriate name for the connection object or accept the default name, and then click OK.

5. Expand the site name in which the standby is located to display the related Servers folder.

6. Expand the related Servers folder to see a list of the servers in that site.

7. Create an inbound connection object from the current operations master on the standby server by doing the following:

   a. Expand the name of the standby server on which you want to create the connection object to display its NTDS Settings object.

   b. Right-click NTDS Settings, click New, and then click Connection.

   c. In the Find Active Directory Domain Controllers dialog box, select the name of the current operations master from which you want to create the connection object, and then click OK.

   d. In the New Object-Connection dialog box, enter an appropriate name for the connection object or accept the default name, and then click OK.

Decommissioning Operations Masters

Before you take an operations master offline permanently, you should transfer any operations master roles that it holds to another domain controller. When you use the Active Directory Domain Services Installation Wizard to decommission a domain controller that currently hosts one or more operations master roles, the wizard automatically reassigns the roles to a different domain controller.

To see how this process works, consider the following example:

1. You run the Active Directory Domain Services Installation Wizard (Dcpromo) on a domain controller. When the wizard starts, it determines whether the domain controller currently hosts any operations master roles.

2. If Dcpromo detects any operations master roles, it queries the directory for other eligible domain controllers and then transfers the roles to

one of the eligible domain controllers. A domain controller is eligible to host the domain-level roles if it is a member of the same domain. A domain controller is eligible to host a forest-level role if it is a member of the same forest.

As you can see, the automated transfer process doesn't allow you to specify the domain controller to assume the operations master roles. Therefore, if you want the operations master role or roles to be assigned to a specific domain controller, you must transfer the roles before decommissioning the current role holder.

Reducing Operations Master Workload

Operations masters can become overloaded while attempting to service client requests on the network, manage their own resources, and perform their unique operations master tasks. If an operations master is overloaded and its performance is affected, you can reconfigure the environment so that some tasks are performed by other, less-used domain controllers. With fewer client requests to process, the operations master can use more resources to perform its unique functions in the forest or domain.

To reduce the workload on an operations master, look for noncritical functions and move these to other servers. If an overloaded operations master is also acting as a DNS server or global catalog server, you can move these functions to other servers to reduce the workload.

You could also adjust the domain controller's weight in the DNS environment so that it processes fewer client requests for a particular service. With fewer requests to process, the domain controller can use more resources to perform operations master services for the domain. For example, to configure the PDC emulator so that it receives only half as many client requests as other domain controllers, set the weight on the LDAP SVR record to 50. Assuming that other domain controllers have the same priority and use the default weight value of 100, DNS would then determine the weight ratio for the PDC emulator to be 50/100 (50 for the PDC emulator and 100 for the other domain controllers). After you reduce this ratio to 50/100, DNS refers clients to the other domain controllers twice as often as it refers to the PDC emulator. When you reduce client referrals for LDAP, the PDC emulator receives fewer client requests and has more resources for other tasks, such as performing tasks related to its operations master role.

> **Real World**   Don't confuse weighting with priority. To prevent clients from sending all requests to a single domain controller, domain controllers are assigned a priority value. The default value is 0. A client uses the priority value to help determine to which domain controller it sends requests. When a client uses DNS to discover a domain controller, the priority value is returned to the client (as is the rest of the DNS information needed to complete the request).
>
> Clients always send requests to the domain controller that has the lowest priority value. If more than one domain controller has the same value, the clients randomly choose from the group of domain controllers with the same value. If no domain controllers with the lowest priority value are available, the clients send requests to the domain controller with the next-highest priority. Because of this, raising the priority value of the LDAP resource record for the PDC emulator can reduce its chances of receiving client requests.
>
> However, although changing the priority of a domain controller also reduces the number of client referrals to it, the change can have an unintended consequence. Rather than reducing access to the domain controller proportionally with regard to the other domain controllers, changing the priority causes Domain Name System (DNS) to stop referring all clients to this domain controller unless all domain controllers with a lower priority setting are unavailable.

To modify the relative priority and weighting for an operations master service in DNS, follow these steps:

1. Click Start, point to Administrative Tools, and then click DNS.
2. Connect to a domain controller in the forest root domain. Right-click DNS, click Connect To DNS Server, and then click The Following

Computer. Enter the name of the domain controller in the forest root domain, and then click OK.

3. Expand Forward Lookup Zones, and then expand the forest root domain.

4. Click the _tcp container. The _ldap records control directory requests. The _gc records control global catalog requests. In the details pane, look for an _ldap or _gc SRV record that has the name of the operations master. The data field lists the priority, weight, and port number assigned to the resource record as well as the name of the server to which the record belongs.

5. Double-click the SRV resource record that you want to modify. This displays a properties dialog box for the record, as shown in Figure 6-6.

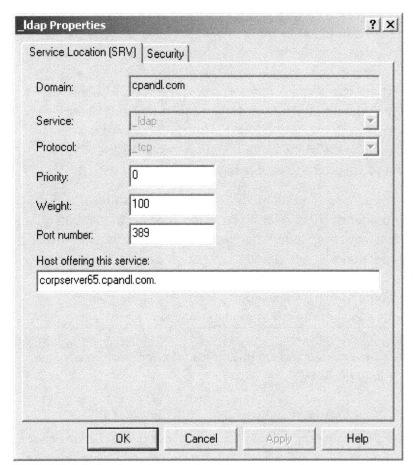

FIGURE 6-6 Set the priority and weight as appropriate.

6. As appropriate, use the Priority box to specify the relative priority of the host with respect to other hosts in the domain that offer the same service. The highest priority goes to a host that has a value of 0. If two or more hosts have the same priority, weighting can be used to determine which host is used.

7. As appropriate, use the Weight box to specify the relative weighting of a host and to load-balance the service. If two or more hosts of a service have the same priority, the weighting can set a preference for one host over another. Hosts with higher weights should be used first.

8. Click OK to save your changes. The changes will be disseminated to other DNS servers during normal zone transfer operations. Depending on the DNS configuration, this process can take several days.

Caution Don't modify service locator records without careful planning with regard to the potential impact on your network. After you modify service locator records, you'll need to carefully monitor your network to ensure proper operations.

Seizing Operations Master Roles

When an operations master fails, you must decide if you need to relocate the operations master role to another domain controller or wait for the domain controller to be returned to service. You can base your decision on the criticality of the role that the domain controller hosts and the expected downtime.

When an operations master fails and is not coming back online, you need to seize the role to forcibly transfer it to another domain controller. Seizing a role is a drastic step that you should perform only when the previous role owner will never be available again. Don't seize an operations master role when you can transfer it gracefully using the normal transfer procedure. Seize a role only as a last resort.

Preparing to Seize Operations Master Roles

Before you seize a role and forcibly transfer it, you should determine how up to date the domain controller that will take over the role is with respect to the previous role owner. Active Directory tracks replication changes using update sequence numbers (USNs). Because of replication latency, domain controllers might not all be up to date. If you compare a domain controller's USN to that of other servers in the domain, you can determine whether the domain controller is the most up to date with respect to changes from the previous role owner. If the domain controller is up to date, you can transfer the role safely. If the domain controller isn't up to date, you can wait for replication to occur and then transfer the role to the domain controller.

Windows Server 2008 and Windows Server 2008 R2 include Repadmin for working with Active Directory replication. To display the highest sequence number for a specified naming context on each replication partner of a designated domain controller, enter the following at a command prompt.

```
repadmin /showutdvec DomainControllerName NamingContext
```

Here, *DomainControllerName* is the fully qualified domain name of the domain controller, and *NamingContext* is the distinguished name of the domain in which the server is located, as in the following code example.

```
repadmin /showutdvec corpserver52 dc=imaginedlands,dc=com
```

The following output shows the highest USN on replication partners for the domain partition.

```
Main-Site\corpserver31    @ USN    678321 @ Time 2008-03-15 12:42:32
Main-Site\corpserver26    @ USN    681525 @ Time 2008-03-15 12:42:35
```

In this example, if CorpServer31 was the previous role owner and the domain controller you are examining has an equal or higher USN for CorpServer31, the domain controller is up to date. However, if CorpServer31 was the previous role owner and the domain controller you are examining has a lower USN for CorpServer31, the domain controller is not up to date, and you should wait for replication to occur before seizing the role. You could also use Repadmin /Syncall to force the domain controller that is the most up to date with respect to the previous role owner to replicate with all of its replication partners.

Seizing Operations Master Roles

You can seize an operations master role by following these steps:

1. Open a command prompt on the console of the server you want to assign as the new operations master. You can do this locally or through Remote Desktop.
2. List current operations masters by entering **netdom query fsmo**.
3. Enter **ntdsutil**. At the ntdsutil prompt, enter **roles**.
4. At the fsmo maintenance prompt, enter **connections**.
5. At the server connections prompt, enter **connect to server** followed by the fully qualified domain name of the domain controller to which you want to assign the operations master role.
6. After you've established a connection to the domain controller, enter **quit** to exit the server connections prompt.
7. At the fsmo maintenance prompt, enter one of the following:

- seize pdc
- seize rid master
- seize infrastructure master
- seize schema master
- seize domain naming master

8. At the fsmo maintenance prompt, enter **quit**.
9. At the ntdsutil prompt, enter **quit**.

After seizing the operations master role, you will need to remove the related data from Active Directory. (For more information, refer to the sections "Performing Forced Removal of Domain Controllers" and "Cleaning Up Metadata in the Active Directory Forest" in Chapter 3, "Deploying Writable Domain Controllers.")

Troubleshooting Operations Masters

All domain controllers, including operations masters, replicate directory data with each other. Replication is how domain controllers stay up to date with directory changes. As part of diagnosing and resolving problems with operations masters, you'll want to ensure replication is occurring normally. Generally, the larger and more extensive the Active Directory environment, the longer it takes for changes to completely replicate to all domain controllers.

You can perform a series of automated tests on an operations master using Dcdiag. Follow these steps:

1. Start an elevated, administrator command prompt by clicking Start, right-clicking Command Prompt, and then clicking Run As Administrator.
2. At the elevated command prompt, enter the following command: **dcdiag /s:ServerName** where *ServerName* specifies the name of the operations master that you want to test. If you are logged on to the operations master already, simply enter **dcdiag** without any parameters.
3. Review the status of each test. If a test fails, note which test failed, and take appropriate corrective steps.

> **Note**   You can run Dcdiag without using an elevated, administrator command prompt. However, if you do this, you'll receive inaccurate test results because tests that require elevation will fail.

Using an elevated, administrator command prompt, you can verify that the operations master is successfully replicating with other domain controllers. At an elevated command prompt, enter the following command: **repadmin /showrepl ServerName** where *ServerName* specifies the name of the operations master that you want to test. If you are logged on to the operations master already, simply enter **repadmin /showrepl**.

Repadmin will then list inbound neighbors for the current or specified domain controller. These inbound neighbors identify the distinguished name of each directory partition for which inbound directory replication has been attempted, the site and name of the source domain controller, and whether replication succeeded.

Additionally, although the PDC emulator typically is the time server for the forest, any administrator could modify this configuration. To determine if the PDC emulator is the default Windows Time service (W32time) time source for the forest, you can use Nltest. At a command prompt, enter the following command: **nltest /server:*ServerName* /dsgetdc:*DomainName*** where *ServerName* specifies the name of the PDC emulator and *DomainName* specifies the name of the domain to which the server belongs. In the following example, you can examine CentralDC89 in the imaginedlands.com domain.

```
nltest /server:centraldc89 /dsgetdc:imaginedlands.com
```

The output will look similar to the following.

```
           DC: \\CENTRALDC89.imaginedlands.com
      Address: \\192.168.15.122
     Dom Guid:
     Dom Name: imaginedlands.com
  Forest Name: imaginedlands.com
 Dc Site Name: Atlanta-First-Site
Our Site Name: NY-First-Site
        Flags: PDC GC DS LDAP KDC TIMESERV GTIMESERV WRITABLE
DNS_FOREST CLOSE_SITE FULL_SECRET
The command completed successfully
```

In the Flags line of the output, if PDC appears, as in the previous sample output, the domain controller is the PDC emulator. If GTIMESERV appears, the domain controller is the global time server for the forest.

Chapter 7. Managing Active Directory Sites, Subnets, and Replication

Understanding how sites, subnets, and replication work is essential to configuring and managing Active Directory Domain Services. Sites and subnets are the physical components of Active Directory, and as such, they typically mirror your organization's network structure. As part of creating a design plan for Active Directory, ongoing maintenance, and planning for any expansion of your network, you should examine your organization's network topology and ensure it is represented effectively and efficiently in Active Directory. Prior to changing your organization's network topology, you should consider whether you need to change the physical representation of the network in Active Directory as well as whether your changes will affect critical logon, authentication, and replication traffic.

Implementing Sites and Subnets

As discussed in "Active Directory Components" in Chapter 1, "Overview of Active Directory," a *subnet* is a subdivision of an IP network, and a *site* is a combination of one or more IP subnets that are connected by fast, highly reliable links. You use sites and subnets to create a directory structure that mirrors the physical structure of your organization.

Working with Sites

The main purpose of a site is to physically group computers to optimize logon, authentication, and replication traffic. Sites help facilitate logon and authentication by determining the nearest domain controller according to site location when a user logs on. Sites help facilitate replication by confining replication traffic to devices within a site as appropriate and by providing mechanisms to control replication between sites.

Replication is handled differently between sites than it is within sites. Replication that occurs within a site is referred to as intrasite replication.

Replication between sites is referred to as intersite replication. Each side of a site link has one or more designated bridgehead servers. Bridgehead servers perform intersite replication with each other. Although bridgehead servers are designated automatically by default, you can designate preferred bridgehead servers in a site.

A key reason to create additional sites at the same physical location is to control replication traffic. Replication traffic between sites is automatically compressed, reducing the amount of traffic passed between sites by 85 to 90 percent. Because network clients try to log on to network resources within their local site first, you can use sites to isolate logon traffic as well.

Each site should have at least one domain controller and one global catalog for client authentication. For name resolution and IP address assignment, each site should have at least one Domain Name System (DNS) server and one Dynamic Host Configuration Protocol (DHCP) server. Then, by creating multiple sites in the same physical location and establishing a domain controller, global catalog, and DNS and DHCP server within each site, you can closely control the logon process.

You might also want to design sites with other network resources in mind, including Distributed File System (DFS) file shares, certificate authorities, and Microsoft Exchange servers. Typically, you will want to configure sites so that clients' network queries can be answered within the site. If every client query for a network resource has to be sent to a remote site, network traffic between sites can be substantial, which can be a problem over slow wide area network (WAN) links.

Setting Site Boundaries

You should use the connectivity between network segments to determine where to locate site boundaries. Any business locations connected over slow or unreliable links should be part of separate sites. This means individual sites typically represent the individual local area networks (LANs) within an organization, and the WAN links between business locations typically mark the boundaries of these sites.

> **Tip** Generally, a fast network has a bandwidth of at least 512 kilobits per second (Kbps). For you to reliably use a network segment within a site for Active Directory replication, the available bandwidth must be at least 128 Kbps. Available bandwidth refers to the amount of bandwidth that is usable during peak traffic after normal network traffic is handled.

As you set site boundaries, you should determine whether placing domain controllers and other network resources at that location is necessary. If you elect not to place a domain controller at a remote location, you must establish the remote location as part of an existing site. Doing this has several advantages because no Active Directory replication will occur between the business locations, and there are no remote domain controllers or additional site infrastructure to manage. However, there are also several disadvantages: all logon traffic must cross the link between the business locations, and users may experience slow logon and authentication to network resources.

In many cases, the decision to establish a separate site may come down to the user experience and the available bandwidth. If you have fast, reliable connections between sites, you may not want to establish a separate site for the remote business location. If you have limited bandwidth between business locations and want to maintain the user experience, you may want to establish a separate site and place domain controllers and possibly other network resources at the site. This should provide better control over the network traffic between sites and improve the logon and authentication processes.

Replication Essentials

Replication is handled differently between sites than it is within sites. Replication that occurs within a site is referred to as intrasite replication. Replication between sites is referred to as intersite replication.

The Replication Model

The Active Directory multimaster replication model is designed to ensure that there is no single point of failure. In this model, every domain controller can access changes to the database and can replicate those changes to all other domain controllers in the forest.

Although more replication is performed within a domain than between domains, replication between domains occurs nonetheless. When a forest is running at the functional level of Windows Server 2003 or higher, the smallest unit of replication is an attribute's updated value. With universal group membership, for example, this means that only the users you've added or removed are updated, rather than the entire group membership.

When any change is made to a domain partition in Active Directory, the change is replicated to all domain controllers in the domain. If the change is made to an attribute of an object tracked by the global catalog, the change is replicated to all global catalog servers in all domains of the forest. Similarly, if you make a change to the forestwide configuration or schema partitions, it is replicated to all domain controllers in all the domains of the forest.

Authentication within and between domains is also handled by domain controllers. If a user logs on to his or her home domain, the local domain controller authenticates the logon. If a user logs on to a domain other than the home domain, the logon request is forwarded through the trust tree to a domain controller in the user's home domain.

The Active Directory replication model is designed for consistency, but at any given moment the information on one domain controller can be different from the information on a different domain controller. This can happen when one domain controller has not yet replicated changes to another domain controller. Over time, however, the changes made to one domain controller are replicated to all domain controllers.

> **Note** With Windows Server 2003 and later, Active Directory can accommodate hundreds of sites per forest. This is possible because the Knowledge Consistency Checker (KCC) has been significantly enhanced.

Replication with Multiple Sites

When multiple sites are involved, the replication model is used to store and then forward changes as necessary between sites. In this case, a domain controller in the site where the changes were originally made forwards the changes to a domain controller in another site. This domain controller in turn stores the changes and then forwards them to all the domain controllers in the second site. In this way, the domain controller on which a change is made doesn't have to replicate directly with all the other domain controllers. It can instead rely on the store-and-forward technique to ensure that the changes are replicated as necessary.

Each side of a site connection has one or more designated bridgehead servers. Bridgehead servers perform intersite replication with each other. Intersite replication traffic is compressed and scheduled by default.

Compression significantly reduces the amount of traffic between sites while simultaneously increasing the processing overhead required on the bridgehead servers to replicate traffic between sites. Because of this, if high processor utilization on bridgehead servers is a concern and you have adequate bandwidth connections between sites, you may want to disable compression, which Windows Server 2003 and later allow you to do.

Scheduling controls the times of the day when replication traffic can flow across site links. With Windows Server 2003 and later, you can enable notification for intersite replication, which allows the bridgehead server in a site to notify the bridgehead server on the other side of a site link that changes have occurred. This allows the other bridgehead server to get more frequent updates by pulling the changes across the site link.

SYSVOL Replication

The Active Directory system volume (SYSVOL) contains domain policy; scripts used for logon, logoff, shutdown, and startup; and other related files. The way domain controllers replicate the SYSVOL depends on the domain functional level. When a domain is running at Windows 2000 native or Windows Server 2003 functional level, domain controllers replicate the SYSVOL using File Replication Service (FRS). When a domain is running at Windows Server 2008 or Windows Server 2008 R2 functional level, domain controllers can replicate the SYSVOL using Distributed File System (DFS).

FRS and DFS are replication services that use the Active Directory replication topology to replicate files and folders in the SYSVOL shared folders on domain controllers. To replicate the SYSVOL, the replication service checks with the KCC to determine the current replication topology and then uses this replication topology to replicate SYSVOL files to all the domain controllers in a domain. When used with Active Directory, DFS has significant advantages over FRS, including faster compression, support for automated recovery from database loss or corruption, replication scheduling, and bandwidth throttling. For detailed information on migrating the SYSVOL on your domain controllers from FRS replication to DFS replication, see *Group Policy Administration: The Personal Trainer*.

Essential Services for Replication

Active Directory replication depends on LDAP, DNS, Kerberos version 5 authentication, and remote procedure call (RPC). These Windows services must be functioning properly to allow directory updates to be replicated. Active Directory also uses either FRS or DFS to replicate files in the system volume (SYSVOL) shared folders on domain controllers. Table 7-1 summarizes the ports that are used.

TABLE 7-1 Ports Used During Active Directory Replication

LDAP	
	UDP: 389, TCP: 389
LDAP Secure Sockets Layer (SSL)	
	TCP: 686
Global catalog (LDAP)	
	TCP: 3268
Kerberos version 5	
	UDP: 88, TCP: 88
DNS	
	UDP: 53, TCP: 53
RPC with FRS	
	TCP: Dynamic
RPC endpoint mapper with DFS	
	TCP: 135
Server Message Block (SMB) over IP	
	UDP: 445, TCP: 445

The User Datagram Protocol (UDP) and TCP ports used during replication are similar regardless of whether FRS or DFS is used. Additionally, note that for intersite replication, two transports are available: RPC over IP and SMTP. SMTP uses TCP port 25.

Intrasite Versus Intersite Replication

When you are planning site structure, keep in mind that the two replication models are handled differently. The intrasite replication model is optimized for high bandwidth connections. The intersite replication model is optimized for limited bandwidth connections.

Intrasite Replication

When replication occurs within a domain, the replication follows a specific model that is very different from the replication model used for intersite replication. With intrasite replication, the focus is on ensuring that changes are rapidly distributed. Intrasite replication traffic is not compressed, and replication is designed so that changes are replicated almost immediately after a change has been made. The main component in Active Directory responsible for the replication structure is the KCC. One of the main responsibilities of the KCC is to generate the replication topology.

As domain controllers are added to a site, the KCC configures a ring topology with pull replication partners. With a ring topology, at least two paths between connected network resources provide redundancy. This configuration ensures that changes can flow from one domain controller to another. With pull replication, two servers are used. One is designated as the push partner, the other as the pull partner. It is the responsibility of the push partner to notify the pull partner that changes are available. The pull partner can then request the changes. Creating push and pull replication partners allows for rapid notification of changes and for updates after a request for changes has been made.

The KCC uses these models to create a replication ring. As domain controllers are added to a site, the size and configuration of this ring changes. When a site includes at least three domain controllers, each domain controller is configured with at least two incoming replication connections.

When a domain controller running Windows Server 2003 or later is updated, it waits approximately 15 seconds before initiating replication. This short wait is implemented in case additional changes are made. The domain controller on which the change is made notifies one of its partners, using an RPC, and specifies that changes are available. The partner can then pull the changes.

After replication with this partner completes, the domain controller waits approximately 3 seconds and then notifies its second partner of changes. The second partner can then pull the changes. Meanwhile, the first partner is notifying its partners of changes as appropriate. This process continues until all the domain controllers have been updated.

The 15-second replication delay can be overridden to allow immediate replication of priority (urgent) changes. Priority replication means that there is no delay to initiate replication. Priority replication is triggered if you perform one of the following actions:

- Change a shared secret password used by the Local Security Authority (LSA) for Kerberos authentication
- Change the domain password policy
- Change the password on a domain controller computer account
- Change the relative ID master role owner
- Lock out an account
- Change the account lockout policy
- Change object attributes in schema

> **Note** If an account is locked out automatically because of failed logon attempts, a priority replication is triggered as well.
>
> **Real World** All nonpriority changes to user and computer passwords are handled by the designated primary domain controller (PDC) emulator in a domain. When a user changes a password, the domain controller to which that user is connected immediately sends the change to the PDC emulator. This ensures the PDC emulator always has the latest password for a user and is why the PDC emulator is checked for a new password if a logon fails initially. After the new password is updated on the PDC emulator, the PDC emulator replicates the change using normal replication. The only exception is when a domain controller contacts the PDC emulator requesting a password for a user. In this case, the PDC emulator immediately replicates the current password to the requesting domain controller so that no additional requests are made for that password.

Intersite Replication

In contrast to intrasite replication, which focuses on speed, intersite replication focuses on efficiency. Intersite replication is designed to transfer replication information between sites while making the most efficient use of the available resources. To do this, Active Directory uses designated bridgehead servers and a default configuration that is scheduled and compressed rather than automatic and uncompressed.

With compression, replication traffic is compressed 85 to 90 percent, meaning that it is 10 to 15 percent of its uncompressed size, allowing replication to be used effectively even on low-bandwidth links. Compression is triggered when the replication traffic is larger than 32 kilobytes (KB).

The main component in Active Directory responsible for the intersite replication structure is the Intersite Topology Generator (ISTG). When you set up a site, Active Directory designates the Knowledge Consistency Checker (KCC) on one of the site's domain controllers as the ISTG. Each site has only one ISTG. Its job is to determine the best way to configure replication between sites.

A key responsibility of the ISTG is to limit the points of replication between sites. Instead of allowing all the domain controllers in one site to replicate with all the domain controllers in another site, the ISTG designates a limited number of domain controllers as bridgehead servers. Replication between sites is always sent from a bridgehead server in one site to a bridgehead server in another site. This ensures that information is replicated only once between sites. As domain controllers are added and removed from sites, the ISTG regenerates the topology automatically.

The ISTG also creates the connection objects that are needed to connect bridgehead servers on either side of a site link. This is how Active Directory logically represents a site link. The ISTG continuously monitors connections and creates new connections when a domain controller acting as a designated bridgehead server is no longer available. In most cases, there will be more than one designated bridgehead server.

Replication through bridgehead servers works like this: Changes made to the directory in one site replicate to the other site via the designated bridgehead servers. The bridgehead servers then initiate replication of the changes exactly (as discussed in the previous section, titled "Intrasite Replication") except that for intersite replication, two transports are available: RPC over IP and SMTP. If you use SMTP as a transport, SMTP uses TCP port 25 by default.

As you can see, intersite replication is really concerned with getting changes from one site to another across a site link. With scheduled replication, you can set the valid times during which replication can occur and the replication frequency within this scheduled interval. By default, when you configure intersite replication, replication is scheduled to occur every 180 minutes, 24 hours a day. In many cases, you will want to change the default schedule to better accommodate the users who also use the link. For example, you might want to set replication to occur every 60 minutes, from 4 A.M. to 7 A.M. and from 9 P.M. to 3 A.M., Monday through Friday, while allowing replication to occur every 180 minutes, 24 hours a day on Saturday and Sunday. This would allow more bandwidth for users during the week and more bandwidth for replication on the weekend.

You can optimize intersite replication in several ways:

- Turn off automatic compression if you have sufficient bandwidth on a link and are more concerned about the processing power used for compression. Turning off compression reduces resource usage on bridgehead servers while substantially increasing the bandwidth used for replication.
- Enable automatic notification of changes to allow domain controllers on either side of the link to indicate that changes are available. Automatic notification allows those changes to be requested rather than making domain controllers wait for the next replication interval.

- Configure site link costs, configure connection objects manually, and designate preferred bridgehead servers.
- Each of these techniques optimizes intersite replication for specific usage scenarios, as I'll discuss in more detail later in the chapter. See the section entitled "Configuring Site Links and Intersite Replication."

Developing Your Site Design

Although site design is relatively independent from domain structure, the replication topology depends on how available domain controllers are and how they are configured. The KCC running on each domain controller monitors domain controller availability and configuration, and it updates replication topology as changes occur. The designated ISTG in a site performs similar monitoring to determine the best way to configure intersite replication. This means that as you implement or change the domain controller configuration, you will change the replication topology.

To develop or revise a site design, you should do the following:

1. Map your network structure and then map this structure to site structure.
2. Design your sites and then associate subnets with these sites.
3. Design the intersite replication topology while considering the impact of site link bridging and planning the placement of servers in sites.

Mapping Your Network Structure

Start by mapping your existing network architecture as well as any planned changes. Include all the business locations in the organization that are part of the forest or forests for which you are developing a site plan.

You must consider whether separate sites are needed. If your organization has multiple locations with limited bandwidth or unreliable connections between locations, you will typically want to create additional sites. You also might want to create additional sites to separate network segments even if they are connected with high-speed links; the reasons for doing this were discussed previously and could include isolating replication traffic between the network segments.

Document the IP subnets on each network segment. Each site in the organization will have separate subnets. Although a single subnet can exist only in one site, a single site can have multiple subnets associated with it. After you create sites, you will create subnet-to-site associations by adding subnets to these sites.

Document the connection speed on the links connecting each network segment as well as other applications that use a lot of bandwidth. The available bandwidth on a connection affects the way you configure site links. Each site link is assigned a link cost, which determines its priority order for replication. If there are several possible routes to a site, the route with the lowest link cost is used first. In the event that a primary link fails, a secondary link can be used.

To map the network structure to site structure, start by examining each network location and the speed of the connections between those locations. In general, if you want to make separate network locations part of the same site, the connections between locations should have at least 512 Kbps of available bandwidth. Small organizations may be able to scale down to dedicated 128-Kbps or 256-Kbps links. Large organizations may need to scale up.

Designing Your Sites

After you determine how many sites you will have, you next need to consider the design of each site. A key part of the site design has to do with naming the sites and identifying the subnets associated with each site.

Site names are used in locator records registered in Domain Name System (DNS). Because of this, site names must use valid DNS names, which include the standard characters A through Z, a through z, 0 through 9, and hyphen (-

). Additionally, the name of a site should reflect its physical location. For example, you might use the following site names: NewYork-First-Site, Chicago-First-Site, and Seattle-First-Site.

Sites do not reflect the Active Directory namespace. Domain and site boundaries are separate. Sites can contain a domain or a portion of a domain. A single site can have one subnet or multiple subnets. However, a single subnet can be in only one site. Therefore, the following rules apply to sites and subnets:

- A single site can contain resources from multiple domains.
- A single domain can have resources spread out among multiple sites.
- A single site can have multiple subnets.

To determine the subnets that you should associate with each site, use the documentation you developed previously. Simply note the IP subnet associations that are needed, and update your site diagram to include the subnets.

Designing Your Intersite Replication Topology

After you name the sites and determine subnet associations, design the intersite replication topology by determining the replication schedule, replication interval, and link cost for each site link. Typically, replication should occur at least every 180 minutes, 24 hours a day, 7 days a week. This is the default replication schedule. If you have limited bandwidth, you may need to alter the schedule to allow user traffic to have priority during peak usage times. Otherwise, if bandwidth isn't a concern or if you have strong concerns about keeping branch locations up to date, you might want to increase the replication frequency. To ensure you understand what's happening on the network, you should monitor site links to get a sense of the bandwidth utilization and the peak usage periods.

When there are multiple links between locations, you need to determine the appropriate cost of each link. Valid link costs range from 1, which assigns the highest possible preference to a link, to 99999, which assigns the lowest possible preference to a link. When you create a new link, the default link cost is set to 100. If you were to set all the links to this cost, all the links would have equal preference for replication. However, low bandwidth links should have different costs from high bandwidth links. Table 7-2 provides an example of how you could use bandwidth to help determine link cost.

TABLE 7-2 Setting Link Cost Based on Link Bandwidth

10 gigabits per second (Gbps) to 2 Gbps	1
2 Gbps to 1 Gbps	2
1 Gbps to 512 megabits per second (Mbps)	4
256 Mbps to 100 Mbps	20
100 Mbps to 10 Mbps	40
10 Mbps to 1.544 Mbps	100
1.544 Mbps to 512 kilobits per second (Kbps)	200
512 Kbps 256 Kbps	400
256 Kbps to 128 Kbps	800
128 Kbps or less	1600

You can use the costs in the table to assign costs to each link you identified previously. Even if there is only one link between all your sites now, you should set an appropriate link cost to ensure that all the links are used in the most efficient way possible if links are added later.

Next, consider the possible impact of site link bridging. By default, Active Directory automatically configures site link bridges, which makes links transitive between sites in much the same way that trusts are transitive between domains.

When a site is bridged, any two domain controllers can make a connection across any consecutive series of links. The site link bridge cost is the sum of all the costs of the links included in the bridge. For example, if the site link cost between Site A and Site B is 100 and the site link cost between Site B and Site C is 200, the link bridge cost using this route from Site A to Site C is 300.

When you know the costs of links and link bridges, you can calculate the effects of a network link failure. For example, if your organization has multiple sites, there may be multiple possible paths between sites. If so, the path used is always the one with the lowest link bridge cost. In case of an outage of a primary link, the path used is the one with the next lowest cost.

Site link bridging can have unintended consequences when you have multiple hubs and spokes on each hub. Here, the same replication traffic could go over the site links twice because of the rule of three hops for optimizing replication topology. The repeat replication over the hub links becomes worse as you add spokes. The solution to the problem of repeat replication traffic is to disable automatic site bridging. Unfortunately, if you disable automatic site link bridging, none of your organization's sites will be able to use this feature. In this case, to bridge site links, you must configure site link bridges manually. You can enable, disable, and manually configure site link bridges as discussed in "Configuring Site Links and Intersite Replication."

> **Note** Another reason to disable automatic site link bridging is to reduce the processing overhead on the designated ISTGs in each site. When you disable bridging, the ISTGs no longer have to create and manage the site link bridges, and this reduces the number of computations required to create the intersite replication topology.

When you finish configuring site links, you should plan the placement of servers in the sites. Consider types of domain controllers you will use and how many of each will be located in a particular site. Determine whether any of the domain controllers host a global catalog or DNS. Determine whether any of the domain controllers have operations master roles and if so, what those roles will be. At minimum, each site should have a domain controller and a global catalog server. This configuration allows intrasite replication to occur without replication traffic having to go across site links. If there is a local DHCP server, clients with dynamic IP addressing will be able to start up and get an IP address assignment without having to go across a site link. If there is a local DNS server, clients will be able to perform DNS queries without having to go across a site link.

Configuring Sites and Subnets

After you've developed a site design or determined how you want to modify your existing site plan, you can use the Active Directory Sites And Services console to configure the necessary sites and subnets as discussed in this section. All sites have one or more subnets associated with them. IP addresses you assign to subnets determine where the site boundaries are established. As you create additional sites, you should identify domain controllers that will be part of the sites and then determine if you need to move the related domain controller objects to the site containers with which they should be associated.

You can start Active Directory Sites And Services by clicking Start, Administrative Tools, and Active Directory Sites And Services. Active Directory Sites And Services connects to a domain controller in your logon domain and forest by default. If your organization has multiple forests, you might need to connect to another forest. To do this, right-click the Active Directory Sites And Services node in the console tree, and then select Change Forest. In the Change Forest dialog box, enter the name of the root domain in the forest to which you want to connect, and then click OK.

Creating Sites

When you install Active Directory Domain Services in a new forest, a new site called Default-First-Site-Name is created. After you install the first domain controller in your Active Directory forest, you can rename the default site.

Although you've renamed this site, it remains the default site for new domain controllers.

Domain controllers you introduce to the forest generally are added to the default site automatically. However, if you have configured other sites and have associated subnets with those sites, domain controllers are added to those additional sites if the IP address you assign matches a subnet in one of the sites. Keep in mind that any domain controller with an IP address that doesn't match a subnet identifier of another previously defined site will be added to the default site.

You can create a site by following these steps:

1. In Active Directory Sites And Services, right-click the Sites container in the console tree and then select New Site.

2. In the New Object–Site dialog box, shown in Figure 7-1, enter a descriptive name for the site. The site name should depict the purpose or physical location of the site.

3. Specify which site link will be used to connect this site to other sites. If the site link you want to use doesn't exist, select the default site link DEFAULTIPSITELINK for now, and then change the site link settings after you've created the necessary site link or links.

4. Click OK. Next, you see a prompt that outlines the steps you must complete to finish the site configuration. Review the recommended steps and then click OK again. These steps include:

   - Ensuring that the site is linked to other sites with appropriate site links.
   - Adding subnets for the site to the Subnets container.

5. Installing one or more domain controllers in the site or moving existing domain controllers into the site.

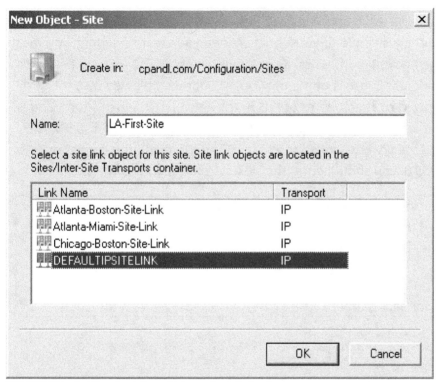

FIGURE 7-1 Use the New Object–Site dialog box to create a new site.

As the prompt states, you should ensure the links to the site are appropriate and, as necessary, create the required site links. After you link the site, you'll need to create subnets and associate them with the site to tell Active Directory the IP addresses that belong to the site. Because each site should have one or more domain controllers, you should install one or more domain controllers in the site or move existing domain controllers into the site.

Creating Subnets

You create subnets and associate them with sites to allow Active Directory to determine the network segments that belong to a site. Any computer with an IP address on a network segment associated with a site is considered to be located in the site. Although a site can have one or more subnets associated with it, an individual subnet can be associated with only one site.

Windows Server 2008 and Windows Server 2008 R2 support both IP version 4 (IPv4) and IP version 6 (IPv6) subnets. When you create a subnet, you must specify the network address by using prefix notation. The address prefix for a network address consists of the network ID address, followed by a forward slash, followed by the number of bits in the network ID. When subnetting is not used, the IPv4 subnet address ends with a 0, such as 192.168.15.0. For example, if the IPv4 network address is 192.168.15.0 and the subnet mask is 255.255.255.0, you should enter the address prefix as 192.168.15.0/24.

> **Note** When you use subnetting, nodes no longer follow the class rules for determining which bits in the IPv4 address are used for the network ID and which bits are used for the host ID. Instead, you set the 32 bits of the IPv4 address to be either network ID bits or host ID bits based on the number of subnets you need, and then you number nodes for each subnet.

You can create a subnet and associate it with a site by completing the following steps:

1. In Active Directory Sites And Services, right-click the Subnets container in the console tree, and then select New Subnet. This displays the New Object–Subnet dialog box, shown in Figure 7-2.

2. In the Prefix field, enter the address prefix for the subnet.

3. Select the site with which the subnet should be associated, and then click OK.

After you create a subnet, you can change its site association. To do so, follow these steps:

1. In Active Directory Sites And Services, double-click the subnet in the Subnets folder.

2. In the General tab of the Properties dialog box, use the Site selection menu to change the site association.

3. Click OK.

> **Tip** If you associate a subnet with a different site, you'll need to ensure the domain controllers in that subnet are moved to the new site. Moving a domain controller from one site to another involves moving the related object in Active Directory from one site container to another. It does not involve installing or demoting a domain controller or physically moving server hardware.

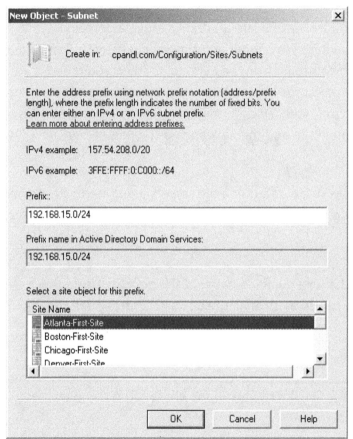

FIGURE 7-2 Use the New Object–Subnet dialog box to create a new subnet.

Adding Domain Controllers to Sites

After you associate subnets with a site, any domain controller you install will automatically be located in the site whenever the domain controller's IP address matches a subnet's network address. However, any domain controllers installed before you established the site and associated subnets with the site will not be located in a site automatically. In this case, you might need to manually move the domain controller to the new site. Keep in mind that moving a domain controller from one site to another involves moving the related object in Active Directory from one site container to another. It does not involve installing or demoting a domain controller or physically moving server hardware.

Don't move a domain controller to a site arbitrarily. Move a domain controller to a site only if it is on a subnet associated with the site. Before you can move a domain controller from one site to another, you must determine in which site the domain controller is currently located. In Active Directory Sites And Services, you can determine the servers associated with a site by expanding the site node and then expanding the related Servers node.

At a command prompt, you can determine the servers associated with a site by entering the following command.

```
dsquery server -domain DomainName
```

Here, *DomainName* is the fully qualified name of the domain. Using the following example, you obtain a list of all the domain controllers in the services.imaginedlands.com domain.

```
dsquery server -domain services.imaginedlands.com
```

If you want a list of all domain controllers in the entire forest, simply enter **dsquery server -forest**.

In either case, the resulting output is a list of distinguished names (DNs) for domain controllers, which includes site configuration information such as the following.

```
"CN=CORPSVR65,CN=Servers,CN=LA-First-Site-
Name,CN=Sites,CN=Configuration,
DC=imaginedlands,DC=com"
```

This additional information specifies the site associated with the server. In this example, the associated site is LA-First-Site-Name.

Sometimes, you'll want to find the domain controllers in a particular site. You can specify a site to examine by using the -site parameter. In the following example, you look for all domain controllers in a site called Seattle-First-Site.

```
dsquery server -site Seattle-First-Site
```

The output of this command is a list of DNs for domain controllers in the specified site.

Before you move a domain controller, you should ensure that the following TCP/IP client values are appropriate for the new location. Check the IP address, including the subnet mask and default gateway, and the DNS server addresses at a minimum. If the domain controller that you are moving is also a DNS server, you must change the TCP/IP settings on any clients that have static references to the domain controller as the preferred or alternate DNS server. You must also update the IP address in any DNS delegations or forwarders that reference the IP address. With dynamic update enabled, DNS updates host (A), host (AAAA), and name server (NS) resource records automatically. However, you must update delegations and forwarders manually:

- Determine whether the parent DNS zone of any zone that is hosted by this DNS server contains a delegation to this DNS server. If the parent DNS zone does contain a delegation to this DNS server, update the IP address in the NS resource record in the parent domain DNS zone that points to this DNS server.
- Determine whether the server acts as a forwarder for any DNS servers. If a DNS server uses this server as a forwarder, change the NS resource record for the forwarder on that DNS server.

Before you move a domain controller, you should also determine whether the server is acting as a preferred bridgehead server for the site, as discussed in "Locating and Designating Bridgehead Servers" later in this chapter. If you move a preferred bridgehead server to a different site, it becomes a preferred bridgehead server in the new site. If other preferred bridgehead servers are not currently in use in this site, the ISTG behavior in this site changes to support preferred bridgehead servers. Because of this, you should either configure the server to not be a preferred bridgehead server or select additional preferred bridgehead servers in the site.

If the server is the last preferred bridgehead server in the original site for its domain and there are other domain controllers for the domain in the site, the ISTG selects a bridgehead server for the site. If you use preferred bridgehead servers, always select more than one server as the preferred bridgehead server for a site. If the server isn't the last preferred bridgehead server, and the move has left only one available preferred bridgehead server, you should either configure the server to not be a preferred bridgehead server or select additional preferred bridgehead servers in the site.

You can move a domain controller to a site by completing the following steps:

1. In Active Directory Sites And Services, domain controllers associated with a site are listed in the site's Servers node. To locate the domain controller that you want to move, expand the site node, and then expand the related Servers node.

2. Right-click the domain controller that you want to work with, and then select Move.

3. In the Move Server dialog box, select the site that should contain the server, and then click OK.

In Windows Server 2008 and Windows Server 2008 R2, you can move a domain controller from one site to another by dragging the related domain controller object from its current site to the Servers node of the target site.

The Net Logon service running on the domain controller will register the new site information in DNS within 60 minutes. Using the Event Viewer, you can review the System log for NETLOGON errors regarding registration of service

(SRV) resource records in DNS that have occurred within the last hour. If there are no errors, the Net Logon service has updated the related SRV resource records in DNS. Otherwise, NETLOGON Event ID 5774 indicates that the dynamic registration of DNS resource records has failed, and you will need to modify the records manually.

Ensuring Clients Find Domain Controllers

When a client requests a domain controller, the DC Locator process tries to locate a domain controller in the site of the client. If no domain controller is available in the site, DC Locator returns any available domain controller in the domain. If the domain controller is located in another site instead of the current site, the client and domain controller may not be able to communicate effectively. With Windows desktop operating systems, the Try Next Closest Site Group Policy setting in the Default Domain Policy can help ensure domain controllers selected are optimized for each site.

The Try Next Closest Site Group Policy setting affects the order in which domain controllers are located and uses site link cost values to determine the next closest site to the site of the client. Using this setting, you may be able to reduce Active Directory traffic on the network by ensuring that clients fail over to the next closest site when they cannot find a domain controller in their site.

With Windows desktop operating systems, you can use the Force Rediscovery Interval Group Policy setting to find a new domain controller that might have been introduced since the last domain controller was located for the client. On domain controllers that are running Windows Server 2008 or later, this setting forces a new domain controller location every 12 hours (43,200 seconds) by default. You can change the time limit for rediscovery by enabling this setting and specifying a new time in seconds.

Both settings are configured in Default Domain Policy. To enable clients to locate a domain controller in the next closest site and modify the forced rediscovery settings, follow these steps:

1. Click Start, click Administrative Tools, and then click Group Policy Management.

2. Double-click the forest node, double-click Domains, and then double-click the domain you want to work with.

3. Right-click Default Domain Policy, and then click Edit.

4. In Group Policy Management Editor, double-click Try Next Closest Site under Computer Configuration/Policies/Administrative Templates/System/Netlogon/DC Locator DNS Records. Click Enabled, and then click OK.

5. In Group Policy Management Editor, double-click Force Rediscovery Interval under Computer Configuration/Policies/Administrative Templates/System/Netlogon/DC Locator DNS Records. Click Enabled, set the desired interval in seconds, and then click OK.

Configuring Site Links and Intersite Replication

You use site links to connect two or more sites for the purpose of replication. When you install Active Directory in a new forest, a new site link called the DEFAULTIPSITELINK is created in the IP container for the first default site. You can separately create any additional links that are needed. You create and manage site links by using the Active Directory Sites And Services console.

Understanding Site Links

Sites you add are included in the default site link unless you have configured other site links. If all of the network connections between sites are the same speed and priority, this default configuration can work without your having to create additional site links. With this configuration, all sites will have the same intersite replication properties. If you were to change these properties, the changes would affect the replication topology for all sites.

To configure different replication properties when the network connections between sites have different speeds and priorities, you can create additional site links. Both endpoints in a site link must exist before you can create a site link. This means you'll need to create the sites at either end of a site link before you can create the site link, and then you can update a site's configuration to include that site link.

When you create additional site links, a site's designated Intersite Topology Generator (ISTG) uses the link properties to prioritize links and determine when a site link should be used. The ISTG generates the intersite replication topology and designates bridgehead servers automatically. Replication traffic between sites always flows from a bridgehead server in one site to a bridgehead server in another site.

Two replication transports are available for site links: IP and Simple Mail Transfer Protocol (SMTP). Bridgehead servers use these replication transports in different ways, for different purposes.

With IP as the transport, domain controllers establish an RPC over IP connection with one replication partner at a time and replicate Active Directory changes. During replication, the bridgehead server establishes a connection using the RPC endpoint mapper port 135 and then determines which port is to be used for replication. The ports used for replication are listed previously in Table 7-1. The same ports are also used for intrasite replication.

Because RPC over IP is synchronous, both replication partners must be available at the time the connection is established. Because of the transitive nature of site links, you must carefully configure site link schedules so that all potential RPC over IP replication partners are available at the time the connection is established. You should use RPC over IP when there are reliable, dedicated connections between sites.

With SMTP as the transport, all replication traffic is converted to e-mail messages that are sent between the sites. Because SMTP replication is asynchronous, both replication partners do not have to be available at the time the connection is established, and replication transactions can be stored until a destination server is available. You should use SMTP when links are unreliable or not always available. Before using SMTP, keep the following in mind:

- You can use SMTP only to replicate information between domain controllers in different domains. Why? You can use SMTP only to replicate the configuration, schema, and global catalog directory partitions. You cannot use SMTP to replicate the domain partition.
- SMTP messages are digitally signed and encrypted to ensure that replication traffic is secure even if replication traffic is routed over the public Internet. All domain controllers that will use SMTP for replication require additional components to create, digitally sign, and then encrypt e-mail messages. Specifically, you must install the SMTP Server feature on each domain controller, and you must install a Microsoft certificate authority (CA) in your organization. The certificates from the CA are used to digitally sign and encrypt the SMTP messages sent between the sites.
- If you plan to use SMTP for replication, you must open related ports on the firewall between sites. Port 25 is the default port used for SMTP.

Creating Site Links

You can create site links between sites to better manage intersite replication. Before you create a site link, determine the transport you want to use. You cannot change the transport after you create a site link; you can only delete the link and then recreate it using the alternate transport.

Each site link must have at least two sites associated with it. These sites establish the endpoints or transit points for the link. For example, after you create NY-First-Site and Boston-First-Site, you can create the NY-Boston-Site-Link. When you do this, the NY and Boston sites are the endpoints for the link, and the ISTG will use the link to create the connection objects that are required to replicate traffic between these sites.

Each site link has a link cost, replication schedule, and replication interval. The cost for a site link determines the priority of the link relative to other site links that might be available. When there are multiple possible routes to a site, the route with the lowest total link cost is used first. In the event a link fails, the route with the next lowest total link cost is used. Typically, you will set the link cost relative to the bandwidth available for a specific connection. However, if the organization has to pay a fee based on bandwidth usage, you could also set the link cost to reflect the actual monetary cost of sending traffic over a particular link.

The replication schedule determines the times during the day that the site link is available for replication. The default replication schedule is 24 hours a day. If you have a limited-bandwidth connection or you want user traffic to have priority at certain times of the day, you might want to configure a different availability schedule.

The replication interval determines the intervals at which the bridgehead servers in each site check to see if directory updates are available. The default interval is 180 minutes. For example, if the replication schedule is configured to allow replication from 9 P.M. to 6 A.M. each day, the bridgehead servers will check for updates at 9 P.M., 12 A.M., 3 A.M., and 6 A.M. daily.

To create a site link between two or more sites, complete the following steps:

1. In Active Directory Sites And Services, expand the Sites container, and then expand the Inter-Site Transports container. Right-click the container for the transport protocol you want to use (either IP or SMTP), and then select New Site Link.

2. In the New Object–Site Link dialog box, shown in Figure 7-3, enter a descriptive name for the site link. The site name serves as a point of reference for administrators and should clearly depict the sites the link connects.

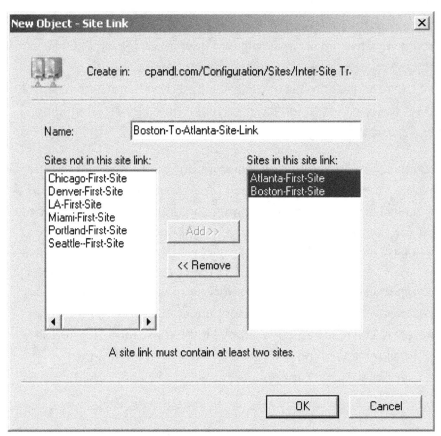

FIGURE 7-3 Create the site link.

3. In the Sites Not In This Site Link list, select a site that should be included in the link, and then click Add to add the site to the Sites In This Site Link list. Repeat this process for each site you want to add to the link. The link must include at least two sites.

4. Click OK to close the New Object–Site Link dialog box.

5. In Active Directory Sites And Services, the site link is added to the appropriate transport folder (IP or SMTP). Select the transport folder in the console tree, and then double-click the site link in the right pane.

6. In the Link Properties dialog box, shown in Figure 7-4, use the Cost combo box to set the relative cost of the link. The default cost is 100. (For more information on setting link cost, see "Designing Your Intersite Replication Topology' earlier in this chapter.

7. Use the Replicate Every combo box to set the replication interval. The default interval is 180 minutes.

8. Click OK to close the site link's Properties dialog box.

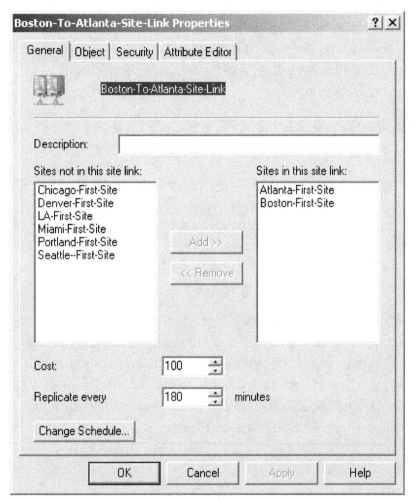

FIGURE 7-4 Set the site link properties.

Note By default, the site link is available for replication 24 hours a day. You can set a different schedule. (To learn more, see the following section, "Configuring Link Replication Schedules.")

Configuring Link Replication Schedules

You can manage the replication schedule for site links either globally or individually. The default configuration for IP links and SMTP links is different. IP site links use individual replication schedules and by default replicate within these schedules according to the replication interval. SMTP site links ignore individual replication schedules and by default replicate only according to the replication interval.

You can control whether global or individual schedules are used by following these steps:

1. In Active Directory Sites And Services, expand the Sites container, and then expand the Inter-Site Transports container. Right-click the container for the transport protocol you want to work with (either IP or SMTP), and then select Properties.

2. In the Properties dialog box, you can now configure global replication for the selected transport by using one of the following techniques:

   ▪ Select the Ignore Schedules check box to ignore individual replication schedules on site links. With this option, bridgehead servers replicate at the designated intervals but ignore any scheduled days or hours.
   ▪ Clear the Ignore Schedules check box to use individual schedules. With this option, bridgehead servers replicate according to the replication interval only during scheduled days and hours.

3. Click OK to apply your settings.

When you use individual schedules, you can manage the times when replication is permitted by setting a replication schedule for each site link. Before you schedule replication hours, you'll want to determine peak usage times and determine whether and how you want to restrict replication. Rather than restrict replication entirely during the workday or during peak usage times on a limited bandwidth link, you might want to allow replication to occur at specific times during these periods. You might also want to create a replication window of several hours to ensure replication can occur.

You can configure a site link's replication schedule by following these steps:

1. In Active Directory Sites And Services, expand the Sites container, expand the Inter-Site Transports container, and then select the container for the transport protocol you want to work with (either IP or SMTP).

2. In the details pane, right-click the site link you want to configure, and then select Properties.

3. Click Change Schedule. As shown in Figure 7-5, use the Schedule For dialog box to set the desired replication schedule. When you are finished, click OK.

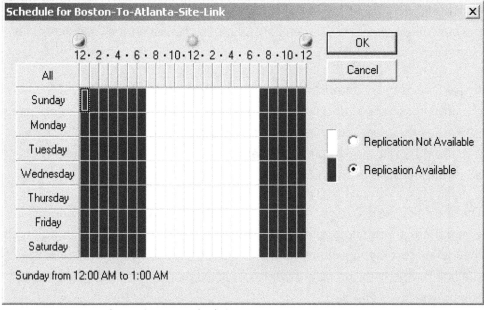

FIGURE 7-5 Set the replication schedule.

In the Schedule For dialog box, each hour of the day or night is a field that you can turn on or off. Hours that are allowed are filled in with a dark bar—you can think of these hours as being turned on. Hours that are disallowed are blank—you can think of these hours as being turned off.

To change the replication setting for a particular hour, click it. Then select either Replication Not Available or Replication Available. Hold down Shift and use the arrow keys to select multiple hours simultaneously. Additionally, keep the following in mind:

- Clicking All allows you to select all the time periods.
- Clicking a "day of the week" button allows you to select all the hours in a particular day.
- Clicking Hourly buttons allows you to select a particular hour for all the days of the week.

Bridging Sites

When more than two sites are linked for replication and use the same transport, all of the site links are bridged by default. Bridging a site link in this way allows any two domain controllers to make a connection across any consecutive series of links.

Active Directory automatically manages site link bridges, and the ISTG monitors for changes and reconfigures the replication topology as necessary. Whenever there are multiple possible routes between sites and a link goes out, the ISTG will allow replication traffic to flow on the alternate route according to the site link bridge cost.

The site link bridge cost is the sum of all the links included in the bridge. When there are multiple routes between linked sites, the site link bridge with the lowest cost is the primary route. If this route becomes unavailable, the site link bridge with the next lowest cost is used automatically as long as site link transitivity is enabled.

You can enable or disable site link bridges on a per-transport basis. By default, both the IP and SMTP transports have site link bridging enabled. If you disable site link bridging, Active Directory will no longer manage site link bridges for the transport. You must then create and manage all site link bridges for that transport. Any sites you manually add to a site link bridge are considered to be transitive with each other. Site links that are not included in the site link bridge are not transitive. (For details on specific scenarios where you might not want to use site link bridges, see "Designing Your Intersite Replication Topology" earlier in this chapter.

To turn off automatic site link bridging and manually configure site link bridges, follow these steps:

1. In Active Directory Sites And Services, expand the Sites container, and then expand the Inter-Site Transports container. Right-click the container for the transport protocol you want to work with (either IP or SMTP), and then select Properties.

2. In the Properties dialog box, clear the Bridge All Site Links check box, and then click OK. If you later want to enable transitive links and have Active Directory ignore the site link bridges you've created, you can select the Bridge All Site Links check box.

After you disable automatic site link bridging, you can manually create site link bridges. To create a site link bridge, you must have at least two site links configured for the transport. A site link bridge must contain at least two site links.

You can create a site link bridge by following these steps:

1. In Active Directory Sites And Services, expand the Sites container, and then expand the Inter-Site Transports container. Right-click the container for the transport protocol you want to use (either IP or SMTP), and then select New Site Link Bridge.

2. In the New Object–Site Link Bridge dialog box, shown in Figure 7-6, enter a descriptive name for the site link bridge. This name serves as a point of reference for administrators and should clearly depict all the site links that are part of the bridge.

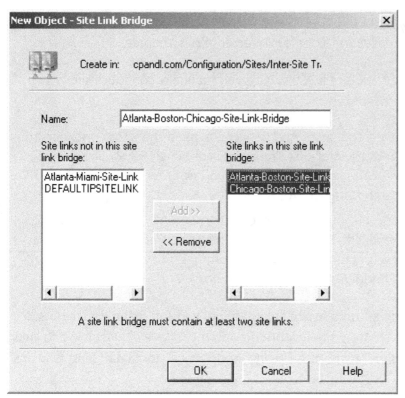

Figure 7-6 Create a site link bridge.

3. In the Site Links Not In This Site Link Bridge list, select a site link that should be included in the bridge, and then click Add to add the site link to the Site Links In This Site Link Bridge list. Repeat this process for each site link you want to add to the bridge. The bridge must include at least two site links.

4. Click OK to create the site link bridge.

Locating and Designating Bridgehead Servers

You can list the bridgehead servers in a site by entering the following command at a command prompt.

```
repadmin /bridgeheads site:SiteName
```

Here, *SiteName* is the name of the site. In the following example, you obtain a list of all the bridgehead servers in the NY-First-Site site.

```
repadmin /bridgeheads site:NY-First-Site
```

If you omit the site:*SiteName* values, the details for the current site are returned.

Operating as a bridgehead server can add a significant load to a domain controller. This load increases with the number and frequency of replication changes. Because of this, the designated bridgehead servers should also be closely monitored to make sure they don't become overloaded.

When a domain controller is overloaded or otherwise not properly equipped to handle the additional load of being a bridgehead server, you might want to control which domain controllers operate as bridgehead servers. You do this by designating preferred bridgehead servers in a site.

After you designate a preferred bridgehead server, the ISTG will use only the preferred bridgehead server for intersite replication. If you decide to designate bridgehead servers, you can and should designate multiple preferred bridgehead servers. If you do not, and the single domain controller acting as the bridgehead server goes offline or is unable to replicate for any reason, intersite replication will stop until the server is again available for replication or you change the preferred bridgehead server configuration options. To change the preferred bridgehead server, you must do one of the following:

- Remove the server as a preferred bridgehead server, and then allow the ISTG to select the bridgehead servers that should be used.
- Remove the server as a preferred bridgehead server, and then specify a different preferred bridgehead server.

You can prevent this situation simply by specifying more than one preferred bridgehead server. When there are multiple preferred bridgehead servers, the ISTG will choose one of the servers you've designated as the preferred bridgehead server. If this server fails, the ISTG chooses another server from the list of preferred bridgehead servers.

You must configure a bridgehead server for each directory partition that needs to be replicated. If you don't do this, replication of the partition will fail, and the ISTG will log an event in the Directory Service event log detailing the failure. Therefore, to ensure proper replication, you must configure at least one domain controller with a replica of each directory partition as a bridgehead server. Active Directory has multiple directory partitions, which are replicated in the following ways:

- On a forestwide basis for configuration and schema directory partitions
- On a domainwide basis for the domain directory partition
- On a select basis for the partition containing global catalog data
- On a select basis for application partitions

When DNS is integrated with Active Directory, a domain controller has ForestDnsZones and DomainDnsZones application partitions. These partitions are used by DNS to store DNS records and other related data.

To configure a domain controller as a preferred bridgehead server, complete the following steps:

1. In Active Directory Sites And Services, domain controllers associated with a site are listed in the site's Servers node. To locate the domain controller you want to work with, expand the site node, and then expand the related Servers node.

2. Right-click the server you want to designate as a preferred bridgehead server, and then select Properties.

3. In the Properties dialog box, shown in Figure 7-7, you have the option of configuring the server as a preferred bridgehead server for either IP or SMTP. Select the appropriate transport in the Transports Available For Inter-Site Data Transfer list, and then click Add. If you later want the server to stop being a preferred bridgehead, select the transport in the This Server Is A Preferred Bridgehead Server For The Following Transports list, and then click Remove.

4. Click OK.

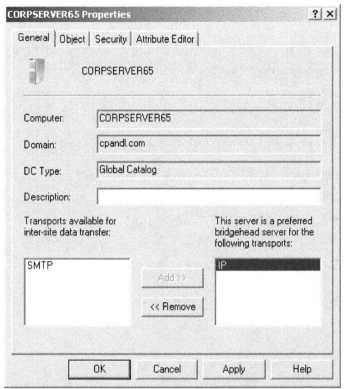

FIGURE 7-7   Designating a preferred bridgehead server.

Locating ISTGs

Each site has an ISTG that is responsible for generating the intersite replication topology. As your organization grows and you add domain controllers and sites, the load on the ISTG can grow substantially because the ISTG must perform additional calculations to determine and maintain the optimal topology. When it is calculating the replication topology, its processor could reach 100 percent utilization. As the topology becomes more and more complex, the process will stay near maximum utilization longer and longer.

Because the ISTG can become overloaded, you should monitor each site's ISTG closely. At the command line, you can determine the ISTG for a particular site by entering the following command.

```
repadmin /istg "site:SiteName"
```

Here, *SiteName* is the name of the site to examine. In the following example, you list the ISTG for the Denver-First-Site site.

```
repadmin /istg "site:Denver-First-Site"
```

You also can determine the ISTG by completing the following steps:

1. In Active Directory Sites And Services, expand the Sites container, and then select the site in which you want to locate the ISTG.

2. In the details pane, double-click NTDS Site Settings.

3. In the NTDS Site Settings Properties dialog box, the current ISTG is listed in the Inter-Site Topology Generator panel (see Figure 7-8).

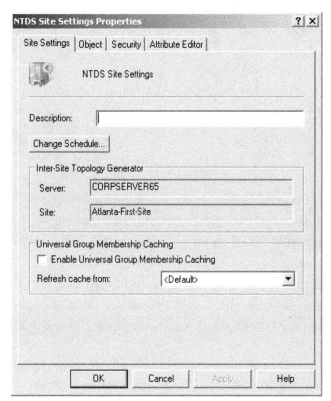

FIGURE 7-8 Locating the ISTG.

Optimizing Site Link Configurations

After you configure sites and site links, you'll want to monitor the flow of traffic between sites and might need to make changes to optimize the configuration. In addition to techniques discussed previously, you can use the following steps to control how compression, synchronization, and notification are used during replication:

1. In Active Directory Sites And Services, expand the Sites container, and then expand the Inter-Site Transports container. In the container for the transport protocol you want to work with (either IP or SMTP), right-click the site link you want to modify, and then select Properties.

2. In the Properties dialog box, click the Attribute Editor tab, as in Figure 7-9. Scroll through the list of attributes until you find the Options attribute. When you find this attribute, select it, and then click Edit.

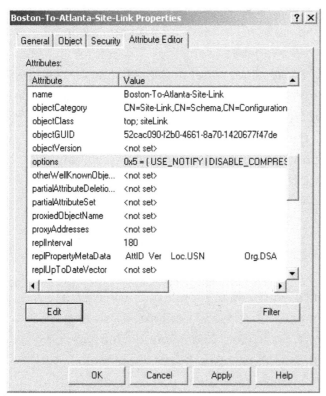

FIGURE 7-9 Locate the Options attribute and determine its current value.

3. In the Integer Attribute Editor dialog box, you can now do the following:

- Enter **1** to enable notification for intersite replication. This means the bridgehead servers on either side of the link can notify each other that changes have occurred. This allows the bridgehead server receiving the notification to pull the changes across the site link and thereby get more frequent updates.
- Enter **2** to enable two-way synchronization for intersite replication. This means bridgehead servers on either side of the link can synchronize changes at the same time. This allows simultaneous synchronization in two directions for faster updates. Use this setting only on links with sufficient bandwidth to handle two-way sync traffic.
- Enter **4** to turn off compression for intersite replication. This means the bridgehead servers on either side of the link will no longer use compression. Use this option only when you have sufficient bandwidth for a site connection and are concerned about high processor utilization on the affected bridgehead servers.
- Use combinations of the flag values to set multiple flags. For example, a value of 5 means compression will be turned off and notification for intersite replication will be enabled.
- Click Clear to reset the Options attribute to its default value of <not set>. When Options is not set, notification for intersite replication is disabled and compression is turned on.

4. Click OK twice.

Monitoring, Verifying, and Troubleshooting Replication

As part of routine maintenance, you need to monitor domain controllers, global catalog servers, bridgehead servers, and site links. If you suspect problems with Active Directory, you should begin your diagnostics and troubleshooting with replication in most cases. By configuring monitoring of Active Directory intrasite and intersite replication, you can diagnose and resolve most replication problems.

Monitoring Replication

Using the Performance Monitor, you can perform in-depth monitoring and analysis of replication and all other Active Directory activities. You open the Performance Monitor by clicking Start, All Programs, Administrative Tools, and then Reliability And Performance Monitor. You can track the performance of multiple domain controllers from a single monitoring server by using Performance Monitor's remote monitoring capabilities.

For monitoring Active Directory, the performance object you'll use is DirectoryServices. With this object, many performance counters are available for selection. Most of these counters have prefixes that reflect the aspect of Active Directory to which the counter relates. These prefixes include the following:

- **AB** AB counters relate to the Address Book in Active Directory.
- **ATQ** ATQ counters relate to the Asynchronous Thread Queue in Active Directory.
- **DRA** DRA counters relate to the Directory Replication Agent in Active Directory.
- **DS** DS counters relate to the Directory Service in Active Directory.
- **LDAP** LDAP counters relate to the Lightweight Directory Access Protocol in Active Directory.
- **SAM** SAM counters relate to the Security Accounts Manager in Active Directory.

You can specify counters to monitor by following these steps:

1. In the Reliability and Performance Monitor console, expand the Monitoring Tools node, and then select the Performance Monitor node.
2. Click the Add (+) button on the toolbar or press Ctrl+L. In the Add Counters dialog box, use the Select Counters From Computer list to select the computer to monitor.

3. Double-click the DirectoryServices or other object to monitor. Specify counters to track by selecting them in the Select Counters From Computer list and then clicking Add. You can learn more about counters by selecting the Show Description check box.

4. Click OK when you are finished adding counters.

> **Note** When Distributed File System (DFS) is used to replicate the SYSVOL files between domain controllers, you can monitor the DFS by using the DFS Replicated Folders, DFS Replication Connections, and DFS Replication Service Volumes objects. When File Replication Service (FRS) is used to replicate the SYSVOL files between domain controllers, you can monitor FRS by using the FileReplicaConn and FileReplicaSet monitoring objects.

In addition to monitoring replication, you will want to check the event logs for specific issues. Events related to Active Directory are logged in the event logs. Events related to Active Directory, including NTDS replication events, are also logged in the Directory Service log on the domain controller.

> **Note** Events related to DFS are recorded in the DFS Replication log on the domain controller, and the primary source for events is DFSR, which is the DFS Service itself. Events related to FRS are recorded in the File Replication Service log on the domain controller, and the primary source for events is NtFrs, which is the File Replication Service itself.

Troubleshooting Replication

Active Directory replication has multiple service dependencies, including LDAP, Domain Name System (DNS), Kerberos v5 authentication, and remote procedure call (RPC). These important services must be functioning properly to allow directory updates to be replicated. During replication, Active Directory relies on various TCP and UDP ports being open between domain controllers. By default, the ports used by Active Directory are those listed previously, in Table 7-1. For replication of files in the system volume (SYSVOL) shared folders on domain controllers, Active Directory uses either the FRS or the DFS Replication Service. The appropriate replication service must be running and properly configured to replicate the SYSVOL.

Active Directory tracks changes using update sequence numbers (USNs). Any time a change is made to the directory, the domain controller processing the change assigns the change a USN. Each domain controller maintains its own local USNs and increments the value each time a change occurs. The domain controller also assigns the local USN to the object attribute that changed. Each object has a related attribute called *uSNChanged*, which is stored with the object. The attribute identifies the highest USN that has been assigned to any of the object's attributes.

Each domain controller tracks its local USN and also the local USNs of other domain controllers. During replication, domain controllers compare the received USN values to what is stored. If the current USN value for a particular domain controller is higher than the stored value, changes associated with that domain controller need to be replicated. If the current value for a particular domain controller is the same as the stored value, changes for that domain controller do not need to be replicated.

You can monitor replication from the command line by using the Replication Administrator (Repadmin) utility. With Repadmin, most command-line parameters accept DCList, which identifies the domain controllers you want to work with. You can specify the values for DCList as follows:

- The asterisk (*) is a wildcard that includes all domain controllers in the enterprise.
- PartialName* is a partial server name that includes a wildcard to match the remainder of the server name, such as DenverDC*.
- Site:SiteName includes only domain controllers in the named site, such as Site:Atlanta-First-Site.
- Gc: includes all global catalog servers in the enterprise.

Using these values, you can perform many tasks with the Replication Administrator. These tasks are summarized in Table 7-3.

TABLE 7-3 Key Replication Administrator Commands

repadmin /bridgeheads *DCList*] [/verbose]	Lists bridgehead servers.
repadmin /failcache *DCList*	Lists failed replication events that were detected by the Knowledge Consistency Checker (KCC).
repadmin /istg *DCList* [/verbose]	Lists the name of the ISTG for a specified site.
repadmin /kcc *DCList* [/async]	Forces the KCC to recalculate the intrasite replication topology for a specified domain controller. By default, this recalculation occurs every 15 minutes. Use the /async option to start the KCC and not wait for it to finish the calculation.
repadmin /latency *DCList* [/verbose]	Lists the amount of time between intersite replications based on the ISTG Keep Alive time stamp.
repadmin /queue *DCList*	Lists tasks waiting in the replication queue.
repadmin /replsummary *DCList*	Displays a summary of the replication state.
repadmin /showcert *DCList*	Displays the server certificates loaded on the specified domain controllers.
repadmin /showconn *DCList*	Displays the connection objects for the specified domain controllers. Defaults to the local site.
repadmin /showctx *DCList*	Lists computers that have opened sessions with a specified domain controller.
repadmin /showoutcalls *DCList*	Lists calls made by the specified server to other servers but that have not yet been answered.
repadmin /showrepl *DCList*	Lists the replication partners for each directory partition on the specified domain controller.
repadmin /showtrust *DCList*	Lists all domains trusted by a specified domain.

Generating Replication Topology

The Knowledge Consistency Checker (KCC) generates the Active Directory replication topology on every domain controller. The KCC runs by default every 15 minutes. You can force the KCC to run on any domain controller. The topology that is generated depends on the domain controller on which you run the command. You can:

- Generate the intersite replication topology by running the KCC on the domain controller in the site that holds the ISTG role.
- Generate the intrasite replication topology by running the KCC on any domain controller in the site that does not hold the ISTG role.

To generate the replication topology on the ISTG, follow these steps:

1. In Active Directory Sites And Services, expand the Sites container, and then expand the site that contains the ISTG on which you want to run the KCC.
2. Expand Servers, and then click the Server object for the ISTG.
3. In the details pane, right-click NTDS Settings, click All Tasks, and then click Check Replication Topology.
4. Click OK to have the server generate the intersite replication topology.

To generate the replication topology on a KCC, follow these steps:

1. In Active Directory Sites And Services, expand the Sites container, and then expand the site that contains the non-ISTG domain controller on which you want to run the KCC.
2. Expand Servers, and then click the Server object for the domain controller.
3. In the details pane, right-click NTDS Settings, click All Tasks, and then click Check Replication Topology.
4. Click OK to have the server generate the intrasite replication topology.

Verifying and Forcing Replication

When you want changes to be replicated from one server to another sooner than the site link schedule allows, you can force replication to occur. To force replication of changes that you've made on a specific domain controller, follow these steps:

1. In Active Directory Sites And Services, expand the Sites container, and then expand the site containing the source server from which you want to replicate changes.

2. Expand Servers, and then expand the Server object.

3. Click the server's NTDS Settings object to display related connection objects in the details pane.

4. In the details pane, right-click the connection object that has the updates that you want to replicate, and then click Replicate Now.

5. When the Replicate Now message box appears, review the information provided, and then click OK.

To force replication of configuration changes to a domain controller that is not receiving replication as a result of configuration errors, follow these steps:

1. In Active Directory Sites And Services, expand the Sites container, and then expand the site containing the domain controller that you want to receive updates.

2. Expand Servers, and then expand the Server object.

3. Right-click the server's NTDS Settings object, and then select Replicate Configuration To The Selected DC.

4. When the Replicate Now message box appears, review the information provided, and then click OK.

To synchronize replication with all replication partners of a domain controller, enter the following command at a command prompt.

```
repadmin /syncall DomainControllerName /e /d /A /P /q
```

Here, *DomainControllerName* is the name of the domain controller for which you want to synchronize replication with all partners. The /e parameter includes partners in all sites. The /d parameter identifies servers by their distinguished names in messages. The /A parameter synchronizes all directory partitions that are held on the source server. The /P parameter pushes changes outward from the source server. The /q parameter runs the command in quiet mode and suppresses callback messages.

> **Note** In the command output, watch for errors. For replication to complete successfully, any errors must be corrected. If no errors occur, replication is successful.

Using an elevated, administrator command prompt, you can verify successful replication on a designated replication partner by entering **repadmin /showrepl**. If you are not running Repadmin on the domain controller whose replication you are checking, you can specify a destination domain controller in the command. For example, if you want to check DomainController53, you enter the following command.

```
repadmin /showrepl DomainController53
```

Repadmin lists inbound neighbors for the current or specified domain controller. These inbound neighbors identify the distinguished name of each directory partition for which inbound directory replication has been attempted, the site and name of the source domain controller, and whether replication succeeded.

Chapter 8. Managing Trusts and Authentication

A trust relationship is a link between two domains in which the trusting domain honors the logon authentication of a trusted domain. Trust relationships can be created manually (explicitly) or automatically (implicitly). Whereas trust relationships created manually need to be managed, trust relationships created automatically do not need to be managed. Both types of trust relationships, however, should be monitored and, as necessary, optimized.

Active Directory Authentication and Trusts

Authentication and trusts are integral parts of Active Directory. Before you implement any Active Directory design or try to modify your existing Active Directory infrastructure, you should have a firm understanding of how both authentication and trusts work in an Active Directory environment.

Trust Essentials

In Active Directory, two-way transitive trusts are established automatically between domains that are members of the same forest. Trusts join parent and child domains in the same domain tree and join the roots of domain trees. Because trusts are transitive, if domain A trusts domain B and domain B trusts domain C, domain A trusts domain C as well. As all trusts in Active Directory are two-way and transitive; by default, every domain in a forest implicitly trusts every other domain. Further, resources in any domain are available to users in every domain in the forest. For example, with the trust relationships in place, a user in the sales.cohovineyard.com domain could access a printer or other resources in the cohovineyard.com domain or even the cs.cohowinery.com domain.

However, the creation of a trust doesn't imply any specific permission. Instead, it implies only the ability to grant permissions. No privileges are automatically implied or inherited by the establishment of a trust relationship. The trust doesn't grant or deny any permission. It exists only to allow administrators to be able to grant permissions.

> **Note** A trust allows users in a trusted domain to access resources in a trusting domain. However, users won't necessarily have the appropriate security permissions to access resources. Users are granted access to a resource when they are assigned the appropriate permissions. That said, keep in mind that users in trusted domains may have implicit access if the resources are accessible to members of the Authenticated Users group.

Domains and forests that are part of trusts are described as being either trusted or trusting. A trusting domain or forest is a domain or forest that establishes a trust. Trusting domains or forests allow access by users from another domain or forest (the trusted domain or forest). A trusted domain or forest is a domain or forest that trusts another domain or forest. Users in trusted domains or forests have access to another domain or forest (the trusting domain or forest).

The *trust path* defines the path that an authentication request must take between the two domains. Authentication requests are passed from a domain controller in the trusted domain to a domain controller in each domain between the trusted domain and the trusting domain. The trust path flows up or down domain trees in the following ways:

- If the trusting domain is below the trusted domain in the same domain tree, authentication requests are passed down the tree through each child domain between the trusted domain and the trusting domain.
- If a trusting domain is above the trusted domain in the same domain tree, authentication requests are passed up the tree through each child domain between the trusted domain and the trusting domain.
- If a trusting domain is in a different domain tree, the trust path flows up the originating domain tree to the root domain of the domain tree. The trust path then flows to the root domain of the target domain tree and then down this tree to the trusting domain.

Thus, a domain controller in the user's local domain would pass a request to a domain controller in the next domain in the trust path. This domain controller would in turn pass the request to a domain controller in the next domain in the trust path, and so on, until finally the request would be passed to a domain controller in the trusting domain. This domain controller would ultimately grant or deny access to the resource.

Because domain structure is separate from your network's physical structure, a resource could actually be located right beside a user's desk, and the user's request would still have to go through this process. If you expand this scenario, you could potentially have many hundreds of users whose requests have to go through a similar process to access resources in a particular domain.

Omitting the fact that the domain design in this scenario is very poor—because if many users are working with resources, those resources are ideally in their own domain or a domain closer in the tree—one solution for this problem would be to establish a shortcut trust between the user's domain and the resource's domain. With a shortcut trust, as long as the domains are in different domain trees, you could specify that the trusted domain explicitly trusts the trusting domain. From then on, when a user in the trusted domain requests a resource in the trusting domain, the local domain controller knows about the trusting domain and can submit the request for authentication directly to a domain controller in the trusting domain.

Shortcut trusts are meant to help make more efficient use of resources on a busy network. On a network with a lot of activity, the explicit trust can reduce the overhead on servers and on the network as a whole. Shortcut trusts shouldn't be implemented without careful planning. They should be used only when resources in one domain will be regularly accessed by users in another domain. They don't need to be used between two domains that have a parent-child relationship, because a default trust already exists explicitly between a parent and a child domain.

With Active Directory, you can also make use of external trusts that work the same way they did in Windows NT 4. External trusts are manually configured and are always nontransitive. One of the primary reasons for establishing an external trust is to create a trust between an Active Directory domain and a legacy Windows NT domain. In this way, existing Windows NT domains continue to be available to users while you are implementing Active Directory. For example, you could upgrade your company's main domain from Windows NT 4 to Windows Server and then create external trusts between any other Windows NT domains. You should create these external trusts as two-way trusts to ensure that users can access resources as their permissions allow.

Authentication Essentials

When a user logs on to a domain, Active Directory looks up information about the groups of which the user is a member to generate a security token for the user. The security token is needed as part of the normal authentication process and is used whenever a user accesses resources on the network. To generate the security token, Active Directory checks the domain local, global, and universal group memberships for the user.

Because of problems authenticating users when global catalog servers are not available, Windows Server 2003 introduced a technique for caching group membership. In a domain with domain controllers running Windows Server 2003 or later, group membership caching can be enabled. After you enable caching, the cache is where domain controllers store group membership information that they have previously looked up. Domain controllers can use this cache for authentication the next time the user logs on to the domain. The cache is maintained indefinitely and updated periodically to ensure that it is current. By default, domain controllers check the consistency of the cache every 8 hours.

The assignment of security tokens is only part of the logon process. The logon process also includes authentication and the assignment of a user principal name (UPN) to the user. Every user account has a UPN, which consists of the user logon name combined with the at symbol (@) and a UPN suffix. The names of the current domain and the root domain are set as the default UPN suffix. You can specify an alternate UPN suffix to use to simplify logon or provide additional logon security.

Active Directory uses Kerberos version 5 as the default authentication protocol. Whenever a client running Windows 2000 or later tries to authenticate with Active Directory, the client tries to use Kerberos. Kerberos supports mutual authentication, which allows for two-way authentication so that not only can a server authenticate a client but a client can also authenticate a server. Thus, mutual authentication ensures that an authorized client is trying to access the network and that an authorized server is the one responding to the client request.

Kerberos uses the following three main components:

- A client that needs access to resources
- A server that manages access to resources and ensures that only authenticated users can gain access to resources
- A key distribution center (KDC) that acts as a central clearinghouse

All domain controllers run the Kerberos key distribution center service to act as KDCs. With Kerberos authentication, a user password is never sent over the network. Instead, Kerberos authentication uses a shared secret authentication model. In most cases, the client and the server use the user's password as the shared secret.

When a user logs on to the network, the client sends the KDC server a message containing the user name, domain name, and a request for access to the network. The message includes a packet of information that has been encrypted using the shared secret information (the user's password), which includes a time stamp.

When the KDC server receives the message, the server reads the user name and then checks the directory database for its copy of the shared secret information (the user's password). The KDC server then decrypts the secret part of the message and checks the message time stamp. As long as the message time stamp is within 5 minutes of the current time on the server, the server can authenticate the user. If the decryption fails or the message time stamp is more than 5 minutes off the current time, the authentication fails. Five minutes is the default value; the allowable time difference can be modified through domain security policy, using the Kerberos policy Maximum Tolerance For Computer Clock Synchronization.

After the user is authenticated, the KDC server sends the client a message that is encrypted with the shared secret information (the user's password). The message includes a session key, which the client will use when communicating with the KDC server from now on, and a session ticket, which grants the user access to the domain controller. The ticket is encrypted with the KDC server's key, which makes it valid only for that domain controller.

When the client receives the message, the client decrypts the message and checks the message time stamp. As long as the message time stamp is within 5 minutes of the current time on the server, the client can authenticate the server and assume that the server is valid. The client then caches the session key so it can be used for all future connections with the KDC server. The session key is valid until it expires or the user logs off. The session ticket is cached as well, but it isn't decrypted.

After initial authentication, the user is granted access to the domain. The only resource to which the user has been granted access is the domain controller. When the user wants to access another resource on the network, the client must request access by sending the KDC server a session ticket request. The message contains the user's name, the session ticket the client was previously granted, the name of the network resource the client is trying to access, and a time stamp that is encrypted with the session key.

When the KDC server receives the message, the server decrypts the session ticket using its key. Afterward, it extracts the original session key from the session ticket and uses it to decrypt the time stamp, which is then validated.

The validation process is designed to ensure that the client is using the correct session key and that the time stamp is valid.

If all is acceptable, the KDC server sends a session ticket to the client. The session ticket includes two copies of a session key that the client will use to access the requested resource. The first copy of the session key is encrypted using the client's session key. The second copy of the session key contains the user's access information and is encrypted with the resource's secret key known only by the KDC server and the network resource.

The client caches the session ticket and then sends it to the network resource to gain access. This request also contains an encrypted time stamp.

The network resource decrypts the second session key in the session ticket, using the secret key it shares with the KDC server. If this is successful, the network resource has validated that the session ticket came from a trusted KDC. It then decrypts the user's access information, using the session key, and checks the user's access permissions. The time stamp sent from the client is also decrypted and validated by the network resource.

If the authentication and authorization are successful (meaning that the client has the appropriate access permissions), the user is granted the type of access to the network resource that the particular permissions allow. The next time the user needs to access the resource, the session ticket in cache is used, as long as it hasn't expired. Using a cached session ticket allows the client to send a request directly to the network resource. If the ticket has expired, however, the client must start over and get a new ticket.

Authentication Across Domain Boundaries

Active Directory uses Kerberos security for server-to-server authentication and the establishment of trusts, while allowing older clients and servers on the network to use NT LAN Manager (NTLM) authentication if necessary. With Active Directory, trusts are automatically configured between all the domains in a forest and are implemented as two-way transitive trusts. As a result, users in one domain in the forest can automatically access resources in any other domain in the forest. Because the trusts are automatically established between all domains in the forest, no setup is involved.

As trusts join parent and child domains in the same domain tree and join the roots of domain trees, the structure of trusts in a forest can be referred to as a trust tree. When a user tries to access a resource in another domain, the trust tree is used, and the user's request has to pass through one domain controller for each domain that is located between the user and the resource. This type of authentication takes place across domain boundaries. Authentication across domain boundaries also applies when a user with an account in one domain visits another domain in the forest and tries to log on to the network from that domain.

A lengthy referral process can be avoided if you establish an explicit trust between two domains. Technically, explicit trusts are one-way transitive trusts, but you can establish a two-way explicit trust by creating two one-way trusts. Thus, unlike standard trusts within the trust tree, which are inherently two-way and transitive, explicit trusts can be made to be two-way if desired. Because they can be used to establish authentication shortcuts between domains, they are also referred to as shortcut trusts.

Authentication Across Forest Boundaries

You can establish authentication and trusts across forest boundaries as well. For example, while you are upgrading your network to implement Active Directory, you can establish external trusts to Windows NT domains to ensure that Windows NT domains continue to be available to users.

One-way external trusts are explicit and nontransitive. This means that if a trust is established between a domain in one forest and a domain in another forest, a user in any domain in the first forest can access a resource in the target domain but cannot access any other domain in the second forest. The reason for this limitation is that the trust doesn't continue past the target domain.

Windows Server 2003 and later support cross-forest transitive trusts, also referred to simply as forest trusts. With this type of trust, you can establish a one-way or two-way transitive trust between forests to share resources and to authenticate users. With a two-way trust, you enable cross-forest authentication and cross-forest authorization that allows users in any domain in both forests to access resources in any domain in both forests. However, before you can use cross-forest trusts, all domain controllers in all domains of both forests must be upgraded to Windows Server 2003 or higher, and the forests must be running at the Windows Server 2003 or higher forest functional level.

Kerberos is the default authentication protocol, but NTLM can also be used. This allows current clients and servers, as well as older clients and servers, to be authenticated. After you establish a two-way cross-forest trust, users get all the benefits of Active Directory regardless of where they sign on to the network. With cross-forest authentication, you ensure secure access to resources when the user account is in one forest and the computer account is in another forest and when the user in one forest needs access to network resources in another trusted forest. As part of cross-forest authorization, administrators can select users and global groups from trusted forests for inclusion in local groups. This ensures the integrity of the forest security boundary while allowing trust between forests.

When you connect two or more forests using cross-forest trusts, the implementation is referred to as a federated forest design. The federated forest design is most useful when you need to join two separate Active Directory structures; for example, when two companies merge, when one company acquires another, or when an organization has a major restructuring. Consider the case in which two companies merge, and, rather than migrate their separate Active Directory structures into a single directory tree, the staff decides to link the two forests using cross-forest trusts. As long as the trusts are two way, users in forest 1 can access resources in forest 2, and users in forest 2 can access resources in forest 1.

Having separate forests with cross-forest trusts between them is also useful when you want a division or group within the organization to have more autonomy but still have a link to the other divisions or groups. By placing the division or group in a separate forest, you ensure strict security and give that division or group ownership of the Active Directory structure. If users in the forest need access to resources in another forest, you can establish a one-way cross-forest trust between the forests. This allows users in the secured forest to gain access to resources in the second forest but will not allow users in the second forest to gain access to the secure forest. Organizations that contain groups or divisions with rigorous security requirements could use this approach.

Working with Domain and Forest Trusts

You can work with trusts using Active Directory Domains and Trusts. To start this tool, click Start, choose Programs or All Programs as appropriate, choose Administrative Tools, and then select Active Directory Domains And Trusts.

Examining Trusts

To examine the existing trusts for a domain, start Active Directory Domains and Trusts, right-click the domain entry, and then select Properties. In the domain's Properties dialog box, click the Trusts tab. As shown in Figure 8-1, the Trust tab has two panels:

- Domains Trusted By This Domain (Outgoing Trusts) This lists the domains that this domain trusts (the trusted domains).
- Domains That Trust This Domain (Incoming Trusts) This lists the domains that trust this domain (the trusting domains).

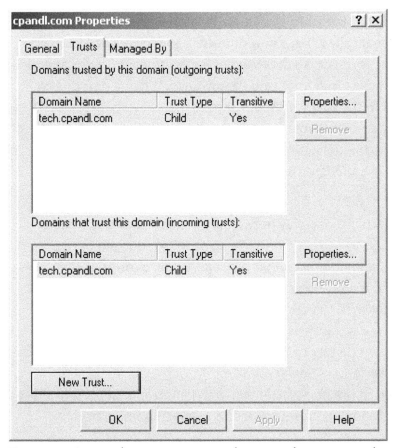

Figure 8-1   Review the existing trusts to determine the trusting and trusted domains for the previously selected domain.

The trust type and transitivity of each trust is listed on the Trusts tab. In Figure 8-1, the trust between the imaginedlands.com domain and the tech.imaginedlands.com domain is a transitive, child trust. This tells you imaginedlands.com is the parent domain and tech.imaginedlands.com is the child domain and there is a transitive trust between them.

You can view information about a particular trust by selecting it and then clicking Properties. As Figure 8-2 shows, the Properties dialog box contains the following information:

- **This Domain**   The domain you are working with.
- **Other/Child Domain**   The domain with which the trust is established.

- **Trust Type**   The type of trust. By default, two-way transitive trusts are created automatically when a new domain is added to a new domain tree within the forest or a subdomain of a root domain. There are two default trust types: Tree Root, and Parent-Child. When a new domain tree is added to the forest, the default trust that is established automatically is a tree-root trust. When a new domain is a subdomain of a root domain, the default trust that is established automatically is a Parent-Child trust. Other trust types that may appear include the following:

  - External, which is a one-way or two-way nontransitive trust used to provide access to resources in a Windows NT 4.0 domain or to a domain in a separate forest that is not joined by a forest trust
  - Forest, which is a one-way or two-way transitive trust used to share resources between forests
  - Realm, which is a transitive or nontransitive trust that can be established as one way or two way between a non-Windows Kerberos realm and a Windows Server domain
  - Shortcut, which is a one-way or two-way transitive trust used to speed up authentication and resource access between domain trees

- **Direction Of Trust**   The direction of the trust. All default trusts are established as two-way trusts. This means that users in the domain you are working with can authenticate in the other domain, and users from the other domain can authenticate in the domain you are working with.
- **Transitivity Of Trust**   The transitivity of the trust. All default trusts are transitive, which means that users from indirectly trusted domains can authenticate in the other domain.

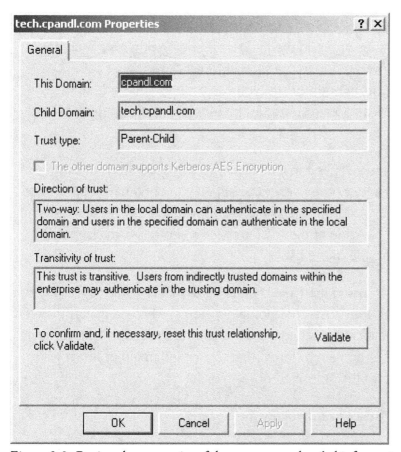

Figure 8-2 Review the properties of the trust to get detailed information.

Establishing Trusts

All trusts, regardless of type, are established in the same way. All trusts have two sides: an incoming trust and an outgoing trust. Both sides of a trust must be established before the trust can be used.

For domain trusts, you need to use two accounts: one that is a member of the Domain Admins group in the first domain and one that is a member of the Domain Admins group in the second domain. If you don't have appropriate accounts in both domains, you can establish one side of the trust and allow an administrator in the other domain to establish the other side of the trust.

For forest trusts, you will need to use two accounts: one that is a member of the Enterprise Admins group in the first forest and one that is a member of the Enterprise Admins group in the second forest. If you don't have appropriate accounts in both forests, you can establish one side of the two-way trust and allow an administrator in the other forest to establish the other side of the trust.

For realm trusts, you will need to establish the trust separately for the Windows domain and for the Kerberos realm. If you don't have appropriate administrative access to both the Windows domain and the Kerberos realm, you can establish one side of the trust and allow another administrator to establish the other side of the trust.

You create trusts by using the New Trust Wizard, which is started from Active Directory Domains and Trusts. The domain or forest where you start the New Trust Wizard is the local domain or forest and is referred to as "this domain or forest." The other domain or forest that the local domain or forest will trust is referred to as the "specified domain or forest."

To start the New Trust Wizard, follow these steps:

1. Click Start, choose Programs or All Programs as appropriate, choose Administrative Tools, and then select Active Directory Domains And Trusts.

2. Right-click the domain for which you want to establish a one-way incoming, one-way outgoing, or two-way trust, and then choose Properties. For a cross-forest trust, the domain you use must be the forest root domain in one of the participating forests.

3. In the domain Properties dialog box, click the Trusts tab. Click the New Trust button to start the New Trust Wizard, as shown in Figure 8-3, and then click Next. When working with the New Trust Wizard, keep in mind the terms listed in Table 8-1.

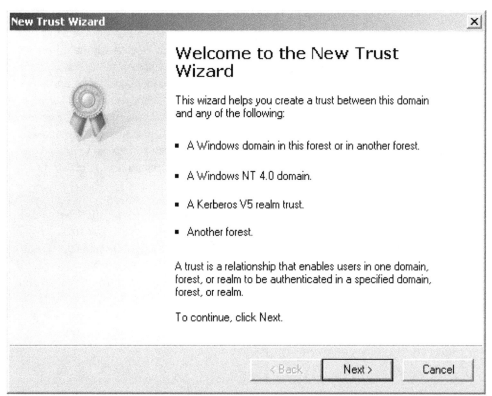

Figure 8-3 The New Trust Wizard.

TABLE 8-1 Important Terms Used by the New Trust Wizard

Trust password	A password stored in the trusted domain object in Active Directory. When you choose this option, a strong trust password is generated automatically for you. You must use the same password when you create a trust relationship between domains.
Both sides of the trust	When you create trusts, you have the option to create each side of the trust separately or both sides of the trust simultaneously. If you choose to create each side of the trust separately, you must run the New Trust Wizard twice— once for each domain—and must supply the same trust password for each domain. If you choose to create both sides of the trust simultaneously, you run the New Trust Wizard once, and the trust password you provide is applied to both sides of the trust. All trust passwords should be strong passwords.

One-way incoming trust	A one-way trust relationship between two domains in which the direction of the trust points toward the domain from which you start the New Trust Wizard. When the direction of the trust points toward a domain, users in that domain can access resources in the specified domain. For example, if you are logged on to domain A and you create a one-way incoming trust to domain B, users in domain A can access resources in domain B. Because this relationship is one way, users in domain B cannot access resources in domain A.
One-way outgoing trust	A one-way trust relationship between two domains in which the direction of the trust points toward the specified target domain. When the direction of trust points toward a specified domain, users in the specified domain can access resources in the domain from which you start the New Trust Wizard. For example, if you are logged on to domain A and you create a one-way outgoing trust to domain B, users in domain B can access resources in domain A. Because this relationship is one way, users in domain A cannot access resources in domain B.
Two-way trust	A trust relationship between two domains in which both domains trust each other. For example, domain A trusts domain B, and domain B trusts domain A. All parent-child trusts are two-way trusts.
Domainwide authentication	An authentication setting that permits unrestricted access by any users in the specified domain to all available shared resources that are located in the local domain. This is the default authentication setting for external trusts.
Forestwide authentication	An authentication setting that permits unrestricted access by any users in the specified forest to all available shared resources located in any of the domains in the local forest. This is the default authentication setting for forest trusts.
Selective authentication	An authentication setting that restricts access over an external trust or forest trust to only those users in a specified domain or specified forest who have been explicitly given authentication permissions to resource computers that reside in the local domain or the local forest. This authentication setting must be enabled manually.

4. On the Trust Name page, shown in Figure 8-4, you must specify the domain name of the other domain. When you click Next, the wizard will attempt to validate the domain name by contacting the domain.

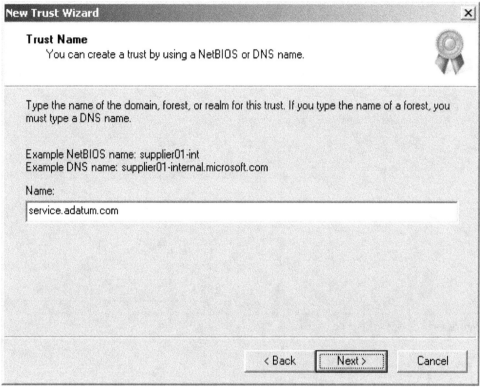

Figure 8-4 Specify the DNS or NetBIOS name of the other domain.

5. If the wizard cannot contact the domain, you'll see the Trust Type page, shown in Figure 8-5, and will need to specify whether you are trying to create a realm trust with an interoperable Kerberos v5 realm or a trust with a Windows domain. With Windows domains, you can retype the domain name before clicking Next to continue, or you can simply click Next to continue.

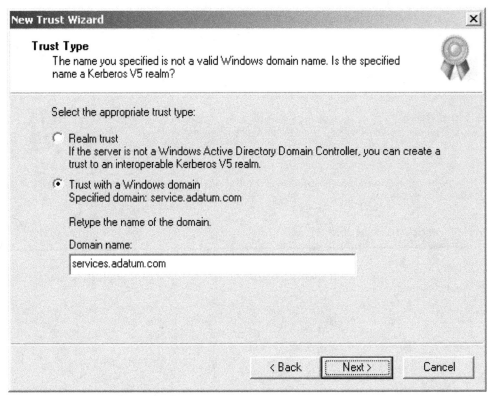

Figure 8-5 Specify the type of trust.

Creating External Trusts

When users need to access resources that are located in a Windows NT 4.0 domain or in a domain that is in a separate Active Directory forest that is not joined by a forest trust, you can create an external trust to form a one-way or two-way nontransitive trust between the domains. Although you can create an external trust between two domains, external trusts cannot be extended implicitly to a third domain. Keep in mind that the forest functional level for both forests must be set to Windows Server 2003 or later. Additionally, if you have the appropriate administrative credentials for each domain, you can create both sides of an external trust at the same time. Otherwise, you will need to create each side of the trust separately.

Real World To create an external trust successfully, you must ensure DNS is configured properly. If you have a root DNS server that you can make the root DNS server for the DNS namespaces of both forests, you should make that server the root DNS server by ensuring that the root zone contains delegations for each of the DNS namespaces. You also should update the root hints of all DNS servers with the new root DNS server. If you have no shared root DNS server, and the root DNS servers for each forest DNS namespace are running Windows Server 2003 or later, configure DNS conditional forwarders in each DNS namespace to route queries for names in the other namespace. If you have no shared root DNS servers, and the root DNS servers for each forest DNS namespace are not running Windows Server 2003 or later, configure DNS secondary zones in each DNS namespace to route queries for names in the other namespace.

Creating a One-Way Incoming External Trust

A one-way incoming external trust allows users in the domain or forest where you start the New Trust Wizard to access resources in a domain outside your forest or in a Windows NT 4.0 domain. With a one-way incoming external trust, one side of a trust will be created, but the new trust will not function until the administrator for the reciprocal domain uses his or her credentials to create the outgoing side of the trust. If you have administrative credentials for both domains involved in the trust, you can create both sides of the trust in one operation.

To create a one-way incoming external trust for one or both sides of the trust, follow these steps:

1. In Active Directory Domains and Trusts, right-click the domain for which you want to establish a one-way incoming external trust, and then click Properties.

2. On the Trusts tab, click New Trust, and then click Next.

3. On the Trust Name page, enter the DNS (or NetBIOS) name of the other external domain, and then click Next.

4. On the Trust Type page, click External Trust, and then click Next.

5. On the Direction Of Trust page, click One-Way: Incoming, and then click Next.

6. On the Sides Of Trust page, click This Domain Only if you are creating one side of the trust, or click Both This Domain And The Specified Domain if you are establishing both sides of the trust. Then click Next.

7. If you are creating one side of the trust, on the Trust Password page, enter and then confirm the trust password, and then click Next three times to begin the trust creation process.

8. If you are establishing both sides of the trust, on the User Name And Password page, enter the user name and password for the appropriate administrator in the specified domain, and then click Next. Afterward, on the Outgoing Trust Authentication Level–Specified Domain page, click Domain-Wide Authentication or Selective Authentication as appropriate, and then click Next three times.

9. On the Confirm Incoming Trust page, do one of the following:

   ▪ Click No if you are establishing one side of the trust and do not want to confirm the incoming trust. For this trust to function, the domain administrator for the specified domain or forest must create a one-way outgoing external trust. The same trust password must be used.

   ▪ Click Yes if you are establishing both sides of the trust and want to confirm the incoming trust. Afterward, provide the appropriate administrative credentials from the specified domain.

10. On the Completing The New Trust Wizard page, click Finish.

Creating a One-Way Outgoing External Trust

A one-way outgoing external trust will allow resources in the domain or forest where you start the New Trust Wizard to be accessed by users in a domain outside your forest or in a Windows NT 4.0 domain. With a one-way outgoing external trust, one side of a trust will be created, but the new trust will not function until the administrator for the reciprocal domain uses his or her credentials to create the incoming side of the trust. If you have administrative credentials for both domains involved in the trust, you can create both sides of the trust in one operation.

To create a one-way outgoing external trust for one or both sides of the trust, follow these steps:

1. In Active Directory Domains and Trusts, right-click the domain for which you want to establish a one-way outgoing external trust, and then click Properties.

2. On the Trusts tab, click New Trust, and then click Next.

3. On the Trust Name page, enter the DNS (or NetBIOS) name of the other external domain, and then click Next.

4. On the Trust Type page, click External Trust, and then click Next.

5. On the Direction Of Trust page, click One-Way: Outgoing, and then click Next.

6. On the Sides Of Trust page, click This Domain Only if you are creating one side of the trust, or click Both This Domain And The Specified Domain if you are establishing both sides of the trust. Then click Next.

7. If you are creating one side of the trust, on the Outgoing Trust Authentication Level–Specified Domain page, click Domain-Wide Authentication or Selective Authentication as appropriate, and then click Next. Afterward, on the Trust Password page, enter and then confirm the trust password, and then click Next three times to begin the trust creation process.

8. If you are establishing both sides of the trust, on the User Name And Password page, enter the user name and password for the appropriate administrator in the specified domain, and then click Next. Afterward, on the Outgoing Trust Authentication Level–Specified Domain page, click Domain-Wide Authentication or Selective Authentication as appropriate, and then click Next three times.

9. On the Confirm Outgoing Trust page, do one of the following:

   ▪ Click No if you are establishing one side of the trust and do not want to confirm the outgoing trust. For this trust to function, the domain administrator for the specified domain or forest must create a one-way incoming external trust. The same trust password must be used.

- Click Yes if you are establishing both sides of the trust and want to confirm the outgoing trust. Afterward, provide the appropriate administrative credentials from the specified domain.

10. On the Completing The New Trust Wizard page, click Finish.

Creating a Two-Way External Trust

A two-way external trust allows users in the domain or forest where you start the New Trust Wizard and users in the reciprocal domain to access resources in either of the two domains. When you create a two-way external trust, you can establish one or both sides of the trust. When you establish one side of the trust, the trust will be created, but the new trust will not function until the administrator for the reciprocal domain uses his or her credentials to create the other side of the trust. If you have administrative credentials for both domains involved in the trust, you can create both sides of the trust in one operation.

To create a two-way external trust for one or both sides of the trust, follow these steps:

1. In Active Directory Domains and Trusts, right-click the domain for which you want to establish a two-way incoming external trust, and then click Properties.
2. On the Trusts tab, click New Trust, and then click Next.
3. On the Trust Name page, enter the DNS (or NetBIOS) name of the other external domain, and then click Next.
4. On the Trust Type page, click External Trust, and then click Next.
5. On the Direction Of Trust page, click Two-Way, and then click Next.
6. On the Sides Of Trust page, click This Domain Only if you are creating one side of the trust, or click Both This Domain And The Specified Domain if you are establishing both sides of the trust. Then click Next.
7. If you are creating one side of the trust, on the Outgoing Trust Authentication Level–Specified Domain page, click Domain-Wide Authentication or Selective Authentication as appropriate, and then click Next. Afterward, on the Trust Password page, enter and then

confirm the trust password, and then click Next three times to begin the trust creation process.

8. If you are establishing both sides of the trust, on the User Name And Password page, enter the user name and password for the appropriate administrator in the specified domain, and then click Next. Afterward, on the Outgoing Trust Authentication Level–Specified Domain page, click Domain-Wide Authentication or Selective Authentication as appropriate, and then click Next three times.

9. On the Confirm Outgoing Trust page, do one of the following:

   ▪ Click No if you are establishing one side of the trust and do not want to confirm the outgoing trust. For this trust to function, the domain administrator for the specified domain or forest must repeat this procedure and establish the outgoing trust for the other side of the trust. The same trust password must be used.

   ▪ Click Yes if you are establishing both sides of the trust and want to confirm the outgoing trust. Afterward, provide the appropriate administrative credentials from the specified domain.

10. On the Confirm Incoming Trust page, do one of the following:

   ▪ Click No if you are establishing one side of the trust and do not want to confirm the incoming trust. For this trust to function, the domain administrator for the specified domain or forest must repeat this procedure and establish the incoming trust for the other side of the trust. The same trust password must be used.

   ▪ Click Yes if you are establishing both sides of the trust and want to confirm the outgoing trust. Afterward, provide the appropriate administrative credentials from the specified domain.

11. On the Completing The New Trust Wizard page, click Finish.

Creating Shortcut Trusts

A shortcut trust is a manually created trust that shortens the trust path to allow users to more quickly access resources in a domain that is in another domain tree in the same forest. How you use shortcut trusts depends on how you implement your Active Directory domains. When your forest contains multiple domain trees, each with many child domains, and authentication delays occur between child domains, you can optimize the authentication process between the child domains by creating shortcut trusts between midlevel domains in each domain tree. When your forest is less extensive and users are experiencing delays while accessing resources in other domains, you may want to establish a shortcut trust directly between the user domain and the resource domain to shorten the trust path.

Creating a One-Way Incoming Shortcut Trust

A one-way incoming shortcut trust allows users in the domain where you start the New Trust Wizard to more quickly access resources in a domain that is in another domain tree in the same forest. With a one-way incoming shortcut trust, one side of a trust will be created, but the new trust will not function until the administrator for the reciprocal domain uses his or her credentials to create the outgoing side of the trust. If you have administrative credentials for both domains involved in the trust, you can create both sides of the trust in one operation.

To create a one-way incoming shortcut trust for one or both sides of the trust, follow these steps:

1. In Active Directory Domains and Trusts, right-click the domain for which you want to establish a one-way incoming shortcut trust, and then click Properties.

2. On the Trusts tab, click New Trust, and then click Next.

3. On the Trust Name page, enter the DNS (or NetBIOS) name of the other domain, and then click Next.

4. On the Direction Of Trust page, click One-Way: Incoming, and then click Next.

5. On the Sides Of Trust page, click This Domain Only if you are creating one side of the trust, or click Both This Domain And The Specified Domain if you are establishing both sides of the trust. Then click Next.

6. If you are creating one side of the trust, on the Trust Password page, enter and then confirm the trust password, and then click Next three times to begin the trust creation process.

7. If you are establishing both sides of the trust, on the User Name And Password page, enter the user name and password for the appropriate administrator in the specified domain, and then click Next three times.

8. On the Confirm Incoming Trust page, do one of the following:

   - Click No if you are establishing one side of the trust and do not want to confirm the incoming trust. For this trust to function, the domain administrator for the specified domain must create a one-way outgoing shortcut trust. The same trust password must be used.
   - Click Yes if you are establishing both sides of the trust and want to confirm the incoming trust. Afterward, provide the appropriate administrative credentials from the specified domain.

9. On the Completing The New Trust Wizard page, click Finish.

Creating a One-Way Outgoing Shortcut Trust

A one-way outgoing shortcut trust will allow resources in the domain where you start the New Trust Wizard to be accessed more quickly by users in a domain that is in another domain tree in the same forest. With a one-way outgoing shortcut trust, one side of a trust will be created, but the new trust will not function until the administrator for the reciprocal domain uses his or her credentials to create the incoming side of the trust. If you have administrative credentials for both domains involved in the trust, you can create both sides of the trust in one operation.

To create a one-way outgoing shortcut trust for one or both sides of the trust, follow these steps:

1. In Active Directory Domains and Trusts, right-click the domain for which you want to establish a one-way outgoing shortcut trust, and then click Properties.

2. On the Trusts tab, click New Trust, and then click Next.

3. On the Trust Name page, enter the DNS (or NetBIOS) name of the other domain, and then click Next.

4. On the Direction Of Trust page, click One-Way: Outgoing, and then click Next.

5. On the Sides Of Trust page, click This Domain Only if you are creating one side of the trust, or click Both This Domain And The Specified Domain if you are establishing both sides of the trust. Then click Next.

6. If you are creating one side of the trust, on the Trust Password page, enter and then confirm the trust password, and then click Next three times to begin the trust creation process.

7. If you are establishing both sides of the trust, on the User Name And Password page, enter the user name and password for the appropriate administrator in the specified domain, and then click Next three times.

8. On the Confirm Outgoing Trust page, do one of the following:

   - Click No if you are establishing one side of the trust and do not want to confirm the outgoing trust. For this trust to function, the domain administrator for the specified domain must create a one-way incoming shortcut trust. The same trust password must be used.
   - Click Yes if you are establishing both sides of the trust and want to confirm the outgoing trust. Afterward, provide the appropriate administrative credentials from the specified domain.

9. On the Completing The New Trust Wizard page, click Finish.

Creating a Two-Way Shortcut Trust

A two-way shortcut trust allows users in the domain where you start the New Trust Wizard and users in a domain that is in another domain tree in the same forest to access resources in either of the two domains more quickly. When you create a two-way shortcut trust, you can establish one or both sides of the trust. When you establish one side of the trust, the trust will be created, but the new trust will not function until the administrator for the reciprocal domain uses his or her credentials to create the other side of the trust. If you have administrative credentials for both domains involved in the trust, you can create both sides of the trust in one operation.

To create a two-way shortcut trust for one or both sides of the trust, follow these steps:

1. In Active Directory Domains and Trusts, right-click the domain for which you want to establish a two-way shortcut trust, and then click Properties.

2. On the Trusts tab, click New Trust, and then click Next.

3. On the Trust Name page, enter the DNS (or NetBIOS) name of the other domain, and then click Next.

4. On the Direction Of Trust page, click Two-Way, and then click Next.

5. On the Sides Of Trust page, click This Domain Only if you are creating one side of the trust, or click Both This Domain And The Specified Domain if you are establishing both sides of the trust. Then click Next.

6. If you are creating one side of the trust, on the Trust Password page, enter and then confirm the trust password, and then click Next three times to begin the trust creation process.

7. If you are establishing both sides of the trust, on the User Name And Password page, enter the user name and password for the appropriate administrator in the specified domain, and then click Next three times.

8. On the Confirm Outgoing Trust page, do one of the following:

   - Click No if you are establishing one side of the trust and do not want to confirm the outgoing trust. For this trust to function, the domain administrator for the specified domain must repeat this procedure and establish the outgoing trust for the other side of the trust. The same trust password must be used.

   - Click Yes if you are establishing both sides of the trust and want to confirm the outgoing trust. Afterward, provide the appropriate administrative credentials from the specified domain.

9. On the Confirm Incoming Trust page, do one of the following:

   - Click No if you are establishing one side of the trust and do not want to confirm the incoming trust. For this trust to function, the domain administrator for the specified domain must repeat this procedure and establish the incoming trust for the other side of the trust. The same trust password must be used.

- Click Yes if you are establishing both sides of the trust and want to confirm the outgoing trust. Afterward, provide the appropriate administrative credentials from the specified domain.

10. On the Completing The New Trust Wizard page, click Finish.

Creating Forest Trusts

When users need to access resources that are located in a disjoined forest, you can create a forest trust to form a one-way or two-way transitive trust relationship. Although you can create a forest trust between two disjoined forests, forest trusts cannot be extended implicitly to a third forest. Keep in mind that the forest functional level for both forests must be set to either Windows Server 2003 or later. Additionally, if you have the appropriate administrative credentials for each forest, you can create both sides of a forest trust at the same time. Otherwise, you will need to create each side of the trust separately.

> **Real World**   To create a forest trust successfully, you must ensure DNS is configured properly. If there is a root DNS server that you can make the root DNS server for the DNS namespaces of both forests, you should make that server the root DNS server by ensuring that the root zone contains delegations for each of the DNS namespaces. You also should update the root hints of all DNS servers with the new root DNS server. If there is no shared root DNS server and the root DNS servers for each forest DNS namespace are running Windows Server 2003 or later, configure DNS conditional forwarders in each DNS namespace to route queries for names in the other namespace. If there are no shared root DNS servers and the root DNS servers for each forest DNS namespace are not running Windows Server 2003 or later, configure DNS secondary zones in each DNS namespace to route queries for names in the other namespace.

Creating a One-Way Incoming Forest Trust

A one-way incoming forest trust allows users in the forest where you start the New Trust Wizard to access resources in another Windows forest. With a one-way incoming forest trust, one side of a trust will be created, but the new trust will not function until the administrator for the reciprocal forest uses his or her credentials to create the outgoing side of the trust. If you have administrative credentials for both forests involved in the trust, you can create both sides of the trust in one operation.

To create a one-way incoming forest trust for one or both sides of the trust, follow these steps:

1. In Active Directory Domains and Trusts, right-click the domain node for the forest root domain of the forest for which you want to establish an incoming forest trust, and then click Properties.

2. On the Trusts tab, click New Trust, and then click Next.

3. On the Trust Name page, enter the DNS (or NetBIOS) name of the forest root domain of the other forest, and then click Next.

4. On the Trust Type page, click Forest Trust, and then click Next.

5. On the Direction Of Trust page, click One-Way: Incoming, and then click Next.

6. On the Sides Of Trust page, click This Domain Only if you are creating one side of the trust, or click Both This Domain And The Specified Domain if you are establishing both sides of the trust. Then click Next.

7. If you are creating one side of the trust, on the Trust Password page, enter and then confirm the trust password, and then click Next three times to begin the trust creation process.

8. If you are establishing both sides of the trust, on the User Name And Password page, enter the user name and password for the appropriate administrator in the specified forest, and then click Next. Afterward, on the Outgoing Trust Authentication Level–Specified Forest page, click Forest-Wide Authentication or Selective Authentication as appropriate, and then click Next three times.

9. On the Confirm Incoming Trust page, do one of the following:

- Click No if you are establishing one side of the trust and do not want to confirm the incoming trust. For this trust to function, the administrator for the specified forest must create a one-way outgoing forest trust. The same trust password must be used.
- Click Yes if you are establishing both sides of the trust and want to confirm the incoming trust. Afterward, provide the appropriate administrative credentials from the specified forest.

10. On the Completing The New Trust Wizard page, click Finish.

Creating a One-Way Outgoing Forest Trust

A one-way outgoing forest trust will allow resources in the forest where you start the New Trust Wizard to be accessed by users in another Windows forest. With a one-way outgoing forest trust, one side of a trust will be created, but the new trust will not function until the administrator for the reciprocal forest uses his or her credentials to create the incoming side of the trust. If you have administrative credentials for both forests involved in the trust, you can create both sides of the trust in one operation.

To create a one-way outgoing forest trust for one or both sides of the trust, follow these steps:

1. In Active Directory Domains and Trusts, right-click the domain node for the forest root domain for which you want to establish an outgoing forest trust, and then click Properties.
2. On the Trusts tab, click New Trust, and then click Next.
3. On the Trust Name page, enter the DNS (or NetBIOS) name of the forest root domain of the other forest, and then click Next.
4. On the Trust Type page, click Forest Trust, and then click Next.
5. On the Direction Of Trust page, click One-Way: Outgoing, and then click Next.
6. On the Sides Of Trust page, click This Domain Only if you are creating one side of the trust, or click Both This Domain And The Specified Domain if you are establishing both sides of the trust. Then click Next.

7. If you are creating one side of the trust, on the Outgoing Trust Authentication Level–Specified Forest page, click Forest-Wide Authentication or Selective Authentication as appropriate, and then click Next. Afterward, on the Trust Password page, enter and then confirm the trust password, and then click Next three times to begin the trust creation process.

8. If you are establishing both sides of the trust, on the User Name And Password page, enter the user name and password for the appropriate administrator in the specified forest, and then click Next. Afterward, on the Outgoing Trust Authentication Level–Specified Forest page, click Forest-Wide Authentication or Selective Authentication as appropriate, and then click Next three times.

9. On the Confirm Outgoing Trust page, do one of the following:

   - Click No if you are establishing one side of the trust and do not want to confirm the outgoing trust. For this trust to function, the administrator for the specified forest must create a one-way incoming forest trust. The same trust password must be used.
   - Click Yes if you are establishing both sides of the trust and want to confirm the outgoing trust. Afterward, provide the appropriate administrative credentials from the specified forest.

10. On the Completing The New Trust Wizard page, click Finish.

Creating a Two-Way Forest Trust

A two-way forest trust allows users in the forest where you start the New Trust Wizard and users in the reciprocal forest to access resources in either of the two forests. When you create a two-way forest trust, you can establish one or both sides of the trust. When you establish one side of the trust, the trust will be created, but the new trust will not function until the administrator for the reciprocal forest uses his or her credentials to create the other side of the trust. If you have administrative credentials for both forests involved in the trust, you can create both sides of the trust in one operation.

To create a two-way forest trust for one or both sides of the trust, follow these steps:

1. In Active Directory Domains and Trusts, right-click the domain node for the forest root domain for which you want to establish a two-way forest trust, and then click Properties.

2. On the Trusts tab, click New Trust, and then click Next.

3. On the Trust Name page, enter the DNS (or NetBIOS) name of the forest root domain of the other forest, and then click Next.

4. On the Trust Type page, click Forest Trust, and then click Next.

5. On the Direction Of Trust page, click Two-Way, and then click Next.

6. On the Sides Of Trust page, click This Domain Only if you are creating one side of the trust, or click Both This Domain And The Specified Domain if you are establishing both sides of the trust. Then click Next.

7. If you are creating one side of the trust, on the Outgoing Trust Authentication Level–Specified Forest page, click Forest-Wide Authentication or Selective Authentication as appropriate, and then click Next. Afterward, on the Trust Password page, enter and then confirm the trust password, and then click Next three times to begin the trust creation process.

8. If you are establishing both sides of the trust, on the User Name And Password page, enter the user name and password for the appropriate administrator in the specified forest, and then click Next. Afterward, on the Outgoing Trust Authentication Level–Specified Forest page, click Forest-Wide Authentication or Selective Authentication as appropriate, and then click Next three times.

9. On the Confirm Outgoing Trust page, do one of the following:

   ▪ Click No if you are establishing one side of the trust and do not want to confirm the outgoing trust. For this trust to function, the administrator for the specified forest must repeat this procedure and establish the outgoing trust for the other side of the trust. The same trust password must be used.

- Click Yes if you are establishing both sides of the trust and want to confirm the outgoing trust. Afterward, provide the appropriate administrative credentials from the specified domain.

10. On the Confirm Incoming Trust page, do one of the following:

- Click No if you are establishing one side of the trust and do not want to confirm the incoming trust. For this trust to function, the administrator for the specified forest must repeat this procedure and establish the incoming trust for the other side of the trust. The same trust password must be used.
- Click Yes if you are establishing both sides of the trust and want to confirm the outgoing trust. Afterward, provide the appropriate administrative credentials from the specified forest.

11. On the Completing The New Trust Wizard page, click Finish.

Creating Realm Trusts

You can create a realm trust to form a one-way or two-way transitive or nontransitive trust relationship between a Windows domain and a non-Windows Kerberos realm. Unlike when you are working exclusively with Windows domains and forests, you will need to create each side of the trust separately.

Creating a One-Way Incoming Realm Trust

A one-way incoming realm trust allows users in the domain where you start the New Trust Wizard to access resources in a Kerberos realm. With a one-way incoming realm trust, the Windows domain side of a trust will be created, but the new trust will not function until the administrator for the Kerberos realm uses his or her credentials to create the outgoing side of the trust.

To create a one-way incoming realm trust for the Windows domain side of the trust, follow these steps:

1. In Active Directory Domains and Trusts, right-click the domain for which you want to establish an incoming realm trust, and then click Properties.

2. On the Trusts tab, click New Trust, and then click Next.

3. On the Trust Name page, enter the DNS (or NetBIOS) name of the Kerberos realm in uppercase letters, and then click Next.

4. On the Trust Type page, click Realm Trust, and then click Next.

5. On the Transitivity Of Trust page, click Nontransitive to form a trust relationship with the domain and the specified realm only, or click Transitive to form a trust relationship with the domain and the specified realm and all trusted realms.

6. On the Direction Of Trust page, click One-Way: Incoming, and then click Next.

7. On the Trust Password page, enter and then confirm the trust password, and then click Next three times to begin the trust creation process.

8. On the Completing The New Trust Wizard page, click Finish.

Creating a One-Way Outgoing Realm Trust

A one-way outgoing realm trust will allow resources in the domain where you start the New Trust Wizard to be accessed by users in a Kerberos realm. With a one-way outgoing realm trust, the Windows domain side of a trust will be created, but the new trust will not function until the administrator for the Kerberos realm uses his or her credentials to create the incoming side of the trust.

To create a one-way outgoing realm trust for the Windows domain side of the trust, follow these steps:

1. In Active Directory Domains and Trusts, right-click the domain for which you want to establish an outgoing realm trust, and then click Properties.

2. On the Trusts tab, click New Trust, and then click Next.

3. On the Trust Name page, enter the DNS (or NetBIOS) name of the Kerberos realm in uppercase letters, and then click Next.

4. On the Trust Type page, click Realm Trust, and then click Next.

5. On the Transitivity Of Trust page, click Nontransitive to form a trust relationship with the domain and the specified realm only, or click Transitive to form a trust relationship with the domain and the specified realm and all trusted realms.

6. On the Direction Of Trust page, click One-Way: Outgoing, and then click Next.

7. On the Trust Password page, enter and then confirm the trust password, and then click Next three times to begin the trust creation process.

8. On the Completing The New Trust Wizard page, click Finish.

Creating a Two-Way Realm Trust

A two-way realm trust allows users in the realm where you start the New Trust Wizard and users in the reciprocal realm to access resources in either of the two realms. When you create a two-way realm trust, you can establish one or both sides of the trust. When you establish one side of the trust, the trust will be created but will not function until the administrator for the reciprocal realm uses his or her credentials to create the other side of the trust. If you have administrative credentials for both realms involved in the trust, you can create both sides of the trust in one operation.

To create a two-way realm trust for one or both sides of the trust, follow these steps:

1. In Active Directory Domains and Trusts, right-click the domain for which you want to establish a two-way realm trust, and then click Properties.

2. On the Trusts tab, click New Trust, and then click Next.

3. On the Trust Name page, enter the DNS (or NetBIOS) name of the Kerberos realm in uppercase letters, and then click Next.

4. On the Trust Type page, click Realm Trust, and then click Next.

5. On the Transitivity Of Trust page, click Nontransitive to form a trust relationship with the domain and the specified realm only, or click Transitive to form a trust relationship with the domain and the specified realm and all trusted realms.

6. On the Direction Of Trust page, click Two-Way, and then click Next.

7. On the Trust Password page, enter and then confirm the trust password, and then click Next three times to begin the trust creation process.

8. On the Completing The New Trust Wizard page, click Finish.

Removing Manually Created Trusts

You can remove manually created trusts when they are no longer needed. You cannot remove default trusts.

To remove a manually created trust, follow these steps:

1. In Active Directory Domains and Trusts, right-click the domain that contains the trust you want to remove, and then click Properties.

2. On the Trusts tab, under either Domains Trusted By This Domain (Outgoing Trusts) or Domains That Trust This Domain (Incoming Trusts), click the trust to be removed, and then click Remove.

3. When prompted, do one of the following:

   - Click No to remove the trust from the local domain only. Repeat this procedure for the reciprocal domain.
   - Click Yes to remove the trust from both the local domain and the other domain. When prompted, enter a user name and password with administrative credentials for the reciprocal domain.

You can remove a trust by running Netdom Trust at an elevated, administrator command prompt. On the Start menu, right-click Command Prompt, and then click Run As Administrator. At the elevated command prompt, enter the following command.

```
netdom trust TrustingDomainName /d:TrustedDomainName /remove
```

Here, *TrustingDomainName* specifies the DNS (or NetBIOS) name of the trusting domain in the trust that is being removed, and *TrustedDomainName* specifies the DNS (or NetBIOS) name of the domain that will be trusted in the trust that is being removed.

Using the /UserO and /PasswordO parameters, you can specify administrator credentials for the trusting domain. Using the /UserD and /PasswordD parameters, you can specify administrator credentials for the trusted domain. With both the /PasswordO and /PasswordD parameters, you will be prompted for the required password when you enter * as the password.

Verifying and Troubleshooting Trusts

By default, Windows validates all incoming trusts automatically. If the credentials used to establish the trust are no longer valid, the trust fails verification. Occasionally, you may want to revalidate trusts. If clients are unable to access resources in a domain outside the forest, the external trust between the domains may have failed. In this case, you should verify the trust for the trusted domain. Note that a primary domain controller (PDC) emulator must be available to reset and verify the external trust.

If clients cannot connect to a domain controller running Windows 2000, check the service pack level on the domain controller. The Windows 2000 domain controller should be running Service Pack 3 or later. If it isn't, upgrade it.

Clients or servers can get trust errors within an Active Directory forest for several reasons. The time on the clients or servers trying to authenticate may be more than 5 minutes off, which is the default maximum time difference allowed for Kerberos authentication. In this case, synchronize the time on the clients and servers. The problem could also be that the domain controller is down or the trust relationship is broken. For the latter case, you can run Netdom to verify or reset the trust.

If clients are experiencing trust errors connecting to a Windows NT 4 domain, the automatic password reset for the trust may not have reached the PDC emulator. You can run Netdom to verify or reset the trust. If this doesn't resolve the problem, see Knowledge Base article 317178 for more information (*http://support.microsoft.com/kb/317178/en-us*).

After upgrading a Windows NT 4 domain that has existing trusts with one or more Active Directory domains, delete and recreate all the previously existing trusts. These trusts are not automatically upgraded from Windows NT 4 trusts. If this doesn't resolve the problem, see Knowledge Base article 275221 for more information (*http://support.microsoft.com/kb/275221/en-us*).

To revalidate or reset a trust, follow these steps:

1. In Active Directory Domains and Trusts, right-click the trusted domain for which you want to verify the incoming trust, then select Properties.
2. In the domain's Properties dialog box, click the Trusts tab, and then click Validate.
3. To validate and reset (if necessary) only the outgoing trust, select No, Do Not Validate The Incoming Trust. To validate and reset (if necessary) both the incoming and outgoing trust, select Yes, Validate The Incoming Trust, as shown in Figure 8-6, and then enter the user name and password for an administrator account in the reciprocal domain.

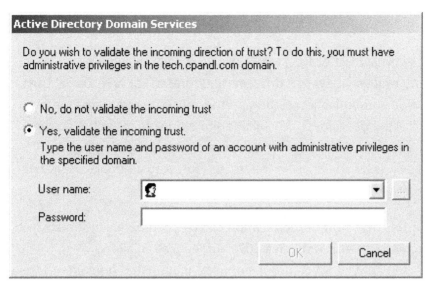

Figure 8-6 Select a validation option.

4. Click OK. If the trust is valid and active, you'll see a prompt confirming this. If the trust is not valid, Active Directory Domains and Trusts will attempt to reset the trust. However, you may need to ensure both sides of the trust have been created and that the trust passwords are set the same.

You can validate a trust by running Netdom Trust at an elevated, administrator command prompt. On the Start menu, right-click Command Prompt, and then click Run As Administrator. At the elevated command prompt, enter the following command.

```
netdom trust TrustingDomainName /d:TrustedDomainName /verify
```

Here, *TrustingDomainName* specifies the DNS (or NetBIOS) name of the trusting domain in the trust that is being created, and *TrustedDomainName* specifies the DNS (or NetBIOS) name of the domain that will be trusted in the trust that is being created.

Configuring Selective Authentication

Creating an external trust or forest trust provides a pathway for all authentication requests between domains and forests. For an external trust, the domainwide authentication setting permits unrestricted access by any users in the trusted domain to all available shared resources in the trusting domain. For a forest trust, the forestwide authentication setting permits unrestricted access by any users in the trusted forest to all available shared resources in any of the domains in the trusting forest.

To enact controls over how authentication can be used between forests, you can use selective authentication. Selective authentication allows administrators to control which groups of users in a trusted domain or forest can access shared resources in a trusting domain or forest.

Enabling or Disabling Selective Authentication for External Trusts

With respect to external trusts, selective authentication restricts access to only those users in a trusted domain who have been explicitly granted authentication permissions to computer objects that reside in the trusting domain. To explicitly give authentication permissions to computer objects in the trusting domain to certain users, you must grant those users the Allowed To Authenticate permission in Active Directory. Therefore, enabling selective authentication for an external trust requires granting the Allowed To Authenticate permission for computer objects in the trusting domain to users in the trusted domain and then turning on selective authentication.

To enable selective authentication for an external trust, follow these steps:

1. In Active Directory Domains and Trusts, right-click the domain that contains the trust you want to configure, and then click Properties.

2. On the Trusts tab, under either Domains Trusted By This Domain (Outgoing Trusts) or Domains That Trust This Domain (Incoming Trusts), click the external trust that you want to configure, and then click Properties.

3. On the Authentication tab, click Selective Authentication to enable selective authentication, or click Domain-Wide Authentication to disable selective authentication. Then click OK.

> **Note** When you use this technique, only the authentication settings for the outgoing trust are displayed. To view the authentication settings for the incoming side of a two-way external trust, connect to a domain controller in the trusted domain, and then use Active Directory Domains and Trusts to view the authentication settings for the outgoing side of the same trust.

Enabling or Disabling Selective Authentication for Forest Trusts

With respect to forest trusts, selective authentication restricts access to only those users in a trusted forest who have been explicitly granted authentication permissions to computer objects that reside in the trusting forest. To explicitly give authentication permissions to computer objects in the trusting forest to certain users, you must grant those users the Allowed To Authenticate permission in Active Directory. Therefore, enabling selective authentication for a forest trust requires granting the Allowed To Authenticate permission for computer objects in the trusting forest to users in the trusted forest and then turning on selective authentication.

To enable selective authentication for a forest trust, follow these steps:

1. In Active Directory Domains and Trusts, right-click the domain node for the forest root domain that contains the trust you want to configure, and then click Properties.

2. On the Trusts tab, under either Domains Trusted By This Domain (Outgoing Trusts) or Domains That Trust This Domain (Incoming Trusts), click the forest trust that you want to configure. Then click Properties.

3. On the Authentication tab, click Selective Authentication to enable selective authentication, or click Forest-Wide Authentication to disable selective authentication. Then click OK.

> **Note** When you use this technique, only the authentication settings for the outgoing trust are displayed. To view the authentication settings for the incoming side of a two-way forest trust, connect to a domain controller in the trusted forest, and then use Active Directory Domains and Trusts to view the authentication settings for the outgoing side of the same trust.

Granting the Allowed To Authenticate Permission

When you enable selective authentication, each user must be explicitly granted access to resources by granting the Allowed To Authenticate permission on computer objects that reside in the trusting domain or forest. To grant the Allowed To Authenticate permission on computers in the trusting domain or forest, follow these steps:

1. In Active Directory Users and Computers, click the Computers container or the container where your computer objects reside.

2. Right-click the computer object that you want users in the trusted domain or forest to access, and then click Properties.

3. On the Security tab, do one of the following:

   - In Group Or User Names, click a user or group name for which you want to grant access to this computer, and then select the Allow check box next to the Allowed To Authenticate permission. Repeat as necessary. Click OK when you finish.
   - Click Add. In Enter The Object Names To Select box, enter the name of the user or group object for which you want to grant access to this resource computer, and then click OK. Select the Allow check box next to the Allowed To Authenticate permission, and then click OK.

Chapter 9. Maintaining and Recovering Active Directory

As an administrator, you'll perform many different tasks to maintain and recover Active Directory Domain Services (AD DS). In other chapters of this book, I've covered most of these tasks. In this chapter, I cover the following additional tasks:

- Protecting items from accidental deletion
- Starting and stopping AD DS
- Setting the functional level of domains and forests
- Configuring deleted item retention
- Configuring the Windows Time service
- Backing up and restoring Active Directory
- Maintaining the directory database

Protecting Objects from Accidental Deletion

When you are working with Windows Server 2008 or later, the Protect Object From Accidental Deletion option is available for objects created in Active Directory Users And Computers, Active Directory Sites And Services, and Active Directory Domains And Trusts. When enabled, this option implements the Deny Delete Subtree permission, which prevents the object from being accidentally deleted.

To protect an object from deletion, follow these steps:

1. Start Active Directory Users And Computers, Active Directory Sites And Services, or Active Directory Domains And Trusts, as appropriate, from the Administrative Tools menu.

2. Enable Advanced Features on the View menu by clicking View and then selecting Advanced Features.

3. When you enable Advanced Features, the Protect Object From Accidental Deletion option is available on the Object tab in the object's

Properties dialog box. Double-click the object you want to work with to open its Properties dialog box.

4. Select the Protect Object From Accidental Deletion option, and then click OK. If you later want to allow the object to be deleted, repeat this procedure and clear the Protect Object From Accidental Deletion option.

If the Protect Object From Accidental Deletion option is enabled and you try to delete the object, the administrator console will appear to let you do this, but the operation will fail with the error "You do not have sufficient privileges to delete X, or this object is protected from accidental deletion."

Starting and Stopping Active Directory Domain Services

On domain controllers that are running Windows Server 2003, you must restart a domain controller in Directory Services Restore Mode (DSRM) to stop AD DS. When you are running in DSRM, you can perform basic database management procedures, including offline defragmentation. When you are finished managing the database, you can restart the domain controller in normal mode to resume normal operations. (For more information, see "Restarting a Domain Controller in Directory Services Restore Mode" in Chapter 3, "Deploying Writable Domain Controllers.")

Domain controllers running Windows Server 2008 or later support restartable AD DS. This feature allows you to start or stop AD DS without having to restart a domain controller in DSRM. Once you've stopped AD DS, you can perform database management procedures as if you were in DSRM. When you are finished managing the database, you can start AD DS to resume normal operations.

You can start or stop AD DS by following these steps:

1. Choose Start, click Administrative Tools, and then click Server Manager. Or click Server Manager on the Quick Launch toolbar.

2. In Server Manager, click the plus sign (+) next to the Configuration node. This expands the node to display its tools.

3. Select the Services node. You should now see a complete list of services installed on the system. By default, this list is organized by service name.

4. Right-click Active Directory Domain Services and then click Start or Stop as appropriate. You can also choose Restart to have Windows stop and then start the service after a brief pause.

Server services that depend on AD DS to function shut down before AD DS shuts down. This means the following services stop when you stop AD DS:

- Distributed File System (DFS) Replication
- DNS Server service
- File Replication Service (FRS)
- Intersite Messaging
- Kerberos Key Distribution Center (KDC)

Other services that are running on the server and that do not depend on AD DS to function, remain available to satisfy client requests while AD DS is stopped.

Setting the Functional Level of Domains and Forests

As discussed in "Establishing Functional Levels" in Chapter 2, "Installing New Forests, Domain Trees, and Child Domains," each forest and each domain within a forest can be assigned a functional level. Functional levels affect the inner workings of Active Directory and are used to enable features that are compatible with the installed server versions of the Windows operating system. For example, with the domain functional level set as Windows Server 2008, the domain can use only domain controllers running Windows Server 2008 or later.

You raise the domain or forest functional level by using Active Directory Domains and Trusts. Although you can raise the functional level of a domain or forest, you can never lower it.

Because raising the forest functional level may require you to raise the functional level of domains, you should predetermine the steps you need to take to raise the forest functional level. To determine the steps you need to take to raise the forest functional level, follow these steps:

1. Click Start, click Administrative Tools, and then click Active Directory Domains And Trusts.

2. Right-click the Active Directory Domains And Trusts node in the console tree, and then click Raise Forest Functional Level. The current forest name and functional level appear in the Raise Forest Functional Level dialog box.

3. Click Save As in the Raise Forest Functional Level dialog box. When you click Save As, a Save As dialog box appears, allowing you to select a save location for a log file. The log file details show the following information:

   - The forest root domain and the current forest functional level.
   - The domains and the domain controllers in those domains that are running earlier versions of Windows Server. These are the servers that need to be upgraded.
   - The domain functional level of each domain for which the functional level must be raised. As long as the domain functional level of all domains is set to at least Windows 2000 native, you can raise the forest functional level—doing so raises the domain functional level in all the domains to Windows Server 2008 or Windows Server 2008 R2 and sets the forest functional level to Windows Server 2008 or Windows Server 2008 R2 as well.

To raise the functional level of a domain, follow these steps:

1. Click Start, click Administrative Tools, and then click Active Directory Domains And Trusts.

2. In the console tree, right-click the domain you want to work with, and then select Raise Domain Functional Level. The current domain name and functional level appear in the Raise Domain Functional Level dialog box.

3. To change the domain functionality, select the new domain functional level in the selection list provided, and then click Raise.

4. When you click OK, the new domain functional level is replicated to each domain controller in the domain. This operation can take several minutes or longer in a large organization.

To raise the functional level of a forest, follow these steps:

1. Click Start, click Administrative Tools, and then click Active Directory Domains And Trusts.

2. Right-click the Active Directory Domains And Trusts node in the console tree, and then click Raise Forest Functional Level. The current forest name and functional level appear in the Raise Forest Functional Level dialog box.

3. To change the forest functional level, select the new forest functional level in the selection list provided, and then click Raise.

4. When you click OK, the new forest functional level is replicated to each domain controller in each domain in the forest. This operation can take several minutes or longer in a large organization.

Configuring Deleted Item Retention

The Deleted Item Retention lifetime, also known as the tombstone lifetime, in an Active Directory forest determines how long deleted objects are retained in Active Directory Domain Services (AD DS). The lifetime is determined by the value of the tombstoneLifetime attribute on the Directory Service object in the configuration directory partition. Because a current backup is required for recovering a domain controller in case of failure and for installing a domain controller from backup media, the Deleted Item Retention lifetime also defines the useful life of a backup that you use for disaster recovery or installation from backup media.

To determine or set the Deleted Item Retention lifetime for the forest, follow these steps:

1. Click Start, click Administrative Tools, and then click ADSI Edit.

2. In ADSI Edit, right-click ADSI Edit, and then click Connect To.

3. For Connection Point, click Select A Well Known Naming Context, and then click Configuration.

4. If you want to connect to a specific domain controller, under Computer, click Select Or Type A Domain Or Server. Enter the server name or the domain name followed by a colon, and then enter the connection port. Port 389 is the default for LDAP.

5. Click OK to connect to the naming context using the specified settings.

6. Navigate to the CN=Services\CN=Windows NT container.

7. Right-click CN=Directory Service, and then click Properties.

8. In the Attribute column, note the value in the Value column for the tombstoneLifetime attribute. If the value is <not set>, the default value is in effect. Normally, this value is 180 days. However, on a domain controller in a forest that was created on a domain controller running Windows Server 2003, the default value is 60 days.

9. If you want to change the lifetime value, click tombstoneLifetime and then click Edit. In the Integer Attribute Editor dialog box, enter the number of days that a domain controller should preserve information about deleted objects, such as 240, and then click OK. Keep in mind that this value also defines the useful life of a backup that you use for disaster recovery or for installation from backup media.

Configuring the Windows Time Service

As discussed in Chapter 8, "Managing Trusts and Authentication," Windows uses Kerberos version 5 (v5) as the primary authentication mechanism. With Kerberos authentication, computers must have their time closely synchronized in order to be properly authenticated. By default, the maximum allowed time difference is 5 minutes. If the time difference is greater than this value, authentication will fail.

Although you could extend the allowable time difference through domain security policy by using the Kerberos policy Maximum Tolerance For Computer Clock Synchronization, doing so doesn't get to the root cause of the time divergence. Whether computers are in a domain or workgroup setting, the root cause of time divergence is a lack of time synchronization, and this is why the Windows Time service (W32time) is essential for proper operations.

The Windows Time service ensures that all computers running current versions of Windows and Windows Server use a common time. To do this, the service synchronizes the date and time using Network Time Protocol (NTP) and time providers. When you deploy your forest root domain, you'll need to configure the Windows Time service as appropriate for your organization. Thereafter, the Windows Time service requires little ongoing management. However, as you expand your network, you might find that you need to modify the time services configuration to make it more efficient.

Understanding Windows Time

Keeping a computer synchronized with world time isn't easy. System clocks can lose time, users can accidentally set the system clock to the wrong time, and other things can also go wrong. To help resolve problems with system time and time synchronization, Windows uses Windows Time service to set a consistent time based on world time.

Windows Time service allows synchronization within 100 milliseconds of world time. Windows Time service uses the Network Time Protocol (NTP) to poll the authoritative time server. The global settings MinPollInterval and MaxPollInterval control the exact rates. If time between the time server and the system differs, the Windows Time service slowly corrects the time. The global settings UpdateInterval and FrequencyCorrectRate control the exact correction rate.

Computers that are not joined to a domain and are running Windows synchronize time with an authoritative, external time source. The default time sources are *time.windows.com*, *time.nist.gov*, *time-nw.nist.gov*, *time-a.nist.gov*, and *time-b.nist.gov*.

Windows computers that are joined to a domain synchronize time with an authoritative time source in the parent domain. The default method of synchronizing time is through the domain hierarchy, in which a client connects to a domain controller in its domain as its time source, and domain controllers in turn get their time from the authoritative time source for the Windows forest. If no domain controller is specifically configured as the authoritative time source in the forest root domain, the domain controller that holds the PDC emulator operations master role is the authoritative time server. The PDC emulator uses its internal clock to provide time to domain controllers throughout the forest.

> **Tip** Because the PDC emulator is the default time source for a forest, you should ensure this domain controller is highly available. If you find that the PDC emulator is overloaded, you might want to make another domain controller the authoritative time source for the forest.

The authoritative time source at the root of a forest acquires its time either by connecting to an installed hardware clock device on the internal network or by connecting to an external time server, which is itself connected to a hardware clock device. Note that if you do not configure the authoritative time server to synchronize time from an external or internal time source, the PDC emulator uses its internal clock and is itself the reliable time source for the forest.

Although a hardware clock, such as a radio or Global Positioning System (GPS) device, is more secure and offers the highest accuracy, you must purchase, install, and maintain the hardware clock. In contrast, when the authoritative time server synchronizes with an external time server, you have good accuracy, and your only cost typically is limited to the cost of network bandwidth used. However, NTP synchronization with an external time source is not authenticated and is therefore less secure than if the time source is inside the network.

> **Tip** All NTP servers need access to UDP port 123. This port must be open for inbound and outbound traffic in order for the Windows Time service to function properly.

Working with W32tm

You can configure settings for the Windows Time service by using the W32tm command-line tool or Group Policy. You can also use W32tm to monitor and troubleshoot the Windows Time service. I'll detail the parameters used with this tool later; let's look at the basics now.

You run W32tm at an elevated command prompt. W32tm works with the local computer by default. You enter **w32tm /register** at a command prompt to register the time service to run as a service and add the default configuration to the registry. You enter **w32tm /unregister** to unregister the time service and remove all configuration information from the registry.

To instruct Windows Time service running on the specified computer to resynchronize its clock and discard accumulated error statistics, you can use the /resync parameter. The basic syntax is as follows.

```
w32tm /resync [/computer:Computer] [/nowait] [/rediscover]
```

Here, *Computer* specifies the computer on which you want to resynchronize time services. If you don't specify a computer, the local computer will resynchronize its time. Use /nowait to have the command return immediately, without waiting for the resynchronization to complete before returning. Use /rediscover to redetect the network configuration and rediscover network sources, and then resynchronize the time.

To monitor time services in a specified domain or for specified computers, or both, you can use the /monitor parameter. The basic syntax is as follows.

```
w32tm /monitor [/domain: DomainName]
[/computers:Computer1,Computer2,…ComputerN] [/threads:N]
```

Here, *DomainName* is the DNS name of the domain to monitor, and computer names are specified by DNS names or IP addresses. If you don't specify a domain or computers to monitor, the current logon domain is used. Be sure to separate computer names by commas, with no spaces. The /threads parameter specifies the number of computers to analyze simultaneously. The default value is 3; the allowed range is 1 to 50.

As part of troubleshooting, you might want to determine the difference between the local computer time and the time on another computer. You can do this by using the /stripchart parameter. You use the /stripchart parameter with the /dataonly parameter to display only the data, without graphics. The basic syntax is as follows.

```
w32tm /stripchart /computer:TargetComputer [/period:RefreshTime]
[/dataonly] [/samples:Count]
```

Here, *TargetComputer* is the designated target computer, *RefreshTime* sets the time between samples, and *Count* sets the number of samples to take. The default time between samples is 2 seconds. Additionally, if you don't set a sample count, samples will be collected until you press Ctrl+C.

To modify the Windows Time service configuration on a target computer, you can use the /config parameter. With this parameter, you use the /update parameter to notify the time service that the configuration has changed, which causes the changes to take effect. You use /reliable:Yes to designate the computer as the reliable time source or /reliable:No to designate the computer as an unreliable time source. Optionally, you can use the /manualpeerlist parameter to specify a manual peer list to use as a space-delimited list of DNS addresses or IP addresses or both. When specifying multiple peers, enclose each value in quote marks.

The syntax for modifying the time service's configuration is as follows.

```
w32tm /config [/computer:TargetComputer] [/update]
[/manualpeerlist:Peers] [/syncfromflags:Flag] [/reliable:(Yes|No)]
```

Here, *TargetComputer* is the computer on which you want to change the configuration of time services, *Peers* lists the manual peers, and *Flag* sets the desired synchronization state. If you don't specify a target computer, the default is the local computer. For the /syncfromflags parameter, enter a value of **manual** when you want the computer to synchronize with peers in the manual peer list. Otherwise, enter a value of **domhier** when you want the computer to synchronize from a domain controller in the domain hierarchy.

Checking the Windows Time Configuration

You use the W32tm command-line tool to configure Windows Time service. To determine whether the computer is configured to synchronize time from the domain or from a manual list of time servers, enter the command **w32tm /query /configuration** at an elevated, administrator command prompt.

In the command output, the Type field identifies the time synchronization method that the client is using. Values you may see include:

- **NoSync**   Indicates that the client does not synchronize time.
- **NTP**   Indicates that the client synchronizes time from an external time source, and the NtpServer field identifies this time source.
- **NT5DS**   Indicates that the client is configured to use the domain hierarchy for its time synchronization.
- **AllSync**   Indicates that the client synchronizes time from any available time source, including domain hierarchy and external time sources.

You can display the time difference between the local computer and a designated time source by entering the following command at an elevated, administrator command prompt.

```
w32tm /stripchart /computer:TimeServer /samples:N /dataonly
```

Here, *TimeServer* sets the Domain Name System (DNS) name or IP address of the time server that you are comparing the local computer's time against, such as *time.windows.com* or *time-nw.nist.gov*, and *N* sets the number of time samples to return. The /stripchart parameter tells W32tm to display the offset between synchronizing computers. This means the results will show the local time and the offset from the designated time server's time.

In Sample 9-1, you compare the local computer's time to the time on the *time.windows.com* time server.

```
w32tm /stripchart /computer:time.windows.com /samples:5 /dataonly
```

SAMPLE 9-1 Positive time offset example.

```
Tracking time.windows.com [207.46.232.182:123].
Collecting 5 samples.
The current time is 9/29/2008 3:12:24 PM.
15:12:24, +16.3861888s
15:12:27, +16.3752471s
15:12:29, +16.3870691s
15:12:31, +16.3837546s
15:12:33, +16.3791971s
```

The output shows the local time is about 16 seconds ahead of time on the time server. If the time is behind, you see a minus sign instead of a plus sign in the offset value. In Sample 9-2, the query on a different computer shows the local time is about 17 seconds behind time on the time server.

SAMPLE 9-2 Negative time offset example.

```
Tracking time.windows.com [207.46.232.182:123].
Collecting 5 samples.
The current time is 9/29/2008 3:08:39 PM.
15:48:39, -17.5644882s
15:48:41, -17.5617493s
15:48:43, -17.5483586s
15:48:45, -17.5705189s
15:48:47, -17.5677411s
```

Before you configure the Windows Time service on any computer, you can use this technique as a basic way to test NTP communications. If the query fails, check the System event log for W32time errors and then refer to the details provided in the More Info link to resolve the problem. If a firewall is blocking access to the Internet time server, you'll need to ensure UDP port 123 is open for outbound and inbound traffic on all routers and firewalls between your authoritative time server and the Internet.

Configuring an Authoritative Time Source

You can configure a domain controller as the authoritative time source and specify the external time sources it should use with W32tm. After you log on or remotely access the domain controller, enter the following command at an elevated command prompt.

```
w32tm /config /manualpeerlist:Peers /syncfromflags:Manual
/reliable:Yes /update
```

Here, you use the /manualpeerlist:*Peers* option to set the external time servers to use for synchronization, /syncfromflags:Manual to specify that the server will synchronize with the manual peer list, /reliable:Yes to specify that the server is the authoritative time server, and /update option to confirm that you want to update the configuration.

When you specify multiple external peers, you use a space as the delimiter and enclose the names of the peers in quotation marks. In the following example, you set the external time servers as *time.windows.com*, *time.nist.gov*, and *time-nw.nist.gov*.

```
w32tm /config /manualpeerlist: "time.windows.com" "time.nist.gov"
"time-nw.nist.gov" /syncfromflags:Manual /reliable:Yes /update
```

You should then synchronize time with an external time server by entering **w32tm /config /update** at an elevated command prompt. After you configure the authoritative time server for the forest, you can log on to a client computer in the forest root domain and check the time service performance by running **w32tm /stripchart**, with the authoritative time server as the computer target in the command. For example, if corpserver65.imaginedlands.com is the authoritative time server, you enter the following.

```
w32tm /stripchart /computer: corpserver65.imaginedlands.com
/samples:5 /dataonly
```

Once you configure another authoritative time server and confirm this designation, you can remove the designation from the PDC emulator. Log on or remotely access the PDC emulator and then enter the following command at an elevated command prompt.

```
w32tm /config /syncfromflags:Domhier /reliable:No /update
```

Here, the /syncfromflags:Domhier option specifies that the PDC emulator's time will be synchronized with the nearest time source in the domain hierarchy, and /reliable:No removes the PDC emulator's status as the reliable time source. You should then attempt to synchronize time with the new authoritative time server by entering **w32tm /config /update** at an elevated command prompt. Because the PDC emulator is in the forest root domain, it will synchronize with a reliable time source in the forest root domain.

Troubleshooting Windows Time Services

Computers that are not joined to a domain may not synchronize time automatically. You can configure these computers to request time from a particular time source, such as a domain controller in a domain. To do this, you must designate a manual time source for the client computer. Enter the command **w32tm /config /manualpeerlist:*Peers* /syncfromflags:Manual /update** where *Peers* is the DNS name or IP address of the domain controller to use as the time source. Next, stop and then start the W32time service by entering **net stop w32time** and then entering **net start w32time**.

If a computer has been manually configured to synchronize from a specific time source and you later want the computer to get its time automatically, you must reconfigure the computer to begin sourcing its time from the domain hierarchy. To do this, log on to the computer and enter the **w32tm /config /syncfromflags:Domhier /update** command at an elevated command prompt. Next, stop and then start the W32time service by entering **net stop w32time** and then entering **net start w32time** at an elevated command prompt.

If you are experiencing problems with the Windows Time service on a client computer, the easiest way to resolve the problem may be to reset the service to its default settings. To restore the local computer's Windows Time service to the default settings, do the following:

1. Open an elevated command prompt.
2. Stop the W32time service by entering **net stop w32time**.
3. Remove the current W32time service settings by entering **w32tm /unregister**.
4. Register the W32time service to use the default settings by entering **w32tm /register**.
5. Start the W32time service by entering **net start w32time**.

Configuring Windows Time Settings in Group Policy

In Group Policy, several policy settings allow you to optimize the way Windows Time service is used. Key policy settings are found under Computer Configuration\Administrative Templates\System\Windows Time Service\Time Providers. These settings include:

- **Enable Windows NTP Client**   When this setting is enabled, this computer can act as an NTP client and synchronize its clock with designated NTP servers.
- **Enable Windows NTP Server**   When this setting is enabled, this computer can act as an NTP server and can service NTP requests from NTP clients.
- **Configure Windows NTP Client**   When you enable this setting, you can set the Windows Time configuration options for clients. Table 9-1 summarizes the available configuration options.

TABLE 9-1 Configuration Settings for Windows NTP Clients

CrossSiteSyncFlags	Determines whether the service chooses synchronization partners outside the domain of the computer. The options and values are 0 (none), 1 (PDC emulator only), or 2 (all). This value is ignored if the NT5DS value is not set. The default value for domain members is 2. The default value for stand-alone clients and servers is 2.
EventLogFlags	Sets the events logged by the Windows Time service.
NtpServer	The peer from which a computer obtains time stamps, consisting of a DNS name or IP address, followed by a comma and a type indicator. The type indicator can be a combination of the following values: 0x1 (special interval), 0x2 (use as fallback only), 0x4 (symmetrical active), and 0x8 (client). There is no default value for this option on domain members. The default value on stand-alone clients and servers is time.microsoft.com,0x1. The default value on the authoritative time server is time.microsoft.com,0x9.
ResolvePeerBackOffMaxTimes	Sets the maximum number of times to double the wait interval when repeated attempts to locate a peer with which to synchronize fail. A value of 0 means that the wait interval is always the minimum. The default value on domain members is 7. The default value on stand-alone clients and servers is 7.
ResolvePeerBackOffMinutes	Sets the initial interval to wait, in minutes, before attempting to locate a peer to synchronize with. The default value on domain members is 15. The default value on stand-alone clients and servers is 15.

SpecialPollInterval	Sets the special poll interval in seconds for manual peers. When the SpecialPollInterval 0x1 flag is enabled for NtpServer, W32time uses this poll interval instead of a poll interval set by the operating system. The default value on domain members is 3,600. The default value on stand-alone clients and servers is 604,800.
Type	Indicates which peers to accept synchronization from. NoSync specifies that the time service does not synchronize with other sources. NTP specifies that the time service synchronizes from the servers specified in the NtpServer registry entry. NT5DS specifies that the time service synchronizes from the domain hierarchy. AllSync specifies that the time service uses all the available synchronization mechanisms. The default value on domain members is NT5DS. The default value on stand-alone clients and servers is NTP.

You can also configure global time services options. Table 9-2 provides detailed information on the most used global settings for the Windows Time service. The related Group Policy settings are under Computer Configuration\Administrative Templates\System\Windows Time Service\Global Configuration Settings. If the Global Configuration Settings policy is enabled, its settings take precedence over local registry settings. The related registry settings are under HKLM\SYSTEM\CurrentControlSet\Services\W32Time\Config. If you change the time services configuration, you can apply the changes by entering the following command at the command prompt.

```
w32tm /config /update
```

TABLE 9-2 Global Configuration Settings for Windows Time Services

AnnounceFlags	Sets the time server classification. A computer must be classified first as a time server to be subsequently classified as a reliable time server. This is why the default flag is 10 (meaning flags 2 and 8 are applied). This setting is used only by domain controllers and determines how the time service is advertised by the Net Logon service. Default value: 10 (8 + 2).
	Accepted values: 10 (default with 8 + 2 flags). 0; the domain controller doesn't advertise time service. 1; the domain controller always advertises time service. 2; the domain controller is a time server and automatically determines whether it should advertise time service. 4; the domain controller will always advertise reliable time service. 8; the domain controller is a reliable time server and automatically determines whether it should advertise time service.
EventLogFlags	Determines the types of events that the time service logs. Default value: 2.
	Accepted values: 1; logs when the time service must make a discontinuous change to the clock. 2; logs when the time service chooses a new time source. 3; logs when the time service hasn't acquired time samples for a period of 1.5 times the maximum poll interval and no longer trusts local clock's accuracy.
FrequencyCorrectRate	Modifies the rate at which the time service corrects (synchronizes) the system clock. The value used is multiplied by the number of clock ticks in 64 seconds to come up with the base gain used to correct system time. Generally, the smaller the value, the more responsive the system is to time changes. However, if the value is too small, the system time can change too frequently to be stable. A value of 3 to 5 is generally a stable range.
	Accepted values: 4 (default).

HoldPeriod	Determines the number of seconds the last consistently read time sample is held. It is essentially designed to prevent frequent time changes caused by inconsistent time samples. During this period, time synchronization (as determined by the FrequencyCorrectRate) and spike detection (for consistent time samples) are switched off to allow for faster time correction (convergence). Accepted values: 5 (default).
LargePhaseOffset	Determines the time offset, in milliseconds, that triggers direct setting of the system clock. If the system clock is off by more than this amount, system time is set directly to the appropriate time rather than using time correction (convergence). Set the offset to a higher value to reduce the likelihood that the system time will be set directly. However, if you do this, it is more likely that bad time samples will be considered good. Accepted values: 128,000 (default).
LocalClockDispersion	Indicates the relative reliability of the local CMOS clock when it's used as a time source for other computers but isn't synchronized with another network time source. The dispersion value is the number of seconds by which the time service should consider the local CMOS clock to be off from the estimated true time at any given time. The higher the reliability by which the local CMOS should be considered, the lower the dispersion value should be set. If the clock is synchronized from a network time source, the dispersion applies to that time source. Accepted values: 10 (default).
MaxAllowedPhaseOffset	Specifies the maximum time correction allowed when convergence is used (rather than direct time setting). If the system clock is off by more than this number of seconds, the time is corrected over multiple convergence intervals. This value is designed to prevent sudden large changes in time. Accepted values: 300 (default for domain controllers); 1 (default for other computers).

MaxNegPhaseCorrection	Specifies the largest negative time correction the time service is allowed to make. If the time is off by more than this amount, the required change is logged rather than corrected. For example, if the clock is set to 5:00 P.M., but it is really 1:59 A.M. on the same day (an earlier time), the required time change will be logged rather than corrected. An administrator will then need to set the time manually. A smaller value is considered more secure because it could prevent malicious time servers from changing system times erroneously. Accepted values: 54,000 (default).
MaxPollInterval	Determines the longest time interval to be used for checking the time. The value is set in units of 2^n seconds, where n is the value for this setting. The default value is 2^{15} (32,768 seconds). The Windows Time service will consider itself to be in an unsynchronized state when 1.5 times the MaxPollInterval has elapsed and it is unable to obtain a time reading from a reliable time server. This value is also referred to as the *maximum clock age*. In NTP, the maximum clock age is 86,400 seconds. Thus, if you set MaxPollInterval to a value greater than 15, the time server may be ignored completely by peers. Accepted values: 15 (default).
MaxPosPhaseCorrection	Specifies the largest positive time correction the time service is allowed to make. If the time is off by more than this amount, the required change is logged rather than corrected. For example, if the clock is set to 1:59 A.M., but it is really 5:00 P.M. on that same day (a later time), the required time change will be logged rather than corrected. An administrator will then need to set the time manually. A smaller value is considered more secure because it could prevent malicious time servers from changing system times erroneously. Accepted values: 54,000 (default).

MinPollInterval	Determines the shortest time interval to be used for checking the time. The value is set in units of 2^n seconds, where n is the value for this setting. The default value for DCs is 2^6 (64 seconds) because time synchronization is more important on DCs, and 2^{10} (1,024 seconds) for other computers, to reduce the number of network accesses. Windows Server 2003 won't poll more frequently than once every 16 seconds, regardless of the MinPollInterval used. Accepted values: 6 (default for DCs); 10 (default for other computers).
PhaseCorrectionRate	Specifies the time correction interval in seconds. This is the interval for time correction when convergence is used. With the default value, the time can be corrected once every second. Accepted values: 1 (default).
PollAdjustFactor	Sets an adjustment interval for polling the time. The value is set in units of 2^n seconds, where n is the value for this setting. Accepted values: 5 (default).
SpikeWatchPeriod	Sets the period in seconds during which suspicious time changes are watched before they are accepted as valid. If you decrease this value, you allow the time server to correct time spikes (sudden changes in time) quickly, but you also increase the likelihood that bad time samples will be considered good. Accepted values: 90 (default).
UpdateInterval	Determines the interval used for phase correction adjustments. The lower the value, the more accurate the time. The higher the value, the more efficient the time sampling. Thus, there is a tradeoff to be made between accuracy and efficiency. On DCs, you want more accuracy and can use more system resources to maintain the system clock because clock accuracy is very important. On other computers, you balance the need for efficiency against the need for accuracy.

Accepted values: 100 (domain controllers); 30,000 (member servers); 360,000 (stand-alone computers).

Using Group Policy, you can configure Windows Time in a domain by completing the following steps:

1. Click Start, click All Programs, and then click Group Policy Management. In Group Policy Management, right-click the policy for the appropriate domain, site, or OU, and then click Edit. This starts the Group Policy Management Editor.

2. If you want to configure global Windows Time settings, expand Computer Configuration, Administrative Templates, System, and Windows Time Service. Double-click Global Configuration Settings, and then select Enabled. Use the fields available to set the desired global settings. Click OK when you are finished.

3. If you want to configure Windows NTP client settings, expand Computer Configuration, Administrative Templates, System, Windows Time Service, and Time Providers. Double-click Configure Windows NTP Client, and then select Enabled. Use the fields available to set the default NTP settings, including the name of the time server to use. Click OK when you are finished.

Backing Up and Recovering Active Directory

Two of the most critically important tasks you'll perform as an administrator are backing up and recovering Active Directory Domain Services. To perform backup and recovery, you must install Windows Server Backup, a feature available for servers running Windows Server. When you install this feature using the Add Feature Wizard in Server Manager, you can run Windows Server Backup from the Administrative Tools menu and access the Wbadmin utility at a command prompt.

Active Directory Backup and Recovery Essentials

In Windows Server, you can perform three types of backup:

- A system state backup, which includes all the files that are required to recover AD DS
- A critical-volumes backup, which includes all the volumes that contain system state files
- A full server backup, which includes all volumes on the server

You can use Windows Server Backup to perform critical-volumes backups and full server backups. You can use the Wbadmin tool at the command line to perform all types of backup, including system state backup.

How often you back up Active Directory depends on the complexity and size of your network. Generally, the more Active Directory objects and domain controllers you have, the more frequently you should back up Active Directory. For example, if you have to recover from the accidental deletion of an organizational unit (OU) by restoring the domain from a backup, you will have to re-create all of the accounts that were created in that OU since the backup was made. To avoid having to re-create accounts and potentially reset large numbers of passwords, you should ensure that recent system state backups are always available to recover related operations that were recently performed.

> **Real World** Computer accounts, including domain controller accounts, change their passwords every 30 days by default. Rolling back the computer password of a domain controller to a former state affects authentication and replication. Changes to user passwords might also be lost as a result of domain controller failure. Because no external record of these changes exists except in AD DS itself, you will find that you need to manually reset computer and user account passwords. Therefore, the more frequently you back up domain controllers, the fewer problems you will encounter if you need to restore the directory. Generally, you will want to create backups of

> each unique directory partition in the forest on two different computers at least daily.

Domain controllers have replication partners with whom they share information. When you have multiple domain controllers in a domain and one fails, the other domain controllers automatically detect the failure and change their replication topology accordingly. You can repair or replace the failed domain controller from a backup. However, the restore doesn't recover Active Directory information stored on the domain controller.

To restore Active Directory on the failed domain controller, you use either a nonauthoritative or authoritative approach. A nonauthoritative restore allows the domain controller to come back online and then get replication updates from other domain controllers. An authoritative restore makes the restored domain controller the authority in the domain, and its data is replicated to other domain controllers.

In most cases, you'll have multiple domain controllers in a domain, giving you flexibility in your disaster-recovery plan. If one of the domain controllers fails, you can install a new domain controller or promote an existing member server so that it can be a domain controller. In either case, the directory on the new domain controller is updated automatically through replication. You could also recover the failed domain controller and then perform a nonauthoritative restore. In this case, you would restore Active Directory on the domain controller and obtain directory updates from other domain controllers in the domain.

In some cases, you might need to perform an authoritative restore of Active Directory. For example, if a large number of objects are deleted from Active Directory, the only way to recover those objects is to use an authoritative restore. In this case, you restore Active Directory on a domain controller and use the recovered data as the master copy of the directory database. This data is then replicated to all other domain controllers.

Real World   When objects have group memberships, recovering the object requires not only restoring the object itself but also restoring group memberships. Group membership is defined by linked attributes on the group object and on the group member object. The member attribute of the group object is a forward link attribute that links to the memberOf attribute of the group member, which can be a user, a computer, or another group.

If you restore a domain controller that is not a global catalog server, only group memberships for groups that are stored in the domain are restored. If you perform the restore on a global catalog server, group memberships in universal groups that are stored in other domains in the forest are also restored. However, restoring memberships in domain local groups that are stored in other domains may require additional recovery steps. (For more information, see the section "Performing an Authoritative Restore of Active Directory" later in this chapter.)

The disaster-recovery strategy you choose for Active Directory might depend on whether you have dedicated or nondedicated domain controllers. When you have dedicated domain controllers that perform no other domain services, you can implement a very simple disaster-recovery procedure for domain controllers. As long as you have multiple domain controllers in each domain, you can restore a failed domain controller by installing a new domain controller and then populating the directory on this new domain controller. You can do so through replication or by recovering the domain controller by using a nonauthoritative restore. You should always back up one or more of the domain controllers, including their system state, so that you always have a current snapshot of Active Directory in the backup archives. If you need to recover from a disaster that has caused all your domain controllers to fail, or if Active Directory has been corrupted, you can recover using an authoritative restore in Directory Services Restore Mode.

When you have nondedicated domain controllers, you should back up the system state whenever you perform a full backup of a domain controller. This stores a snapshot of Active Directory along with the other pertinent system information that can be used to fully recover the domain controller. If a domain controller fails, you can recover it the way you recover any server. You then have the option of restoring the system state data and Active Directory to allow the server to resume operating as a domain controller, by using a nonauthoritative restore in Directory Services Restore Mode. If you need to recover from a disaster that has caused all your domain controllers to fail, or if Active Directory has been corrupted, you also have the option of using an authoritative restore in Directory Services Restore Mode.

> **Real World** When planning backups of Active Directory, you should remember the tombstone lifetime. Active Directory doesn't actually delete objects when you remove them from the directory. Instead, objects are tombstoned (marked for deletion), and the tombstone is replicated to all the other domain controllers. By default, the tombstone lifetime is 180 days, meaning that a tombstone will remain in the directory for 180 days before it is deleted. To ensure that you don't accidentally restore objects that have actually been removed from Active Directory, you are prevented from restoring Active Directory if the backup archive is older than the tombstone lifetime. This means that, by default, you cannot restore a backup of Active Directory that is older than 180 days.

Backing Up and Restoring the System State

With Wbadmin, you can use the Start SystemStateBackup command to create a backup of the system state and the Start SystemStateRecovery command to restore the system state. You must be in the Directory Services Restore Mode to restore the system state on a domain controller.

Whenever you make major changes to the directory environment, you should create a new system state backup. You can back up a server's system state by entering the following at an elevated command prompt.

```
wbadmin start systemstatebackup -backupTarget:VolumeName
```

Here, *VolumeName* is the storage location for the backup, such as X:. By default, the target volume for a system state backup cannot be the same as a source volume that has files that are included in the backup. Therefore, the target volume cannot be any volume that hosts the operating system, the Ntds.dit file, Ntds log files, or the SYSVOL directory.

> **Real World** You can change the target restriction on source volumes by adding the AllowSSBToAnyVolume registry entry to the server under HKLM\SYSTEM\CurrentControlSet\Services\wbengine\SystemStateBackup in the registry. The value type should be set as DWORD. A value of 0 prevents the storing of system state backups on a source volume. A value of 1 allows the storing of system state backups on a source volume. Keep in mind, however, that a backup to the source volume might not work, because the backup can be modified during the backup process.

You can restore a server's system state by entering the following at an elevated command prompt.

```
wbadmin start systemstaterecovery -backupTarget:VolumeName
```

Here, *VolumeName* is the storage location that contains the backup you want to recover, such as X:.

You can use other parameters to manage recovery operations as well. Use the -recoveryTarget parameter to restore to an alternate location. Use the -machine parameter to specify the name of the computer to recover if the original backup location contains backups for multiple computers. Use the -authorSysvol parameter to perform an authoritative restore of the SYSVOL.

The system state contains other system information besides Active Directory. Therefore, any restore of Active Directory includes all that information, and that information will be restored to its previous state as well. If a server's configuration has changed since the backup, the configuration changes will be lost.

> **Note** A system state backup and recovery includes Active Directory–integrated Domain Name System (DNS) zones but does not include

file-based DNS zones. To back up and restore file-based DNS zones, you should back up and recover the entire volume that hosts the files.

Performing a Nonauthoritative Restore of Active Directory

When a domain controller fails, you can restore it the way you restore any other server, except when it comes to Active Directory. With this in mind, first fix the problem that caused the server to fail. After you've restored the server, you can then work to restore Active Directory.

You recover Active Directory by restoring the system state on the domain controller, using a special recovery mode called Directory Services Restore Mode. If you have made changes to Active Directory since the backup, the system state backup will not contain those changes. However, other domain controllers in the domain will have the most recent changes, and the domain controller will be able to obtain those changes through the normal replication process.

When you want to restore Active Directory on a domain controller and have the domain controller get directory updates from other domain controllers, you perform a nonauthoritative restore. A nonauthoritative restore allows the domain controller to come back online and then get replication updates from other domain controllers.

Schedule a full server backup of a domain controller to ensure recovery of the server operating system and application data in the event of a hardware failure. Schedule a separate backup of critical volumes to ensure timely recovery of Active Directory. To guard against unforeseen issues, schedule backups on at least two different domain controllers for each domain, and schedule additional backups on any domain controller with a unique application partition.

A full server backup is a backup of every volume on the server. You can use this type of backup to recover a domain controller onto new hardware. On a domain controller, critical volumes include the boot volume and the volumes that contain operating system files, Active Directory database and log files, and the SYSVOL folders.

You can use critical-volume backups to restore Active Directory on a domain controller. Critical-volume backups can also be restored and copied to transferrable media to install a new domain controller in the same domain.

The procedure to perform a full server or critical-volume recovery of a domain controller is the same as for any server. When you do this, you will also be performing a nonauthoritative restore of Active Directory. After the recovery is complete, restart the domain controller in the standard operations mode and then verify the installation. When you restart the domain controller, Active Directory automatically detects that it has been recovered from a backup. Active Directory will then perform an integrity check and will re-index the database. From that point on, the server can act as a domain controller, and it has a directory database that is current as of the date of the backup. The domain controller then connects to its replication partners and begins updating the database so that any changes since the backup are reflected.

After you log on to the server, check Active Directory and verify that all of the objects that were present in the directory at the time of the backup are restored. The easiest way to confirm this is to browse Active Directory Users And Computers, Active Directory Domains And Trusts, and Active Directory Sites And Services.

Performing an Authoritative Restore of Active Directory

An authoritative restore is used when you need to recover Active Directory to a specific point in time and then replicate the restored data to all other domain controllers. Consider the following example: someone accidentally deleted the Marketing organizational unit (OU) and all the objects it contained. Because the changes have already been replicated to all domain controllers in the domain, the only way to restore the OU and the related objects would be to use an authoritative restore. Similarly, if Active Directory were somehow corrupted, the only way to recover Active Directory fully would be to use an authoritative restore.

When performing authoritative restores, you should consider several significant issues. The first and most important issue has to do with passwords used for computers and Windows NT LAN Manager (NTLM) trusts. These passwords are changed automatically every 7 days. If you perform an authoritative restore of Active Directory, the restored data will contain the passwords that were in use when the backup archive was made. If you monitor the event logs after the restore, you might see related events, or you might hear from users who are experiencing problems accessing resources in the domain.

Computer account passwords allow computers to authenticate themselves in a domain using a computer trust. If a computer password has changed, the computer may not be able to reauthenticate itself in the domain. In this case, you may need to reset the computer account password by right-clicking on the computer account in Active Directory Users And Computers, and then selecting Reset Account. If the password doesn't reset, you might need to remove the computer account from the domain and then add it back.

NTLM trusts are trusts between Active Directory domains and Windows NT domains. If a trust password has changed, the trust between the domains may fail. In this case, you might need to delete the trust and then re-create it, as discussed in Chapter 8.

Another significant issue you should consider when performing an authoritative restore has to do with group membership. After an authoritative restore, problems with group membership can occur for several reasons.

In the first case, an administrator might have updated a group object's membership on a domain controller that has not yet received the restored data. Because of this, the domain controller might replicate the changes to other domain controllers, causing a temporary inconsistency. The changes shouldn't be permanent, however, because when you perform an authoritative restore, the update sequence number (USN) of all restored objects is incremented by 100,000. This ensures that the restored data is authoritative and overwrites any existing data.

Another problem with group membership can occur if group objects contain user accounts that do not currently exist in the domain. In this case, if group objects are replicated before these user objects are, the user accounts that do not currently exist in the domain will be seen as invalid user accounts. As a result, the user accounts will be deleted as group members. When the user accounts are later replicated, the user accounts will not be added back to the groups.

Although there is no way to control which objects are replicated first, there is a way to correct this problem. You must force the domain controller to replicate the group membership list along with the group object. You can do this by creating a temporary user account and adding it to each group that contains user accounts that are currently not valid in the domain. Here's how this would work: You authoritatively restore and then restart the domain controller. The domain controller begins replicating its data to other domain controllers. When this initial replication process finishes, you create a temporary user account and add it to the requisite groups. The group membership list will then be replicated. If any domain controller has removed previously invalid user accounts as members of these groups, the domain controller will return the user accounts to the group.

Global catalog servers are best suited for recovering group memberships after an authoritative restore. If possible, you should perform the authoritative restore on a global catalog server in the domain where the objects were deleted, to recover security principals and group memberships. Global catalog servers store a single, writable domain partition replica and a partial, read-only replica of all other domains in the forest. A partial replica means that the global catalog stores all objects, but with a limited set of attributes on each object.

Specifically, global catalog servers can restore global group memberships for the recovery domain and recover universal group memberships for all domains in the forest. Although memberships in domain local groups in the recovery domain are restored automatically during an authoritative restore, the global catalog does not store the member attribute for domain local group objects from other domains. Therefore, for restored security principals that have memberships in domain local groups in other domains, you must recover these memberships by using the files that Ntdsutil generates during an authoritative restore. Specifically, you must use the .txt file that Ntdsutil generates during an authoritative restore to generate an .ldf file in each additional domain that has groups in which restored security principals have memberships.

> **Tip** Keep in mind that if you can isolate a domain controller (or preferably a global catalog server) in the domain where the deletion occurred, before the server receives replication of the deletion, you might be able to avoid performing a restore from a backup and having to extend the restore process to other domains. To do so, you restart the domain controller in Directory Services Restore Mode and then perform an authoritative restore to recover only the deletions.

You can perform an authoritative restore by completing the following steps:

1. Perform a full server or critical-volume recovery of the domain controller. After you've repaired or rebuilt the server, restart the server and press F8 during startup to access the Windows Advanced Options menu. You must press F8 before the Windows splash screen appears.

2. On the Windows Advanced Options menu, select Directory Services Restore Mode (Windows Domain Controllers Only). Windows will then restart in safe mode without loading Active Directory components.

3. You will next need to choose the operating system you want to start.

4. Log on to the server by using the local Administrator account, with the Directory Services Restore Mode password that was configured on the domain controller when Active Directory was installed.

5. The Desktop prompt warns you that you are running in safe mode, which allows you to fix problems with the server but makes some of your devices unavailable. Click OK.

6. Open an elevated command prompt. Next, at the command prompt, enter **ntdsutil**. This starts the Directory Services Management Tool.

7. At the Ntdsutil prompt, enter **authoritative restore**. You should now be at the Authoritative Restore prompt, where you have the following options:

   - You can authoritatively restore the entire Active Directory database by entering **restore database**. If you restore the entire Active Directory database, a significant amount of replication traffic will be generated throughout the domain and the forest. You should restore the entire database only if Active Directory has been corrupted or there is some other significant reason for doing so.

   - You can authoritatively restore a container and all its related objects (referred to as a subtree) by entering **restore subtree *ObjectDN***, where *ObjectDN* is the distinguished name of the container to restore. For example, if someone accidentally deleted the Marketing OU in the imaginedlands.com domain, you could restore the OU and all the objects it contained by entering the command **restore subtree ou=marketing,dc=imaginedlands,dc=com**.

   - You can authoritatively restore an individual object by entering **restore object *ObjectDN***, where *ObjectDN* is the distinguished name of the object to restore. For example, if someone accidentally deleted the Sales group from the default container for users and groups (cn=users) in the imaginedlands.com domain, you could restore the group by entering the command **restore object cn=sales,cn=users,dc=imaginedlands,dc=com**.

8. When you type a restore command and press Enter, the Authoritative Restore Confirmation dialog box appears, which prompts you to click Yes if you're sure you want to perform the restore action. Click Yes to perform the restore operation.

9. Enter **quit** twice to exit Ntdsutil, and then restart the server.

> **Note** Every object that is restored will have its USN incremented by 100,000. When you are restoring the entire database, you cannot override this behavior, which is necessary to ensure that the data is properly replicated. For subtree and object restores, you can override this behavior by setting a different version increment value, using the Verinc option. For example, if you wanted to restore the Sales group in the imaginedlands.com domain and increment the USN by 500 rather than 100,000, you could do this by entering the command **restore object cn=sales,cn=users,dc=imaginedlands,dc=comverinc 500**.

Restoring Sysvol Data

The Sysvol folder is backed up as part of the system state information and contains critical domain information, including Group Policy objects, Group Policy templates, and scripts used for startup, shutdown, logging on, and logging off. If you restore a domain controller, the Sysvol data will be replicated from other domain controllers. Unlike Active Directory data, Sysvol data is replicated using the File Replication Service (FRS).

When you perform a nonauthoritative restore of a domain controller, the domain controller's Sysvol data is not set as the primary data. This means that the restored Sysvol would not be replicated and could instead be overwritten by Sysvol data from other domain controllers.

When you perform an authoritative restore of a domain controller, the domain controller's Sysvol data is set as the primary data for the domain. This means that the restored Sysvol will be replicated to all other domain controllers. For example, if someone deletes several scripts used for startup or logon, and there are no backups of these scripts, these can be restored by performing an authoritative restore and allowing the restored, authoritative domain controller's Sysvol data to be replicated.

You can prevent a restored, authoritative domain controller's Sysvol data from overwriting the Sysvol on other domain controllers. To do this, you should back up the Sysvol in the desired state on another domain controller before performing the authoritative restore. After you complete the authoritative restore, you can restore the Sysvol in the desired state to the authoritative domain controller.

Recovering by Installing a New Domain Controller

Sometimes you won't be able to or won't want to repair a failed domain controller and may instead elect to install a new domain controller. You can install a new domain controller by promoting an existing member server so that it is a domain controller or by installing a new computer and then promoting it. Either way, the domain controller will get its directory information from another domain controller.

Installing a new domain controller is the easy part. When you finish that, you need to clean up references to the old domain controller so that other computers in the domain don't try to connect to it anymore. You need to remove references to the server in DNS.

To clean up DNS, you need to remove all records for the server in DNS. These include SRV records that designate the computer as a domain controller and any additional records that designate the computer as a global catalog server or PDC emulator, if applicable.

You need to examine any roles that the failed server played. If the failed server was a global catalog server, designate another domain controller as a global catalog server. (For information on designating another server as a global catalog server, see Chapter 5, "Configuring, Maintaining, and Troubleshooting Global Catalog Servers.")

If the failed server held an operations master role, you will need to seize the role and give it to another domain controller (as discussed in Chapter 6, "Configuring, Maintaining, and Troubleshooting Operations Masters"). After seizing the operations master role, you will need to remove the related data from Active Directory. (For more information, refer to the sections "Performing Forced Removal of Domain Controllers" and "Cleaning Up

Metadata in the Active Directory Forest" in Chapter 3, "Deploying Writable Domain Controllers".)

Working with Active Directory Recycle Bin

Active Directory Recycle Bin is available when your Active Directory forest is operating in the Windows Server 2008 R2 mode. The Active Directory Recycle Bin adds an easy-to-use recovery feature for Active Directory objects. With this feature enabled, all link-valued and non-link-valued attributes of a deleted object are preserved, allowing you to restore the object to the same state it was in before it was deleted.

You also can recover objects from the recycle bin without having to initiate an authoritative restore. This differs substantially from the previously available technique, which used an authoritative restore to recover deleted objects from the Deleted Objects container. Previously, when you deleted an object, most of its non-link-valued attributes were cleared and all of its link-valued attributes were removed, which meant that although you could recover a deleted object, it was not restored to its previous state.

Getting Schema Ready for the Recycle Bin

To use Active Directory Recycle Bin, the forest must be using schema for Windows Server 2008 R2 or later. As discussed in "Deploying Windows Server 2008 and R2," you can update schema using Adprep.exe as part of your preparations for deploying Windows Server 2008 R2. When you update schema, every object in the forest is updated with the recycle bin attributes as well. Keep in mind this process is irreversible once it is started.

After you prepare Active Directory schema, you need to upgrade all domain controllers in your Active Directory forest to Windows Server 2008 R2 and then raise the domain and forest functional levels to the Windows Server 2008 R2 level. You'll then be able to enable and access the recycle bin. However, keep in mind, that once the recycle bin has been enabled it cannot be disabled.

With the recycle bin enabled, when an Active Directory object is deleted, the object is put in a state referred to as logically deleted, moved to the Deleted Objects container, and its distinguished name is altered. A deleted object remains in the Deleted Objects container for the period of time set in the delete object lifetime value, which is 180 days by default.

> **Tip** The msDS-deletedObjectLifetime attribute replaces the tombstoneLifetime attribute. However, when msDS-deletedObjectLifetime is set to $null, the lifetime value comes from the tombstoneLifetime. If the tombstoneLifetime is also set to $null, the default value is 180 days.

Enabling Active Directory Recycle Bin

Any account that is a member of Enterprise Admins can be used to enable Active Directory Recycle Bin throughout your Active Directory forest. To enable the recycle bin using Windows PowerShell, complete the following steps:

1. Click Start, click Administrative Tools, right-click Active Directory Module for Windows PowerShell, and then click Run As Administrator. If you do not use the Active Directory Module for Windows PowerShell, you must import the Active Directory cmdlet by using **import-module activedirectory**.

2. At the PowerShell prompt, type the following command, and then press ENTER:

```
Enable-ADOptionalFeature -Identity 'CN=Recycle Bin
Feature,CN=Optional Features,CN=Directory Service,CN=Windows NT,
CN=Services,CN=Configuration,DC=yourdomain,DC=yourdomainsuffix'
-Scope ForestOrConfigurationSet -Target 'ForestRootDomain'
```

> Where DC=*yourdomain*,DC=*yourdomainsuffix* are set as appropriate for your forest root domain and ***ForestRootDomain*** is the full name of the forest root domain, such as:

```
Enable-ADOptionalFeature -Identity 'CN=Recycle Bin
Feature,CN=Optional Features,CN=Directory Service,CN=Windows NT,
CN=Services,CN=Configuration,DC=imaginedlands,DC=.com'
-Scope ForestOrConfigurationSet -Target 'imaginedlands.com'
```

Recovering Deleted Objects

You can recover deleted objects from the Deleted Objects container by using an authoritative restore. The procedure has not changed from previous releases of Windows Server. What has changed, however, is the fact that the objects are restored to their previous state with all link-valued and non-link-valued attributes preserved. To perform an authoritative restore, the domain controller must be in Directory Services Restore Mode.

Rather than using an authoritative restore and taking a domain controller offline, you can recover deleted objects by using the Ldp.exe administration tool or the Active Directory cmdlets for Windows PowerShell. Keep in mind that Active Directory blocks access to an object for a short while after it is deleted. During this time, Active Directory processes the object's link-value table to maintain referential integrity on the linked attribute's values. Active Directory then permits access to the deleted object.

Recovery Using Ldp.exe

You can use Ldp.exe to display the Deleted Objects container and recover a deleted object by following these steps:

1. Click Start, type **Ldp.exe** in the Search box, and then press Enter.
2. On the Options menu, click Controls. In the Controls dialog box, select Return Deleted Objects in the Load Predefined list, and then click OK.
3. Bind to the server that hosts the forest root domain by choosing Bind from the Connection menu. Next, select the Bind type, and then click OK.
4. On the View menu, click Tree. In the Tree View dialog box, use the BaseDN list to select the appropriate forest root domain name, such as DC=ImaginedLands,DC=Com, and then click OK.
5. In the console tree, double-click the root distinguished name and locate the CN=Deleted Objects container.
6. Locate and right-click the Active Directory object that you want to restore, and then click Modify. This displays the Modify dialog box.

7. In the Edit Entry Attribute text box, type **isDeleted**. Don't enter anything in the Values text box.

8. Under Operation, click Delete, and then click Enter.

9. In the Edit Entry Attribute text box, type **distinguishedName**. In Values, type the original distinguished name of this Active Directory object.

10. Under Operation, click Replace. Select the Extended check box, click Enter, and then click Run.

Recovery Using Windows PowerShell

The Active Directory cmdlets for Windows PowerShell can also help you recover deleted objects. You use Get-ADObject to retrieve the object or objects you want to restore, pass that object or objects to Restore-ADObject, and then Restore-ADObject restores the object or objects to the directory database.

> **Note** The Active Directory module is not imported into Windows PowerShell by default. You need to import the module by using **import-module activedirectory**.

Get started by opening an elevated, administrator PowerShell prompt by right-clicking the Windows PowerShell entry on the menu and clicking Run As Administrator. The basic syntax for recovering an object is as follows:

```
Get-ADObject -Filter {ObjectId} -IncludeDeletedObjects |
Restore-ADObject
```

where **ObjectId** is a filter value that identifies the object you want to restore. For example, you could restore a deleted user account by display name or SAM account name as shown in these examples:

```
Get-ADObject -Filter {DisplayName -eq "Tom Smith"}
-IncludeDeletedObjects | Restore-ADObject

Get-ADObject -Filter {SamAccountName -eq "toms"}
-IncludeDeletedObjects | Restore-ADObject
```

Keep in mind nested objects must be recovered from the highest-level of the deleted hierarchy to a live parent container. For example, if you accidentally deleted an OU and all its related accounts, you need to restore the OU before you can restore the related accounts.

The basic syntax for restoring container objects such as an OU is as follows:

```
Get-ADObject -ldapFilter:"(msDS-LastKnownRDN=ContainerID)"
-IncludeDeletedObjects | Restore-ADObject
```

where **ContainerID** is a filter value that identifies the container object you want to restore. For example, you could restore the Managers OU as shown in this example:

```
Get-ADObject -ldapFilter:"(msDS-LastKnownRDN=Managers)"
-IncludeDeletedObjects | Restore-ADObject
```

If the OU contains accounts you also want to restore, you can now restore the accounts by using the technique discussed previously, or you can restore all accounts at the same time. The basic syntax requires that you establish a search base and associate the accounts with their last known parent, as shown here:

```
Get-ADObject -SearchBase "CN=Deleted Objects,ForestRootDN"
-Filter {lastKnownParent -eq "ContainerCN,ForestRootDN"}
-IncludeDeletedObjects | Restore-ADObject
```

where **ForestRootDN** is the distinguished name of the forest root domain, such as DC=ImaginedLands,DC=Com, and **ContainerCN** is the common name of the container, such as OU=Managers or CN=Users. The following example restores all the accounts that were in the Managers OU when it was deleted:

```
Get-ADObject -SearchBase "CN=Deleted Objects,DC=ImaginedLands,DC=com"
-Filter {lastKnownParent -eq "OU=Managers,DC=ImaginedLands,DC=com"}
-IncludeDeletedObjects | Restore-ADObject
```

Maintaining the Directory Database

The Active Directory database is stored in the Ntds.dit file. In addition to this file, the directory service uses log files, which store transactions before they are committed to the database file. Other than regular backup, the directory files require no daily maintenance.

Understanding Directory Database Operations

During regular operation, you will delete objects from AD DS. When you delete an object, free space becomes available in the database. AD DS regularly consolidates this free disk space through a process called online defragmentation, and the consolidated free space is reused when you add new objects to the directory. Although this automatic online defragmentation redistributes and retains free disk space for use by the database, it does not release the disk space to the file system. Therefore, the database size does not shrink, even though objects might have been deleted. This is to be expected, and you do not normally need to correct this.

You may have to manage the database to resolve low disk space, hardware failure, or fragmentation issues caused by deleting objects. To resolve low disk-space issues, you can move the files to a different location permanently or replace the disk on which the database or log files are stored. To resolve a hardware failure, you can replace the disk on which the database or log files are stored. To recover physical disk space, you can defragment the database after bulk deletion of objects or after removing the global catalog.

Bulk deletion or removal of the global catalog can significantly decrease the used space in the directory, but the unused (free) space is not automatically returned to the file system. Although this condition does not affect database operation, it does result in large amounts of free disk space in the database. To decrease the size of the database file by returning free disk space in the database to the file system, you can perform an offline defragmentation of the database. Whereas online defragmentation occurs automatically while AD DS is running, offline defragmentation requires stopping AD DS or taking the domain controller offline and then using the Ntdsutil.exe command-line tool to perform the procedure.

Checking for Free Space in the Directory Database

Garbage collection in Active Directory Domain Services (AD DS) is the process of removing deleted objects from the directory database. This process results in unused (free) disk space in the directory database. By default, this free space is not returned to the file system or reported in Event Viewer. To see the amount of free disk space that could be made available to the file system by offline defragmentation, you can change the garbage-collection logging level so that the free disk space is reported in the Directory Service event log. After you change the logging level, you can check the Directory Service event log for Event ID 1646. This event reports the amount of disk space that you can recover by performing offline defragmentation.

The Registry entry you use to control garbage-collection logging is Garbage Collection under HKEY_LOCAL_MACHINE\SYSTEM\CurrentControlSet\Services\NTDS\Diagnostics. When this key entry has a value of 0, garbage-collection logging is disabled. When this key entry has a value of 1, garbage-collection logging is enabled. You can determine the current value for this key entry by entering the following command at a command prompt.

```
reg query HKLM\SYSTEM\CurrentControlSet\Services\NTDS\Diagnostics
```

The key path can also include the UNC path of a remote computer that you want to examine, such as \\CorpServer15 or \\192.168.16.125. In the following example, you examine the NTDS configuration on Server26.

```
reg query
\\Server26\HKLM\SYSTEM\CurrentControlSet\Services\NTDS\Diagnostics
```

To change the garbage-collection logging level, follow these steps:

1. Log on locally or remotely to the domain controller you want to configure. Start the Registry Editor by clicking Start, typing **regedit** in the Search box, and then pressing Enter.

2. In Registry Editor, navigate to HKEY_LOCAL_MACHINE\SYSTEM\CurrentControlSet\Services\NTDS\Diagnostics.

3. Double-click Garbage Collection. In the Value data box, enter **1**, and then click OK. If you later want to disable garbage-collection logging, repeat this procedure and enter a value of **0**.

Performing Offline Defragmentation

Performing offline defragmentation creates a new, compacted version of the database file in a different location. Although this location can be on a network drive, it is best to perform this procedure on a local file system if possible. You can use locally attached external storage devices to provide additional disk space for defragmentation of the database. After you compact the directory file to the temporary location, you can copy the compacted directory file back to its original location.

The source drive on which the database currently resides should have at least 15 percent of the current size of the directory database file for temporary storage during the index rebuild process. The destination drive for the compacted file should have free space equivalent to at least the current size of the database. Therefore, if the source and destination path are on the same drive, you should have free space equivalent to at least 115 percent of the current size of the directory database file.

Before you perform offline defragmentation of the directory database file, you should make a copy of the file. If the compaction of the database does not work properly, you can then easily restore the database by copying back the copy of the file that you made. Do not delete this copy of the file until you have verified that the AD DS starts and runs properly.

You can perform offline defragmentation of the directory database by following these steps:

1. Stop AD DS. At an elevated, administrator command prompt, enter the following command: **net stop ntds**. When prompted, enter **Y** to stop additional services.

> **Note** For Windows Server 2003, you restart the domain controller in Directory Services Restore Mode (DSRM) to stop AD DS. Then you start the domain controller in normal mode to start AD DS.

2. At the elevated command prompt, enter **ntdsutil**.
3. At the Ntdsutil prompt, enter **activate instance ntds**.
4. At the Ntdsutil prompt, enter **files**.
5. If you are compacting the database to a local drive, at the File Maintenance prompt, enter **compact to *LocalDirectoryPath*** where *LocalDirectoryPath* is the path to a location on the local computer that includes the drive path, such as D:\Database. If the path contains any spaces, enclose the entire path in quotation marks (for example, **compact to "c:\DbFolder"**). If the directory does not exist, Ntdsutil.exe creates the directory and then creates in that location the file named Ntds.dit.
6. If you mapped a drive to a shared folder on a remote computer, type the drive letter only; for example, **compact to X:\.**
7. If defragmentation completes successfully, enter **quit** to quit the File Maintenance prompt. Enter **quit** again to quit Ntdsutil.exe.
8. If defragmentation has errors, copy the original version of the Ntds.dit file to the original database location, and repeat the offline defragmentation procedure.
9. If defragmentation succeeds with no errors, you can:

▪ Delete all the log files in the log directory by entering the following command: **del *PathToLogFiles**.log**. Be sure to include the drive path and the full file path. Ntdsutil provides the correct path to the log files in the on-screen instructions. Do not delete the copy of the Ntds.dit file until you have at least verified that the domain controller starts properly.

▪ Manually copy the compacted database file to the original location by entering the following command: **copy "*TemporaryPath*\Ntds.dit"**

"OriginalPath\Ntds.dit". Ntdsutil provides the correct paths to the temporary and original locations of the Ntds.dit file in the on-screen instructions.

Once you successfully defragment the database, you should check the integrity of the compacted database file. To do this, follow these steps:

1. At an elevated command prompt, enter **ntdsutil**.
2. At the Ntdsutil prompt, enter **files**.
3. At the File Maintenance prompt, enter **integrity**.
4. If the integrity check fails, an error likely occurred during the copy operation. Manually copy the compacted database file to the original location again, and then repeat the integrity check.
5. If the integrity check succeeds, enter **quit** to quit the File Maintenance prompt, and then enter **quit** again to quit Ntdsutil.exe.
6. Restart AD DS. For Windows Server 2008 or later, at the command prompt, enter **net start ntds**. For Windows Server 2003, restart the server in normal mode.

If errors appear when you restart AD DS, stop AD DS by entering **net stop ntds**. Enter **Y** to stop additional services. Use Event Viewer to identify errors logged in the Directory Service log. If you find Event ID 1046 "The Active Directory database engine caused an exception with the following parameters" or Event ID 1168 "Internal error: An Active Directory error has occurred," you must restore from backup media.

> **Real World** If the integrity check repeatedly fails, you may need to revert to the original copy of the database file. You can also attempt to perform semantic database analysis with fixup to resolve the problem. To do this, follow these steps:
>
> 1. At an elevated command prompt, enter **ntdsutil**.
>
> 2. At the Ntdsutil prompt, enter **activate instance ntds**.
>
> 3. At the Ntdsutil prompt, enter **semantic database analysis**.
>
> 4. At the Semantic Checker prompt, enter **verbose on**.
>
> 5. At the Semantic Checker prompt, enter **go fixup**.
>
> 6. If errors are reported during the semantic database analysis Go Fixup phase, you'll need to perform directory database recovery. Enter **files** to go to the File Maintenance prompt, and then enter **recover**.
>
> 7. If semantic database analysis with fixup succeeds, at the Semantic Checker prompt, enter **quit**, and then enter **quit** again to close Ntdsutil.exe.
>
> 8. Restart AD DS. At the command prompt, enter **net start ntds**.

Moving the Directory Database

In some cases, you may need to move the Active Directory database file and logs. For example, if the physical disk on which the database or log files are stored requires upgrading or maintenance, you will need to move the files. If the database file or logs are causing the disk to run low on free space, you will need to free up space or move the file or logs to a disk that has more space.

If the path to the database file or log files will change as a result of moving the files, you must use Ntdsutil.exe to move the files so that the registry is updated with the new path. Even if you are moving the files only temporarily, you should use Ntdsutil.exe to move files locally so that the registry remains current. When you finish, you should perform a system state backup or a critical-volume backup to ensure you can recover the directory in the new location. You should also verify that the correct permissions are applied on the destination folder after the move. If necessary, modify the permissions to protect the files.

Before you attempt to move the database file or logs, you should determine their size and location. By default, the database file and associated log files are stored in the %SystemRoot%\NTDS directory. If you change to the appropriate directory, you can use the Dir command to list the contents and determine the size of the Ntds.dit file and .log files.

With AD DS offline, you also can examine the database and log files. To do this, follow these steps:

1. Stop AD DS. At an elevated, administrator command prompt, enter the following command: net stop ntds. When prompted, enter Y to stop additional services.

    > **Note** In Windows Server 2003, restart the domain controller in Directory Services Restore Mode (DSRM) to stop AD DS. Then start the domain controller in normal mode to start AD DS.

2. At the elevated command prompt, enter **ntdsutil**.

3. At the Ntdsutil prompt, enter **activate instance ntds**.

4. At the Ntdsutil prompt, enter **files**.

5. At the File Maintenance prompt, enter **info**. As shown in the following example, the output indicates the free space on drives, storage locations for directory data, and the space used by directory files.

```
Drive Information:

        C:\ NTFS (Fixed Drive  ) free(142.7 Gb) total(232.8 Gb)
        D:\ NTFS (Fixed Drive  ) free(112.6 Gb) total(232.8 Gb)

DS Path Information:

   Database   : D:\Windows\NTDS\ntds.dit - 1423.1 Mb
   Backup dir : D:\Windows\NTDS\dsadata.bak
   Working dir: D:\Windows\NTDS
```

```
Log dir    : D:\Windows\NTDS - 40.0 Mb total
                edbres00002.jrs - 10.0 Mb
                edbres00001.jrs - 10.0 Mb
                edb00001.log - 10.0 Mb
                edb.log - 10.0 Mb
```

6. Enter **quit** to quit the File Maintenance prompt. Enter **quit** again to quit Ntdsutil.exe.

7. Restart AD DS. At the command prompt, enter **net start ntds**.

When you move the directory files to a local folder on the domain controller, you can move them permanently or temporarily. For example, you could move files to a temporary destination if you need to reformat the original location, or you could move the directory files to a permanent location if you have additional space on another disk. When you move files temporarily, you can use the same procedure to move the files back. Ntdsutil updates the registry for you when you move files locally.

To move the directory database and log files to a local drive, follow these steps:

1. Stop AD DS. At an elevated, administrator command prompt, enter the following command: **net stop ntds**. When prompted, enter **Y** to stop additional services.

> **Note** For Windows Server 2003, you restart the domain controller in Directory Services Restore Mode (DSRM) to stop AD DS. Then you start the domain controller in normal mode to start AD DS.

2. At the elevated command prompt, change directories to the current location of the directory database file (Ntds.dit) or the log files, whichever you are moving.

3. Run the Dir command, and note the current size and location of the Ntds.dit file.

4. At the elevated command prompt, enter **ntdsutil**.

5. At the Ntdsutil prompt, enter **activate instance ntds**.

6. At the Ntdsutil prompt, enter **files**.

7. To move the Ntds.dit file, enter **move db to *DirPath*** where *DirPath* specifies the path to the new location and also specifies the drive designator. If the directory does not exist, Ntdsutil.exe creates it.

8. To move the log files, enter **move logs to *DirPath*** where *DirPath* specifies the path to the new location and also specifies the drive designator. If the directory does not exist, Ntdsutil.exe creates it.

9. When the move operation is complete, enter **quit** to quit the File Maintenance prompt. Enter **quit** again to quit Ntdsutil.exe.

10. At the elevated command prompt, change to the destination directory and run the Dir command. Confirm that the file or files were copied. If you copied the Ntds.dit file, confirm that it is the right size.

11. If you are moving the database file or log files temporarily, you can now perform any required updates to the original drive. After you update the drive, repeat steps 4 through 10 to move the files back to the original location.

12. If you are moving the database file or log files permanently, keep in mind that Ntdsutil updates the registry automatically when you move files locally. You should use Windows Explorer to check the permissions on the destination folder. Verify that the Administrators group has Allow Full Control, that SYSTEM has Allow Full Control, that the Include Inheritable Permissions From This Object's Parent check box is cleared, and that No Deny permissions are selected.

Note If Include Inheritable Permissions From This Object's Parent is selected, click Edit, clear the setting, and then click OK. When you are prompted, click Copy to copy previously inherited permissions to this object.

---

13. Once you successfully move files and check permissions as necessary, check the integrity of the database. The procedure is the same as the one discussed in the previous section, "Performing Offline Defragmentation."

14. Restart AD DS. At the command prompt, enter **net start ntds**.

If you do not have space on the domain controller to move the files temporarily, you can copy files to a remote share, but you must then restore the files to their original locations. To copy files to a remote share, follow these steps:

1. Stop AD DS. At an elevated, administrator command prompt, enter the following command: **net stop ntds**. When prompted, enter **Y** to stop additional services.

2. At the elevated command prompt, change directories to the current location of the directory database file (Ntds.dit) or the log files, whichever you are moving.

3. Run the Dir command, and note the current size and location of the Ntds.dit file.

4. Use the Xcopy command to copy the database, to copy the log files, or to copy both to the remote location.

5. When Xcopy completes, change drives to the remote directory and run the Dir command to compare the file sizes to the original file sizes.

6. You can now perform any required updates to the original drive. After you update the drive, xcopy the database or log files or both to their original locations.

7. Once you successfully move files, check the integrity of the database. The procedure is the same as the one discussed in the previous section, "Performing Offline Defragmentation."

8. Restart AD DS. At the command prompt, enter **net start ntds**.

Appendix A. Active Directory Utilities Reference

In this book, I've discussed many command-line tools and scripts. This appendix is intended to provide a quick reference to the syntax and usage of these tools as well as other commands and utilities that you may find helpful when working with Active Directory. These tools are listed alphabetically by tool name. Unless otherwise noted, these tools work the same way on both Windows Server and Windows desktop operating systems. In addition, if a tool is not included in both server and desktop operating systems, the source of the tool is listed, such as "Windows Server 2008 or later only" for the tools available only on Windows Server 2008 or later by default.

DCDIAG

Performs diagnostics testing on a domain controller.

```
dcdiag [/s:Server[:LDAPPort]] [/u [Domain\]UserName]
[/p {Password | * | ""}] [/h | /?] [/xsl] [/a | /e]
[/I] [/fix] [/c] [/q | /v] [/n:NamingContext]
[/skip:TestName] [/test:TestName] [/f:TextLogName]
[/x:XmlLogName]
```

This command applies only to Windows Server 2003 and later.

DCGPOFIX

Restores default group policy objects.

```
dcgpofix [/ignoreschema]
[/target: {domain | dc | both}]
```

This command applies only to Windows Server 2003 and later.

DISKPART

Invokes a text-mode command interpreter so that you can manage disks, partitions, and volumes using a separate command prompt and commands that are internal to DISKPART.

```
diskpart
```

DSADD COMPUTER

Creates a computer account in the Active Directory directory service.

```
dsadd computer ComputerDN [-samid SAMName]
[-desc Description] [-loc Location]
[-memberof GroupDN ...] [{-s Server | -d Domain}]
[-u UserName] [-p {Password | *}] [-q]
[{-uc | -uco | -uci}]
```

This command is available in business and enterprise editions of Windows desktop operating systems if Remote Server Administration Tools Pack has been installed.

DSADD GROUP

Creates a group account in Active Directory.

```
dsadd group GroupDN [-secgrp {yes | no}]
[-scope {l | g | u}] [-samid SAMName]
[-desc Description] [-memberof Group ...]
[-members Member ...] [{-s Server | -d Domain}]
[-u UserName] [-p {Password | *}] [-q]
[{-uc | -uco | -uci}]
```

This command is available in business and enterprise editions of Windows desktop operating systems if Remote Server Administration Tools Pack has been installed.

DSADD USER

Creates a user account in Active Directory.

```
dsadd user UserDN [-samid SAMName] [-upn UPN]
[-fn FirstName] [-mi Initial]    [-ln LastName]
[-display DisplayName] [-empid EmployeeID]
[-pwd {Password | *}] [-desc Description]
[-memberof Group ...] [-office Office]
[-tel PhoneNumber] [-email EmailAddress]
[-hometel HomePhoneNumber] [-pager PagerNumber]
```

```
[-mobile CellPhoneNumber] [-fax FaxNumber]
[-iptel IPPhoneNumber] [-webpg WebPage]
[-title Title] [-dept Department] [-company Company]
[-mgr Manager] [-hmdir HomeDirectory]
[-hmdrv DriveLetter:] [-profile ProfilePath]
[-loscr ScriptPath] [-mustchpwd {yes | no}]
[-canchpwd {yes | no}] [-reversiblepwd {yes | no}]
[-pwdneverexpires {yes | no}] [-acctexpires NumberOfDays]
[-disabled {yes | no}]
[{-s Server | -d Domain}] [-u UserName]
[-p {Password | *}] [-q] [{-uc | -uco | -uci}]
[-fnp FirstNamePhonetic] [-lnp LastNamePhonetic]
[-displayp DisplayNamePhonetic]
```

This command is available in business and enterprise editions of Windows desktop operating systems if Remote Server Administration Tools Pack has been installed.

DSGET COMPUTER

Displays the properties of a computer account using one of two syntaxes. The syntax for viewing the properties of multiple computers is

```
dsget computer ComputerDN ... [-dn] [-samid] [-sid]
[-desc] [-loc] [-disabled] [{-s Server | -d Domain}]
[-u UserName] [-p {Password | *}] [-c] [-q] [-l]
[{-uc | -uco | -uci}] [-part PartitionDN [-qlimit]
[-qused]]
```

The syntax for viewing the membership information of a single computer is

```
dsget computer ComputerDN [-memberof [-expand]]
[{-s Server | -d Domain}] [-u UserName]
[-p {Password | *}] [-c] [-q] [-l]
[{-uc | -uco | -uci}]
```

This command is available in business and enterprise editions of Windows desktop operating systems if Remote Server Administration Tools Pack has been installed.

DSGET GROUP

Displays the properties of group accounts using one of two syntaxes. The syntax for viewing the properties of multiple groups is

```
dsget group GroupDN ... [-dn] [-samid] [-sid]
[-desc] [-secgrp] [-scope] [{-s Server | -d Domain}]
[-u UserName] [-p {Password | *}] [-c] [-q] [-l]
[{-uc | -uco | -uci}] [-part PartitionDN [-qlimit]
[-qused]]
```

The syntax for viewing the group membership information for an individual group is

```
dsget group GroupDN [{-memberof | -members}
[-expand]] [{-s Server | -d Domain}] [-u UserName]
[-p {Password | *}] [-c] [-q] [-l]
[{-uc | -uco | -uci}]
```

This command is available in business and enterprise editions of Windows desktop operating systems if Remote Server Administration Tools Pack has been installed.

DSGET SERVER

Displays the various properties of domain controllers using any of three syntaxes. The syntax for displaying the general properties of a specified domain controller is

```
dsget server ServerDN ... [-dn] [-desc] [-dnsname]
[-site] [-isgc] [{-s Server | -d Domain}]
[-u UserName] [-p {Password | *}] [-c]
[-q] [-l] [{-uc | -uco | -uci}]
```

The syntax for displaying a list of the security principals who own the largest number of directory objects on the specified domain controller is

```
dsget server ServerDN [{-s Server | -d Domain}]
[-u UserName] [-p {Password | *}] [-c] [-q] [-l]
[{-uc | -uco | -uci}]
[-topobjowner NumberToDisplay]
```

The syntax for displaying the distinguished names of the directory partitions on the specified server is

```
dsget server ServerDN [{-s Server | -d Domain}]
[-u UserName] [-p {Password | *}] [-c] [-q] [-l]
[{-uc | -uco | -uci}] [-part]
```

This command is available in business and enterprise editions of Windows desktop operating systems if Remote Server Administration Tools Pack has been installed.

DSGET USER

Displays the properties of user accounts using one of two syntaxes. The syntax for viewing the properties of multiple users is

```
dsget user UserDN ... [-dn] [-samid] [-sid] [-upn]
[-fn] [-mi] [-ln] [-display] [-fnp] [-lnp]
[-displayp] [-effectivepso] [-empid] [-desc]
[-office] [-tel] [-email] [-hometel] [-pager]
[-mobile] [-fax] [-iptel] [-webpg] [-title] [-dept]
[-company] [-mgr] [-hmdir] [-hmdrv] [-profile]
[-loscr] [-mustchpwd] [-canchpwd] [-pwdneverexpires]
[-disabled] [-acctexpires] [-reversiblepwd]
[{-uc | -uco | -uci}] [-part PartitionDN [-qlimit]
[-qused]] [{-s Server | -d Domain}] [-u UserName]
[-p {Password | *}] [-c] [-q] [-l]
```

The syntax for viewing the group membership for users is

```
dsget user UserDN [-memberof [-expand]]
[{-uc | -uco | -uci}] [{-s Server | -d Domain}]
[-u UserName] [-p {Password | *}] [-c]
[-q] [-l]
```

This command is available in business and enterprise editions of Windows desktop operating systems if Remote Server Administration Tools Pack has been installed.

DSMGMT

Invokes a text-mode command interpreter so that you can manage directory services using a separate command prompt and commands that are internal to DSMGMT.

```
dsmgmt
```

DSMOD COMPUTER

Modifies attributes of one or more computer accounts in the directory.

```
dsmod computer ComputerDN ... [-desc Description]
[-loc Location] [-disabled {yes | no}] [-reset]
[{-s Server | -d Domain}] [-u UserName]
[-p {Password | *}] [-c] [-q]
[{-uc | -uco | -uci}]
```

This command is available in business and enterprise editions of Windows desktop operating systems if Remote Server Administration Tools Pack has been installed.

DSMOD GROUP

Modifies attributes of one or more group accounts in the directory.

```
dsmod group GroupDN ... [-samid SAMName]
[-desc Description] [-secgrp {yes | no}]
[-scope {l | g | u}] [{-addmbr | -rmmbr | -chmbr} MemberDN ...]
[{-s Server | -d Domain}]
[-u UserName] [-p {Password | *}] [-c] [-q]
[{-uc | -uco | -uci}]
```

This command is available in business and enterprise editions of Windows desktop operating systems if Remote Server Administration Tools Pack has been installed.

DSMOD SERVER

Modifies properties of a domain controller.

```
dsmod server ServerDN ... [-desc Description]
[-isgc {yes | no}] [{-s Server | -d Domain}]
[-u UserName] [-p {Password | *}] [-c] [-q]
[{-uc | -uco | -uci}]
```

This command is available in business and enterprise editions of Windows desktop operating systems if Remote Server Administration Tools Pack has been installed.

DSMOD USER

Modifies attributes of one or more user accounts in the directory.

```
dsmod user UserDN ... [-upn UPN] [-fn FirstName]
[-mi Initial] [-ln LastName] [-display DisplayName]
[-empid EmployeeID] [-pwd {Password | *}]
[-desc Description] [-office Office]
[-tel PhoneNumber] [-email EmailAddress]
[-hometel HomePhoneNumber] [-pager PagerNumber]
[-mobile CellPhoneNumber] [-fax FaxNumber]
[-iptel IPPhoneNumber] [-webpg WebPage]
[-title Title] [-dept Department] [-company Company]
[-mgr Manager] [-hmdir HomeDirectory]
[-hmdrv DriveLetter:] [-profile ProfilePath]
[-loscr ScriptPath] [-mustchpwd {yes | no}]
[-canchpwd {yes | no}] [-reversiblepwd {yes | no}]
[-pwdneverexpires {yes | no}]
[-acctexpires NumberOfDays] [-disabled {yes | no}]
[{-s Server | -d Domain}] [-u UserName]
[-p {Password | *}] [-c] [-q] [{-uc | -uco | -uci}]
[-fnp FirstNamePhonetic] [-lnp LastNamePhonetic]
[-displayp DisplayNamePhonetic]
```

This command is available in business and enterprise editions of Windows desktop operating systems if Remote Server Administration Tools Pack has been installed.

DSMOVE

Moves or renames Active Directory objects.

```
dsmove ObjectDN [-newname NewName]
[-newparent ParentDN] [{-s server | -d Domain}]
[-u UserName] [-p {Password | *}] [-q]
[{-uc | -uco | -uci}]
```

This command is available in business and enterprise editions of Windows desktop operating systems if Remote Server Administration Tools Pack has been installed.

DSQUERY COMPUTER

Searches for computer accounts matching criteria.

```
dsquery computer [{StartNode | forestroot | domainroot}]
[-o {dn | rdn | samid}]
[-scope {subtree | onelevel | base}] [-name Name]
[-desc Description] [-samid SAMName]
[-inactive NumberOfWeeks] [-stalepwd NumberOfDays]
[-disabled] [{-s server | -d Domain}]
[-u UserName] [-p {Password | *}] [-q]    [-r] [-gc]
[-limit NumberOfObjects] [{-uc | -uco | -uci}]
```

This command is available in business and enterprise editions of Windows desktop operating systems if Remote Server Administration Tools Pack has been installed.

DSQUERY CONTACT

Searches for contacts matching criteria.

```
dsquery contact [{StartNode | forestroot | domainroot}] [-o {dn |
rdn}] [-scope {subtree | onelevel | base}] [-name Name] [-desc
Description]
[{-s Server | -d Domain}] [-u UserName]
[-p {Password | *}] [-q] [-r] [-gc]
[-limit NumberOfObjects] [{-uc | -uco | -uci}]
```

This command is available in business and enterprise editions of Windows desktop operating systems if Remote Server Administration Tools Pack has been installed.

DSQUERY GROUP

Searches for group accounts matching criteria.

```
dsquery group [{StartNode | forestroot | domainroot}] [-o {dn | rdn |
samid}]
[-scope {subtree | onelevel | base}]
[-name Name] [-desc Description] [-samid SAMName]
[{-s Server | -d Domain}] [-u UserName]
[-p {Password | *}] [-q] [-r] [-gc]
[-limit NumberOfObjects] [{-uc | -uco | -uci}]
```

This command is available in business and enterprise editions of Windows desktop operating systems if Remote Server Administration Tools Pack has been installed.

DSQUERY PARTITION

Searches for Active Directory partitions matching criteria.

```
dsquery partition [-o {dn | rdn}] [-part Filter]
[-desc Description] [{-s Server | -d Domain}]
[-u UserName] [-p {Password | *}] [-q] [-r]
[-limit NumberOfObjects] [{-uc | -uco | -uci}]
```

This command is available in business and enterprise editions of Windows desktop operating systems if Remote Server Administration Tools Pack has been installed.

DSQUERY QUOTA

Searches for disk quotas matching criteria.

```
dsquery quota {domainroot | ObjectDN} [-o {dn | rdn}] [-acct Name] [-
qlimit Filter] [-desc Description] [{-s Server | -d Domain}]
[-u UserName] [-p {Password | *}] [-q] [-r]
[-limit NumberOfObjects] [{-uc | -uco | -uci}]
```

This command is available in business and enterprise editions of Windows desktop operating systems if Remote Server Administration Tools Pack has been installed.

DSQUERY SERVER

Searches for domain controllers matching criteria.

```
dsquery server [-o {dn | rdn}] [-forest]
[-domain DomainName] [-site SiteName] [-name Name]
[-desc Description] [-hasfsmo {schema | name | infr | pdc | rid}]
[-isgc] [-isreadonly] [{-s Server | -d Domain}] [-u UserName] [-p
{Password | *}] [-q] [-r] [-gc] [-limit NumberOfObjects] [{-uc | -uco
| -uci}]
```

This command is available in business and enterprise editions of Windows desktop operating systems if Remote Server Administration Tools Pack has been installed.

DSQUERY SITE

Searches for Active Directory sites matching criteria.

```
dsquery site [-o {dn | rdn}] [-name Name]
[-desc Description] [{-s Server | -d Domain}]
[-u UserName] [-p {Password | *}] [-q] [-r] [-gc]
[-limit NumberOfObjects] [{-uc | -uco | -uci}]
```

This command is available in business and enterprise editions of Windows desktop operating systems if Remote Server Administration Tools Pack has been installed.

DSQUERY USER

Searches for user accounts matching criteria.

```
dsquery user [{StartNode | forestroot | domainroot}]
[-o {dn | rdn | upn | samid}] [-scope {subtree | onelevel | base}]
[-name Name] [-namep NamePhonetic]
[-desc Description] [-upn UPN] [-samid SAMName]
```

```
[-inactive NumberOfWeeks] [-stalepwd NumberOfDays]
[-disabled] [{-s Server | -d Domain}] [-u UserName]
[-p {Password | *}] [-q] [-r] [-gc] [-limit NumberOfObjects]
[{-uc | -uco | -uci}]
```

This command is available in business and enterprise editions of Windows desktop operating systems if Remote Server Administration Tools Pack has been installed.

DSQUERY *

Searches for any Active Directory objects matching criteria.

```
dsquery * [{StartNode | forestroot | domainroot}]
[-scope {subtree | onelevel | base}] [-filter LDAPFilter]
[-attr {AttributeList | *}] [-attrsonly]
[-l] [{-s Server | -d Domain}] [-u UserName]
[-p {Password | *}] [-q] [-r] [-gc]
[-limit NumberOfObjects] [{-uc | -uco | -uci}]
```

This command is available in business and enterprise editions of Windows desktop operating systems if Remote Server Administration Tools Pack has been installed.

DSRM

Deletes Active Directory objects.

```
dsrm ObjectDN ... [-subtree [-exclude]] [-noprompt]
[{-s Server | -d Domain}] [-u UserName]
[-p {Password | *}] [-c] [-q] [{-uc | -uco | -uci}]
```

This command is available in business and enterprise editions of Windows desktop operating systems if Remote Server Administration Tools Pack has been installed.

ESENTUTL

Manages Extensible Storage Engine (ESE) databases, including those used by Active Directory Domain Services (AD DS).

Syntax for defragmentation:

```
esentutl /d DatabaseName /s [StreamingFileName] /t [TempDBName]
/f [TempStreamingFileName] /i /p /b [BackupFileName] /8 /o
```

Syntax for recovery:

```
esentutl /r LogFileBaseName /l [LogDirectory] /s
[SystemFilesDirectory] /i /t /u [Log] /d [DBFileDirectory] /n
Path1[:Path2] /8 /o
```

Syntax for checking integrity:

```
esentutl /g DatabaseName /s [StreamingFileName] /t [TempDBName]
/f [TempStreamingFileName] /i /8 /o
```

Syntax for performing a checksum:

```
esentutl /k FileToCheck /s [StreamingFileName] /t [TempDBName]
/p PauseRateForThrottling /e /i /8 /o
```

Syntax for repair:

```
esentutl /p DatabaseName /s [StreamingFileName] /t [TempDBName]
/f [ReportPrefix] /i /g /createstm /8 /o
```

Syntax for dumping a file:

```
esentutl /m [h|k|l|m|s|u] FileName /p PageNumber /s
[StreamingFileName] /t TableName /v /8 /o
```

Syntax for copying a file:

```
esentutl /y SourceFile /d DestinationFile /o
```

GET-EVENTLOG

A Windows PowerShell command for displaying information about event logs or entries stored in event logs.

```
get-eventlog -list
```

```
get-eventlog [-logname] LogName [-newest NN]
```

GET-PROCESS

A Windows PowerShell command for displaying information about running processes.

```
get-process -id [ID1,ID2,...]

get-process -inputobject ProcessName1, ProcessName2,...

get-process [-name] [ProcessName1, ProcessName2,...]
```

GET-SERVICE

A Windows PowerShell command for displaying information about configured services.

```
get-service [-displayname [ServiceName1, ServiceName2,...]]
 -include [ServiceName1, ServiceName2,...]
 -exclude [ServiceName1, ServiceName2,...]

get-service [-name] [ServiceName1, ServiceName2,...]
 -include [ServiceName1, ServiceName2,...]
 -exclude [ServiceName1, ServiceName2,...]

get-service [-inputobject ServiceName1, ServiceName2,...]
 [-include [ServiceName1, ServiceName2,...]
 [-exclude [ServiceName1, ServiceName2,...]
```

GPUPDATE

Forces a background refresh of group policy.

```
gpupdate [/target:{computer | user}] [/force] [/wait:<Value>]
[/logoff] [/boot] [/sync]
```

IPCONFIG

Displays TCP/IP configuration.

```
ipconfig [/allcompartments] {/all}

ipconfig [/release [Adapter]
  | /renew [Adapter]
  | /release6 [Adapter] | /renew6 [Adapter]]

ipconfig /flushdns | /displaydns | /registerdns

ipconfig /showclassid Adapter
```

```
ipconfig /setclassid Adapter [ClassIDToSet]]
```

NET ACCOUNTS

Manages user account and password policies.

```
net accounts [/forcelogoff:{Minutes | no}]
  [/minpwlen:Length]
  [/maxpwage:{Days | unlimited}]
  [/minpwage:Days]
  [/uniquepw:Number] [/domain]
```

NET COMPUTER

Adds or removes computers from a domain.

```
net computer \\ComputerName {/add | /del}
```

NET CONFIG SERVER

Displays or modifies configuration of server service.

```
net config server [/autodisconnect:Time]
   [/srvcomment:"Text"] [/hidden:{yes | no}]
```

NET CONFIG WORKSTATION

Displays or modifies configuration of workstation service.

```
net config workstation [/charcount:Bytes]
[/chartime:MSec]
[/charwait:Sec]
```

NET CONTINUE

Resumes a paused service.

```
net continue Service
```

NET FILE

Displays or manages open files on a server.

```
net file [ID [/close]]
```

NET GROUP

Displays or manages global groups.

```
net group [GroupName [/comment:"Text"]]
   [/domain]

net group GroupName {/add [/comment:"Text"]
   | /delete} [/domain]

net group GroupName UserName [...]
   {/add | /delete} [/domain]
```

NET LOCALGROUP

Displays local group accounts.

```
net localgroup [GroupName [/comment:"Text"]] [/domain]
```

Creates a local group account.

```
net localgroup GroupName {/add [/comment:"Text"]} [/domain]
```

Modifies local group accounts.

```
net localgroup [GroupName Name [ ...] /add [/domain]
```

Deletes a local group account.

```
net localgroup GroupName /delete  [/domain]
```

NET PAUSE

Suspends a service.

```
net pause Service
```

NET PRINT

Displays or manages print jobs and shared queues.

```
net print \\ComputerName\ShareName

net print [\\ComputerName] JobNumber
[/hold | /release | /delete]
```

NET SESSION

Lists or disconnects sessions.

```
net session [\\ComputerName] [/delete]
```

NET SHARE

Displays or manages shared printers and directories.

```
net share [ShareName]

net share ShareName[=Drive:Path] [/users:Number | /unlimited]
[/remark:"Text"] [/cache:Flag]

net share {ShareName | DeviceName | Drive:Path} /delete
```

NET START

Lists or starts network services.

```
net start [Service]
```

NET STATISTICS

Displays workstation and server statistics.

```
net statistics [workstation | server]
```

NET STOP

Stops services.

```
net stop Service
```

NET TIME

Displays or synchronizes network time.

```
net time [\\ComputerName | /domain[:DomainName] |
 /rtsdomain[:DomainName]] [/set]

net time [\\ComputerName] /querysntp

net time [\\ComputerName] /setsntp[:ServerList]
```

NET USE

Displays or manages remote connections.

```
net use [DeviceName | *] [\\ComputerName\ShareName[\Volume]
[Password | *]] [/user:[DomainName\]UserName]
[/user:[UserName@DomainName]] [[/delete] | [/persistent:{yes | no}]]
[/smartcard] [/savecred]

net use [DeviceName | *] [Password | *]] [/home]

net use [/persistent:{yes | no}]
```

NET USER

Creates local user accounts.

```
net user UserName [Password | *] /add
[/active:{no | yes}] [/comment:"DescriptionText"]
[/countrycode:NNN]
[/expires: {{MM/DD/YYYY | DD/MM/YYYY | MMM,DD,YYYY} | never}]
[/fullname:"Name"] [/homedir:Path]
[/passwordchg:{yes | no}] [/passwordreq:{yes | no}]
[/profilepath:[Path]] [/scriptpath:Path]
[/times:{Day[-Day][,Day[-Day]] ,Time[-Time][,Time[-Time]] [;...] |
all}] [/usercomment:"Text"]
[/workstations:{ComputerName[,...] | *}] [/domain]
```

Modifies local user accounts.

```
net user [UserName [Password | *] [/active:{no | yes}]
[/comment:"DescriptionText"]
[/countrycode:NNN] [/expires:{{MM/DD/YYYY | DD/MM/YYYY | MMM,DD,YYYY}
| never}] [/fullname:"Name"]
[/homedir:Path] [/passwordchg:{yes | no}]
[/passwordreq:{yes | no}] [/profilepath:[Path]]
[/scriptpath:Path] [/times:{Day[-Day][,Day[-Day]] ,Time[-Time]
```

```
[,Time[-Time]] [;...] | all}] [/usercomment:"Text"]
[/workstations:{ComputerName[,...] | *}]] [/domain]
```

Deletes local user accounts.

```
net user UserName [/delete] [/domain]
```

NET VIEW

Displays network resources or computers.

```
net view [\\ComputerName [/cache] | [/all] |
 /domain[:DomainName]]
```

```
net view /network:nw [\\ComputerName]
```

NETDOM ADD

Adds a workstation or server account to the domain.

```
netdom add Computer [/domain:Domain] [/userd:User]
[/passwordd:[Password | *]] [/server:Server]
[/ou:OUPath] [/dc] [/securepasswordprompt]
```

NETDOM COMPUTERNAME

Manages the primary and alternate names for a computer. This command can safely rename a domain controller or a server.

```
netdom computername Computer [/usero:User] [/passwordo:[Password |
*]]
[/userd:User]
[/passwordd:[Password | *]] [/securepasswordprompt]
/add:NewAlternateDNSName | /remove:AlternateDNSName
 | /makeprimary:ComputerDNSName
 | /enumerate[:{alternatenames | primaryname | allnames}] | /verify
```

NETDOM JOIN

Joins a workstation or member server to the domain.

```
netdom join Computer /domain:Domain [/ou:OUPath] [/userd:User]
[/passwordd:[Password | *]]
```

```
[/usero:User] [/passwordo:[Password | *]]
[/reboot[:TimeInSeconds]]
[/securepasswordprompt]
```

NETDOM MOVE

Moves a workstation or member server to a new domain.

```
netdom move Computer /domain:Domain [/ou:OUPath]
[/userd:User] [/passwordd:[Password | *]]
[/usero:User] [/passwordo:[Password | *]]
[/userf:User] [/passwordf:[Password | *]]
[/reboot[:TimeInSeconds]]
[/securepasswordprompt]
```

NETDOM MOVENT4BDC

Moves Windows NT 4.0 backup domain controllers to a new domain.

```
netdom movent4bdc Computer [/domain:Domain] [/reboot[:TimeInSeconds]]
```

NETDOM QUERY

Queries a domain for information.

```
netdom query [/domain:Domain] [/server:Server]
[/userd:User] [/passwordd:[Password | *]]
[/verify] [/reset] [/direct] [/securepasswordprompt]
{workstation | server | dc | ou | pdc | fsmo | trust}
```

NETDOM REMOVE

Removes a workstation or server from the domain.

```
netdom remove Computer [/domain:Domain] [/userd:User]
[/passwordd:[Password | *]]
[/usero:User] [/passwordo:[Password | *]]
[/reboot[:TimeInSeconds]] [/force]
[/securepasswordprompt]
```

NETDOM RENAMECOMPUTER

Renames a computer. If the computer is joined to a domain, the computer object in the domain is also renamed. Do not use this command to rename a domain controller.

```
netdom renamecomputer Computer /newname:NewName
[/userd:User [/passwordd:[Password | *]]]
[/usero:User [/passwordo:[Password | *]]]
[/force] [/reboot[:TimeInSeconds]]
[/securepasswordprompt]
```

NETDOM RESETPWD

Resets the machine account password for the domain controller on which this command is run.

```
netdom resetpwd /server:DomainController /userd:User
/passwordd: [Password | *] [/securepasswordprompt]
```

NETDOM RESET

Resets the secure connection between a workstation and a domain controller.

```
netdom reset Computer [/domain:Domain] [/server:Server] [/usero:User]
[/passwordo:[Password | *]] [/securepasswordprompt]
```

NETDOM TRUST

Manages or verifies the trust relationship between domains.

```
netdom trust TrustingDomainName /domain:TrustedDomainName
[/userd:User]
[/passwordd:[Password | *]] [/usero:User]
[/passwordo:[Password | *]] [/verify] [/reset]
[/passwordt:NewRealmTrustPassword]
[/add] [/remove] [/twoway] [/realm] [/kerberos]
[/transitive[:{yes | no}]]
[/oneside:{trusted | trusting}] [/force]
[/quarantine[:{yes | no}]]
[/namesuffixes:TrustName [/togglesuffix:#]]
```

```
[/enablesidhistory[:{yes | no}]]
[/foresttransitive[:{yes | no}]]
[/crossorganization[:{yes | no}]]
[/addtln:TopLevelName]
[/addtlnex:TopLevelNameExclusion]
[/removetln:TopLevelName]
[/removetlnex:TopLevelNameExclusion]
[/securepasswordprompt]
```

NETDOM VERIFY

Verifies the secure connection between a workstation and a domain controller.

```
netdom verify Computer [/domain:Domain]
[/usero:User] [/passwordo:[Password | *]]
[/securepasswordprompt]
```

NETSH

Invokes a separate command prompt that allows you to manage the configuration of various network services on local and remote computers.

```
netsh
```

NSLOOKUP

Shows the status of Domain Name System (DNS).

```
nslookup [-Option] [Computer]
```

```
nslookup [-Option] [Computer Server]
```

PATHPING

Traces routes and provides packet-loss information.

```
pathping [-n] [-h MaxHops] [-g HostList]
[-i Address] [-p Period]
[-q NumberOfQueries] [-w TimeOut]
TargetName [-4] [-6]
```

PING

Determines whether a network connection can be established.

```
ping [-t] [-a] [-n Count] [-l Size] [-f]
[-i TTL] [-v TOS] [-r Count] [-s Count]
[[-j HostList] | [-k HostList]]
[-w TimeOut] [-R} [-S SourceAddress]
[-4] [-6] DestinationList
```

> **Note** This command uses case-sensitive switches.

ROUTE

Manages network routing tables.

```
route [-f] [-p] [-4|-6] Command [Destination]
[mask NetMask] [Gateway] [metric Metric]
[if Interface]
```

SC CONFIG

Configures service startup and logon accounts.

```
sc [\\ServerName] config ServiceName
[type= {own | share|{interact type = {own | share}}
| kernel | filesys |rec | adapt}]
[start= {boot | system | auto | demand | disabled
 | delayed-auto}]
[error= {normal | severe | critical | ignore}]
[binpath= BinaryPathName]
[group= LoadOrderGroup]
[tag= {yes | no}]
[depend= Dependencies]
[obj= {AccountName | ObjectName}]
[displayname= DisplayName]
[password= Password]
```

SC CONTINUE

Resumes a paused service.

```
sc [\\ServerName] continue ServiceName
```

SC FAILURE

Displays the actions that will be taken if a service fails.

```
sc [\\ServerName] failure ServiceName
[reset= ErrorFreePeriod]
[reboot= BroadcastMessage] [command= CommandLine]
[actions= FailureActionsAndDelayTime]
```

SC PAUSE

Pauses a service.

```
sc [\\ServerName] pause ServiceName
```

SC QC

Displays configuration information for a named service.

```
sc [\\ServerName] qc ServiceName [BufferSize]
```

SC QFAILURE

Sets the action to take upon failure of a service.

```
sc [\\ServerName] qfailure ServiceName [BufferSize]
```

SC QUERY

Displays the list of services configured on the computer.

```
sc [\\ServerName] query ServiceName
[type= {driver | service | all}]
[type= {own | share | interact | kernel | filesys
 | rec | adapt}]
[state= {active | inactive | all}]
[bufsize= BufferSize] [ri= ResumeIndex]
[group= GroupName]
```

SC START

Starts a service.

```
sc [\\ServerName] start ServiceName [ServiceArgs]
```

SC STOP

Stops a service.

```
sc [\\ServerName] stop ServiceName
```

SCHTASKS /CHANGE

Changes the properties of existing tasks.

```
schtasks /change /tn TaskName
[/s System [/u [Domain\]User
[/p [Password]]]] {[/ru [Domain\]User]
[/rp Password]  [/tr TaskToRun]} [/st StartTime]
[/ri RunInterval] [{/et EndTime | /du Duration}
[/k]] [/sd StartDate] [/ed EndDate]
[enable | disable] [/it] [/z]
```

SCHTASKS /CREATE

Creates scheduled tasks.

```
schtasks /create [/s System [/u [Domain\]User
[/p [Password]]]] [/ru [Domain\]UserName
[rp Password]] /tn TaskName /tr TaskToRun
/sc ScheduleType [/mo Modifier] [/d Day]
[/i IdleTime] [/st StartTime] [/m Month [, Month [...]]] [/sd
StartDate] [/ed EndDate] [/ri RunInterval] [{/et EndTime | /du
Duration}
[/k]] [/it | /np] [/z] [/f] [/xml XMLFile]
```

SCHTASKS /DELETE

Removes scheduled tasks that are no longer wanted.

```
schtasks /delete /tn {TaskName | *} [/f]
[/s Computer [/u [Domain\]User [/p [Password]]]]
```

SCHTASKS /END

Stops a running task.

```
schtasks /end /tn TaskName [/s Computer [/u [Domain\]User
[/p [Password]]]]
```

SCHTASKS /QUERY

Displays scheduled tasks on the local or named computer.

```
schtasks /query [/s Computer [/u [Domain\]User [/p [Password]]]]
[/fo {table | list | csv} | /xml] [/nh] [/v] [/tn {TaskName]
```

SCHTASKS /RUN

Starts a scheduled task.

```
schtasks /run /tn TaskName [/s Computer [/u [Domain\]User
[/p [Password]]]]
```

SERVERMANAGERCMD

Installs and removes roles, role services, and features. Also lists installed roles, role services, and features.

Syntax for queries:
```
servermanagercmd -query [QueryFile.xml] [-logPath LogFile.txt]
```

```
servermanagercmd -version
```

Syntax for installations:
```
servermanagercmd -install Component [-resultPath ResultFile.xml [-
restart] | [-whatif]] [-logPath LogFile.txt] [-allSubFeatures]
```

Syntax for removals:
```
servermanagercmd -remove Component [-resultPath ResultFile.xml [-
restart] | [-whatif]] [-logPath LogFile.txt]
```

Syntax for installations or removals using an answer file:
```
servermanagercmd -inputPath AnswerFile.xml
[-resultPath ResultFile.xml
[-restart] | [-whatif]] [-logPath LogFile.txt]
```

SET

Displays or modifies Windows environment variables. Also used to evaluate numeric expressions at the command line.

```
set [Variable=[String]]
set /a Expression
set /p Variable=[PromptString]
```

SET-SERVICE

A Windows PowerShell command for modifying the configuration of system services.

```
set-service [-name] ServiceName [-displayname DisplayName]
[-description Description]
[-startuptype {Automatic | Manual | Disabled}]
[-whatif] [-config] [Parameters]
```

SHUTDOWN

Shuts down or restarts a computer.

```
shutdown [/i | /l | /s | /r | /g | /a | /p | /h | /e] [/f]
[/m \\ComputerName] [/t NN] [/d [p|u:]N1:N2 [/c "CommentText"]]
```

STOP-PROCESS

A Windows PowerShell command for stopping one or more running processes.

```
stop-process -id [ID1, ID2,...] [-confirm]
[-passthru] [-whatif] [Parameters]

stop-process -inputobject ProcessName1, ProcessName2,... [-passthru]
[-whatif] [-config]
[Parameters]
stop-process -name ProcessName1, ProcessName2,...
[-confirm] [-passthru] [-whatif] [Parameters]
```

STOP-SERVICE

A Windows PowerShell command for stopping one or more running services.

```
stop-service [-displayname [ServiceName1, ServiceName2,...]]
-include [ServiceName1, ServiceName2,...]
-exclude [ServiceName1, ServiceName2,...]

stop-service [-name] [ServiceName1, ServiceName2,...]
-include [ServiceName1, ServiceName2,...]
-exclude [ServiceName1, ServiceName2,...]
```

> **Note** Windows PowerShell also has commands for starting (start-service), restarting (restart-service), suspending (suspend-service), and resuming (resume-service) services. These commands have the same syntax as stop-service.

SYSTEMINFO

Displays detailed configuration information.

```
systeminfo [/s Computer [/u [Domain\]User
[/p [Password]]]] [/fo {table|list|csv}] [/nh]
```

TASKKILL

Stops running processes by name or process ID.

```
taskkill [/s Computer] [/u [Domain\]User
[/p Password]]] {[/fi Filter1 [/fi Filter2 [ ... ]]]
[/pid ID|/im ImageName]} [/f][/t]
```

TASKLIST

Lists all running processes by name and process ID.

```
tasklist [/s Computer [/u [Domain\]User
[/p [Password]]]] [{/m Module | /svc | /v}]
[/fo {table | list | csv}] [/nh]
[/fi FilterName [/fi FilterName2 [ ... ]]]
```

TRACERPT

Generates trace reports from trace logs.

```
tracerpt {[-l] LogFile1 LogFile2 ... | [-o OutputFile] | -rt
SessionName1 SessionName2 ...} [-of <CSV | EVTX | XML>] [-lr]
[-summary SummaryReportFile] [-report ReportFileName]
[-f <XML | HTML>] [-df SchemaFile] [-int DumpEventFile] [-rts]
[-tmf TraceDefinitionFile] [-tp TraceFilePath] [-gmt] [-i ImagePath]
[-pdb SymbolPath] [-rl N] [-export SchemaExportFile]
[-config ConfigFile] [-y]
```

TRACERT

Displays the path between computers.

```
tracert [-d] [-h MaxHops] [-j HostList]
[-w TimeOut] [-r] [-s SourceAddrress] [-4] [-6]
TargetName
```

WBADMIN

Performs or schedules backup and recovery operations. This command applies only to Windows Server 2008 and to business and enterprise editions of Windows desktop operating systems.

Syntax for enabling backups:
```
wbadmin enable backup
[-addtarget:{BackupTargetDisk}]
[-removetarget:{BackupTargetDisk}]
[-schedule:TimeToRunBackup]
[-include:VolumesToInclude]
[-allCritical] [-quiet]
```

Syntax for disabling backups:
```
wbadmin disable backup [-quiet]
```

Syntax for starting backups:
```
wbadmin start backup
[-backuptarget:{TargetVolume | TargetNetworkShare}]
[-include:VolumesToInclude] [-allCritical]
```

```
[-noverify] [-user:UserName] [-password:Password]
[-noinheritacl] [-vssFull] [-quiet]
```

Syntax for stopping the current backup job:

```
wbadmin stop job [-quiet]
```

Syntax for listing available disks:

```
wbadmin get disks
```

Syntax for getting the status of the current backup job:

```
wbadmin get status
```

Syntax for getting a list of available backups:

```
wbadmin get versions
[-backuptarget:{VolumeName | NetworkSharePath}]
[-machine:BackupMachineName]
```

Syntax for starting a system state backup:

```
wbadmin start systemstatebackup
-backuptarget:{VolumeName} [-quiet]
```

Syntax for starting a system state recovery:

```
wbadmin start systemstaterecovery
-version:VersionIdentifier -showsummary
[-backuptarget:{VolumeName | NetworkSharePath}]
[-machine:BackupMachineName]
[-recoverytarget:TargetPathForRecovery]
[-authsysvol] [-quiet]
```

Syntax for deleting a system state backup:

```
wbadmin delete systemstatebackup
-keepVersions: NumberOfCopiesToKeep | -version VersionID | -
deleteOldest
[-backuptarget:{VolumeName}]
[-machine:BackupMachineName] [-quiet]
```

About the Author

William R. Stanek (http://www.williamstanek.com/) has more than 20 years of hands-on experience with advanced programming and development. He is a leading technology expert, an award-winning author, and a pretty-darn-good instructional trainer. Over the years, his practical advice has helped millions of programmers, developers, and network engineers all over the world. His current and books include *Windows 8.1 Administration Pocket Consultant*, *Windows Server 2012 R2 Pocket Consultant* and *Windows Server 2012 R2 Inside Out*.

William has been involved in the commercial Internet community since 1991. His core business and technology experience comes from more than 11 years of military service. He has substantial experience in developing server technology, encryption, and Internet solutions. He has written many technical white papers and training courses on a wide variety of topics. He frequently serves as a subject matter expert and consultant.

William has an MS with distinction in information systems and a BS in computer science, magna cum laude. He is proud to have served in the Persian Gulf War as a combat crewmember on an electronic warfare aircraft. He flew on numerous combat missions into Iraq and was awarded nine medals for his wartime service, including one of the United States of America's highest flying honors, the Air Force Distinguished Flying Cross. Currently, he resides in the Pacific Northwest with his wife and children.

William recently rediscovered his love of the great outdoors. When he's not writing, he can be found hiking, biking, backpacking, traveling, or trekking in search of adventure with his family!

Find William on Twitter at www.twitter.com/WilliamStanek and on Facebook at www.facebook.com/William.Stanek.Author.